Debt–Proof
Your
Marriage

Other Books by Mary Hunt

Cheaper, Better, Faster
Debt-Proof Your Christmas
The Financially Confident Woman
Live Your Life for Half the Price
Raising Financially Confident Kids
7 Money Rules for Life
The Smart Woman's Guide to Planning for Retirement
Debt-Proof Living

Debt–Proof
Your
Marriage

How to Manage
Your Money Together

Mary Hunt

Revell
a division of Baker Publishing Group
www.RevellBooks.com

© 2016 by Mary Hunt

Published by Revell
a division of Baker Publishing Group
P.O. Box 6287, Grand Rapids, MI 49516-6287
www.revellbooks.com

Printed in the United States of America

Library of Congress Cataloging-in-Publication Data is on file at the Library of Congress, Washington, DC.

ISBN 978-0-8007-2683-6

Unless otherwise indicated, Scripture quotations are from the Holy Bible, New International Version®. NIV®. Copyright © 1973, 1978, 1984, 2011 by Biblica, Inc.™ Used by permission of Zondervan. All rights reserved worldwide. www.zondervan.com

Scripture quotations labeled KJV are from the King James Version of the Bible.

Scripture quotations labeled NCV are from the New Century Version®. Copyright © 1987, 1988, 1991 by Word Publishing, a division of Thomas Nelson, Inc. Used by permission. All rights reserved.

Scripture quotations labeled NLT are from the *Holy Bible*, New Living Translation, copyright © 1996, 2004, 2007 by Tyndale House Foundation. Used by permission of Tyndale House Publishers, Inc., Carol Stream, Illinois 60188. All rights reserved.

Scripture quotations labeled TLB are from *The Living Bible*, copyright © 1971. Used by permission of Tyndale House Publishers, Inc., Wheaton, Illinois 60189. All rights reserved.

Scripture quotations labeled CEV are from the Contemporary English Version © 1991, 1992, 1995 by American Bible Society. Used by permission.

Cheapskate Monthly, Debt-Proof Living, rapid debt-repayment plan, rapid debt-repayment plan calculator, and Tiptionary are registered trademarks owned by Mary Hunt.

16 17 18 19 20 21 22   7 6 5 4 3 2 1

For Harold, the love of my life and companion
through all the stages of marriage

Contents

Introduction   11

Part 1: Get Your Relationship Ready for Financial Harmony

1. This Is My Story and I'm Sticking to It   17
   A Story of Financial Discord

2. A Stiff Dose of Reality   33
   Money and Marriage

3. Marriage Is like a Dirt Road   39
   Money and the Stages of Marriage

4. The Currency of Life   49
   Why Money Is Hard for Couples

5. News Flash: You Are Different   71
   His Needs Are Not Her Needs

6. For Wives Only   85
   Real Men Don't Ask for Directions

7. For Husbands Only   91
   You Can Have What You Want

8. Getting It Together   97
   Honey, Let's Talk about Our Relationship

Contents

Part 2: How to Debt-Proof Your Marriage

9. Debt-Proof Living   105
   An Overview

10. Till Debt Do Us Part   115
    The Trouble with Debt

11. You Are Here   123
    Discovering Your Worth

12. Getting Where You Want to Be   141
    The Basic Elements of Your Financial Plan

13. A Life-Changing Formula   145
    The 80 Percent Solution

14. Knowledge Is a Powerful Thing   155
    The Spending Record

15. You Want Security? I'll Show You Security!   171
    The Contingency Fund

16. You Want Freedom? I'll Show You Freedom!   181
    The Freedom Account

17. You Can Get Out of Debt   197
    The Rapid Debt-Repayment Plan

18. Telling Your Money Where to Go   207
    The Spending Plan

Part 3: Unique Solutions for Common Dilemmas

19. Finding Money You Didn't Know You Had   223
    Forty Ways to Live below Your Means

20. Credit: The Good, the Bad, the Ugly   243
    *Credit Cards, Credit Reports, Credit Scores,
    and Credit Repair*

Contents

21. Tell the Middleman Thanks but No Thanks   259
    How to Pay Off Your Mortgage Early

22. How to Stay on Track with a Roller-Coaster
    Income   267
    The Thrill and the Agony of Self-Employment

23. What to Do When You've Fallen and You Can't
    Get Up   273
    Credit Counseling and Debt Negotiation

24. A Call to Faithfulness   285
    An Eternal Perspective on Wealth

    Epilogue   291
    Acknowledgments   293
    Notes   295

Introduction

Imagine how dull and boring our lives would be without harmony. Quilts would be pieced from the same fabric. The rainbow would be a series of seven red stripes. The a cappella group Take 6 would be reduced to Take 1, and you and your spouse would have exactly the same personality, temperament, and taste. Yawn. Harmony blends colors into the rainbow, creates the visual warmth of a quilt, combines the tones of the scale, and weaves the differences between a husband and wife into a satisfying and intimate relationship.

If you have money issues in your marriage—big troubles, small problems, or something in between—this book will help you bring harmony to that most challenging part of your marriage. However, I am not going to force you into a one-size-fits-all budget or even tell you how to spend your money.

What I will do is teach you everything I know about how to get out of debt. I'm going to tell you how to step away from the edge of fear and panic, how to live beneath your means, and how to prepare for the future. You've probably tried several times to manage your money and discovered it is not easy. You may have read books, purchased software, attended seminars, or enrolled in a program at your church or in your community. Your attempts may have worked in the beginning, but then, like you do after a failed diet, you went back to the old ways and experienced the equivalent of gaining back all the weight you lost, plus some.

Information alone cannot change your financial situation. That's because in a marriage, money is not simply about money. If it were, you could pick up any basic financial information and have no trouble following it. Nonmoney decisions, like what color to paint the bedroom or when to mow the lawn, are what I characterize as surface matters. Easily resolved. But money issues? Whoa, baby! That's a completely different story because matters of money are deeply emotional and affect us in ways we may not even be aware of. Money-related issues in a marriage are not surface matters.

Before you can develop financial harmony in your marriage, you and your spouse need a deep emotional connection. Length of marriage has absolutely nothing to do with whether you can connect at this level. The best word I know to describe this connection is *intimacy*, and I'm not talking about sex.

The kind of intimacy that is a precondition for the development of financial harmony in your marriage has nothing to do with sex or physical attraction. It has everything to do with respect and trust. It is that safe place where the two of you are free to be who you are without pretending, without being ashamed, and without fear of rejection. Emotional intimacy is the secret ingredient you need to develop financial harmony in your marriage.

Have you ever wondered why two couples can face the same life-challenging situation—unemployment, health problems, bankruptcy, or even the loss of a child—and one couple comes through the ordeal stronger and more devoted than ever, while the other marriage crumbles under the strain? I believe it has to do with the intimacy I just described. Intimacy is the insurance for all the stages of marriage and the promise of safe passage through the storms of life. Without that deep connection between spouses, just about anything can set them up for discord and financial disaster.

If you are discouraged because you're sure your spouse is not interested in reading this book or even talking about its contents, don't worry. The only person necessary to begin to move your relationship toward a place of intimacy and financial harmony is you. You can begin to make a significant change in your marriage, and if necessary, you can do it single-handedly.

I don't know everything, but I do know a lot about how to manage personal income, how to get out of debt (and stay out), and how to get rid of your financial fear and anxiety. Learning to manage money well in your marriage is worth the effort because doing so will help your relationship to grow and mature. It's also a proven fact that a healthy marriage contributes to financial success in life.

I am not a certified financial planner or a licensed marriage therapist. I have a degree, but you would not be impressed. What I offer you comes from experience and real life—my real life. I know the fear of being swept out to sea on the waves of financial turmoil. Worry overtakes your mind. It's hard to fall asleep; it hurts to wake up. Every aspect of your marriage falls under the shadow of impending doom. I've known all of that—and I know the way out.

If you're ready to get serious, I'm ready to take the guesswork out of personal money management for you. Even though we've never met, you'll be surprised at how well I know you and the issues with which you've been struggling.

You've prayed for help to turn around your personal finances, and here you are several paragraphs into the answers you've been looking for. No matter your current situation or how badly you may be feeling about your finances right now, take heart, my friend. Help is on the way.

Stop worrying . . . and start reading.

Part 1

Get Your Relationship Ready for Financial Harmony

1

This Is My Story and I'm Sticking to It

A Story of Financial Discord

When something happens to you, you have two choices in how to deal with it. You can either get bitter, or get better.

Donald Miller[1]

It was a typical hot summer day in California. I needed to get away to think things through. In desperation, I grabbed the car keys and took off, no particular destination in mind. I wandered around for a while, hoping the pain would go away, but it didn't. I ended up at my in-laws' home, relieved to discover no one there. I didn't feel much like talking.

I found the key, slipped in through the back door, and fell into the closest chair. I could hardly breathe and not because of the heat. To call this "anxiety" would be a serious understatement.

Never before in my thirty-four years had I known such loss, fear, and dread. I was out of options. I had nowhere to turn, no help, and worse, no hope.

From my earliest recollections, my life centered on a simple goal, which became my secret promise: when I grow up, I am going to be rich. Very rich. I wasn't going to be like my family, which I perceived to be poor. I blamed our poverty for the cloud of sadness and despair that hung over my life. How I would become rich wasn't important, only that I would.

In time, that promise turned into the light at the end of a dark tunnel. I saw wealth as my ticket to happiness, as the way to fill a void deep inside me. On this fictional foundation, I built all my hopes and dreams. I fixed my eyes and set my heart on that "someday" when I would grow up, leave home, have lots of money, and be happy.

I went away to college, a scared freshman reduced to something between bewilderment and embarrassment. I didn't fit in. My clothes were all wrong; my hair wasn't right. I didn't have a car. I was backward, small-town, sheltered, and naive. I was an oddball. Everything about me was weird, and I was devastated.

I wanted to fit in and be accepted. I knew I could learn. I was confident I could change, provided I had a plan. There was just one tiny problem: I needed money.

It's not as though I was broke. I'd worked through high school, saving all that I could, but that was mostly earmarked for tuition and books. I landed a part-time campus job, taught piano lessons, and played the organ in a local church on the weekends. While my cash flow was barely a trickle, I did have limited funds. And I had a checking account.

Along with new friendships came new expenses. Going out to eat, mall shopping, and keeping up with my stylish friends came with a price tag. I couldn't stand keeping track of my checking account but hated even more not having money. Even when I was short, if I could figure out a way to purchase things, I felt like I had money. Writing a check on a Wednesday even though I couldn't cover it until I got paid on Friday seemed perfectly logical, provided I could get away with it. And I did. Over and over. Having stuff now and paying for it later gave me a kind of rush, a sense of beating the system. It was my little secret. No one needed to know how often I spent money before I actually received it. And when I bounced a check and overdrew my account, no one knew that either.

My pattern of life became one of deceit and manipulation. Every time I wrote a check, I'd hold my breath until I could figure out a way to cover it. Over and again, I'd try to reform. Somehow I'd cover everything and promise myself that I'd never write another bad check. Until the next time.

Knowing that my state of poverty was only a temporary condition gave me some kind of weird comfort. It also justified my actions. I was a poor, starving student waiting for Prince Charming to arrive. While I didn't know the particulars—like his name—I knew he'd be along someday. Then my money problems would be over because I'd be sure to marry well. I'd finally be rich, and all this nonsense with scraping by, juggling my checking account, and worrying about irate phone calls would end.

Harold and I married shortly after I graduated. We had a lot in common, and he had great earning potential. Things were falling nicely into place. I was sure I'd be rich. Harold was in management training with one of the country's most prestigious banks. Our future was bright.

In the years we dated, I never tipped my hand about my spending problem. He might think poorly of me. Besides, there was no need. Once we were married and the money started rolling in, that would be behind me. Marriage was my chance to start over. I wasn't bringing much debt or an overdrawn account with me. I'd have a brand-new, unblemished, joint checking account with someone who actually knew how to reconcile it. I was living the dream I had designed. Life was wonderful.

I was a little surprised that my new husband wasn't as rigid with the money as I had anticipated. I knew he was opposed to incurring debt, and overdrawing our checking account was unthinkable, but beyond that, we didn't have a plan to save or to budget. He wasn't even worried about balancing the account, which came as a big relief to me. He would check the balance at work, and as long as it wasn't in the red, that's all that mattered. We shared a cavalier attitude about our money. We got it; we spent it. Our dual incomes and low overhead gave us plenty of opportunities to do lots of the latter.

Sometime during those first few months, I suggested we should get a credit card. Harold didn't particularly care for that suggestion, so I bided my time. I was fairly certain I could get him to change his mind. He needed to be more progressive. With only mild persistence, he agreed to a Texaco gasoline charge card that required full payment every month. Success!

In retrospect, that first card was pathetic as credit cards go but a significant milestone for me. My first charge card filled me with pride and status. I was somebody when I drove in for a fill-up. I had a rather inflated opinion of how much dignity and respect the card afforded me each time I used it. But the best part was that I could use my gas money for something else. Harold paid the charge card bill at the end of the month, and it felt great to have a man take care of me. For the first time in my life, I felt protected and nurtured. I soaked it up like a sponge.

The first time I overdrew the bank account was an honest mistake. Harold hit the roof. We didn't communicate well when it came to money, so I wouldn't understand for years how serious it was for the bank branch manager's personal account to show up on the rejected debit report. My screwup was a double violation: first at home, then at the office. Of course, I was repentant. I promised it would never happen again, and I meant it.

Imagine my surprise when I learned that with a valid credit card I could get a Sears card. No permission needed. I could sign for it all by myself, a detail that was more significant to me than actually getting the card. And it wasn't as if I would ever use it. Something seemed right, almost wise, about being prepared in this way for big things such as tools or appliances.

Soon other department stores began sending their credit cards without request (a practice halted by law in the years to come). With all my heart, I believed credit was evidence of an excellent evaluation of my character and self-worth. If these companies were willing to trust me with credit, surely they knew I could afford it.

Getting our first bank card was a defining moment that would reshape my life, and not for the better. Harold could hardly balk about getting a MasterCharge account (forerunner of MasterCard) because it was issued by his employing bank. He'd been through all the training and employee brainwashing about the benefits of consumer credit. He helped direct inner-branch campaigns to get all customers on board and into "perma-debt" (carrying a revolving balance forever). Our dual cards and accompanying credit limit (a whopping $300) were now part of his benefit package. While he still opposed the idea of a revolving balance, he seemed to be softening a bit.

Having my own bank card gave me a sense of prestige. I felt modern and well-to-do. I could shop in all kinds of places and know that Harold would take care of the payments later. I loved the minimum payment option. It was like a gift, a special entitlement I surely deserved. A $100 outfit was more like $10 a month. Quite affordable.

Living from paycheck to paycheck worked as long as we had two of them every week and as long as the cars didn't break down, or Christmas didn't come, or our wisdom teeth didn't scream for extraction. Spending all that we had just as quickly as we got it left no margin for the unexpected. It wasn't long before our credit

21

cards became necessary solutions. Harold hated them; I thought they were blessings.

I learned quickly that we had a lot more peace in our home if I was judicious about how much information I shared with my husband. I knew what would upset him and what he didn't really need to know. I could buy all kinds of things, and he wouldn't notice. I figured out ways to do things that would create the least volatility.

Our differences became very clear during those first years. For example, he was vehemently opposed (do you hear me when I say vehemently?) to spending more than we made, to bouncing checks, and to revolving debt. I participated in all three. I had to because we simply did not make enough money to pay for everything we needed plus all our regular expenses.

When Harold attempted to restrict my spending, I was resentful. He had asked me to marry him; he had promised to love me and to share his life with me. To me, that meant he would protect, provide for, and nourish me too. Of course, he didn't have a clue about that thing inside of me that was driven to be rich, but it was very real. And each time he tried to squelch it, inwardly I rebelled. Buying things and spending money, even if I didn't actually have cash, gave me feelings of power and prestige. I felt equal to those I admired and superior to those I pitied.

I began collecting credit cards the way kids collect baseball cards. I didn't plan to use them, but things came up, and I felt I had no other choice. Paying the full balances every month just wasn't happening. Harold had to resort to making minimum payments. But the cumulative payments depleted our cash flow so severely that using the cards regularly and allowing the balances to grow became the norm where once it had been the exception. Harold hated it, and I hated hearing about it. Every time he gave me a little talking to about our tenuous financial situation, I felt small and diminished—like I'd been called to the principal's office or lectured by my father. I would always repent and promise to do better—anything to bring the conversation to a quick conclusion.

I had promises to keep, plans to work. My happiness hinged on becoming rich. Now I was grown up. I'd done everything right. I had graduated from college and married well; I went to church; I worked very hard; I was a good person. I could not bear the thought of this not turning out right. It had to work. I'd do better. I'd make more money. I'd join another multilevel marketing company. I'd be the best, climb to the top. I'd start my own business. I'd start five businesses. I had to be rich. The more I had, the more I wanted. Nothing satisfied for long, and more was never enough.

After five years of marriage, we had two boys. While certainly not unexpected events, children brought with them a new level of expense we hadn't anticipated. We bought a bigger house; we needed new cars. Our boys needed to fit the images and plans I'd been making for them. I found myself reliving my own childhood through theirs. I gave them everything I thought would make them happy. I wanted them to fit in at school, at church, on the playground, and on the sports teams in all the ways I'd wanted to fit in at their age.

Many times during those years, Harold came to the end of his rope with our financial situation. Reluctantly, he'd agree to refinance our home. Because real estate values were increasing at unprecedented rates, we had equity—a fact that was always at the forefront of my mind. I knew that equity was an asset, and it was our asset. It was a lifeboat tied to the side of our ship always at the ready if we needed it. We were young, retirement was a lifetime away, and if we needed our money now, we should not hesitate to gain access to it. Even if the worst happened and we lost everything, we could just start over. I had an answer for everything.

Each time we took a ride in the lifeboat, we weren't improving anything at all. We were only moving our rapidly accumulating debt from credit cards to mortgage companies and banks. But in some strange way, I believed the hype and ads that insisted we were being wise and responsible by paying down our debts. It felt that way. We'd walk away from the bank with a big fat check, bring everything current, pocket the difference, if there was any, and feel righteous. Another clean slate. Ceremoniously, I would cut up all my plastic and pledge never to charge again, just like at Thanksgiving when I would promise never to overeat again. My credit card pledges lasted about as long as my never-overeat-again promises . . . until I got hungry.

Our home equity consolidation bailouts were never the solution. They eased the pain for a time, but the cruel reality was that with our other living expenses and payments, we never had enough. Always the answer was more credit, higher limits, bigger payments, more credit, juggling balances, cash advances from one card to make the payment on another.

It's not like I wasn't willing to help make money. I taught piano lessons. I worked temporary jobs, dabbled in crafts, and made other efforts to earn money. But it was never enough. Without fail, I would start using the cards again. I would touch the first domino, and the others would fall. Within a couple of years, we'd be right back where we were with the credit cards maxed out, our finances in shambles. But now there were equity loans too.

Riding a financial roller coaster became our way of life. We'd run everything up, then scramble to find a way to refinance, calm things down for a while, then head right back to where we'd been and higher. I became a master at hiding, juggling, and manipulating my husband and our creditors.

Harold's career with the bank was going well. By bank standards, his future was bright. But not by my standards. I thought he deserved so much more. He simply did not make enough money, and given the banking industry, I doubted he ever would. I told him so. I didn't trust him to be the leader in our marriage. He needed my intervention. There were so many areas in

24

which I believed he could improve. I took him on as an improvement project. I "encouraged" him to think about a new career, something that would pay us what he was worth. I nagged and pleaded. He resisted. I suggested and directed. He withdrew. I wouldn't give up.

We were the quintessential financially mismatched couple. I spent to feel good, to prove that I could, and to prove to myself that we were not poor. His inclination was to not spend to make sure we didn't become poor. Despite all our differences and the horrible financial strain on our marriage, he never gave up on me. Neither of us ever left, not even for a day, a fact I can only attribute to the mercy of God and the undying commitment of my husband. A lesser man might have left, and with good reason.

In my heart, I was sure that incredible wealth was right around the next bend. For my life to make sense, I had to believe that. My job, I determined, was to find it and to just hold on by any means until I did. And I knew I could change my husband's mind so that he would be as driven as I was to be successful.

Just as I'd planned, I found it. Wealth. Well, at least the promise for how we could be wealthy.

One of Harold's clients at the bank was a young, hip, Florida-based distribution company. They'd recently opened operations in Southern California. It became obvious to Harold that this was what one might call a "cash intensive" business. Their daily deposits of cash were so large that Harold, as the branch manager, had to handle them. I know what you're thinking, and to this day I don't believe the business involved contraband or illegal activities, although we'll probably never know for certain.

What Harold knew for sure was that they had a very active distribution operation of ordinary household goods. These guys had the good fortune (and I use the term loosely) of getting in on the infamous ground level of the country's latest multilevel marketing opportunity. They were slick and very friendly. They appeared to be authentic. They dressed to the hilt, drove fancy cars, lived in gorgeous beach homes, and, to my utter joy, befriended us.

One weekend, they said the words I'd been waiting a lifetime to hear: they were willing to share their dream with us! Their opportunity would become our opportunity. I was ecstatic.

I convinced Harold to say good-bye to his sixteen-year banking career, full tenure, and regular paychecks. Blinded by greed and my insatiable desire to get rich quickly, we took our deepest financial plunge yet, into a business we knew nothing about. Worse, we did it with borrowed funds.

It's no wonder that in only four months our first entrepreneurial endeavor ended in an abrupt and devastating failure and the loss of all the money we'd borrowed plus all that we'd poured into this bogus venture. Those newly found friends of ours disappeared more quickly than the money.

Our debts were enormous, our income nonexistent. Harold and I were unemployed, and the anxiety and turmoil became unbearable. We had no income, no liquid assets. We were beginning to hear the rumblings of foreclosure on our mortgage, which was now four months in arrears.

That day as I sat in the silence and emptiness of my in-laws' house, I could see no way out. I was terrified and desperate. This strong, take-charge, I-can-do-anything wife and mother was hanging on by a thread.

I'd run out of options and clever schemes. The pain in the pit of my stomach was worse than anything I'd ever known. I'd brought together all the elements that frequently prompt divorce, bankruptcy, the loss of a home, and the destruction of a family. I completely fell apart. I could not go on. There was no way out, no hope. I'd ruined everything—Harold's life, my life, our boys' lives.

I don't know how long I sat there that day. But I know I hit rock bottom, and it was only then at that dark, lonely, painful place that I was willing to look inside myself and find where the real problem resided. It wasn't in my husband or in our failed business or in our miserable marriage.

I learned something that day. When you're at the bottom, there's only one way to look, and that is up. It was as if God turned on the floodlight of heaven to illuminate the dark caverns of my life. For the first time, I saw the magnitude of the mess I'd made, the ugliness of my greed and secret plans. I saw how deceptive, deceitful, and manipulative I'd been. I'd lied to have things my way, and I was certain that I'd destroyed my husband's life. The enormity of that was almost more than I could bear.

As I began to deal honestly with my situation, I fell to my knees and begged for God's forgiveness for the horrible mess I'd created and for help to rebuild my life. I made a new promise: I would stop my irrational spending and would do whatever it took to pay back what we owed. When I said I was willing to do anything, I meant it more than I'd ever meant it in my life. I asked God to help me change.

Somehow I went home that day. Nothing radical happened; we were still not speaking to each other. The pain of what we were going through was so enormous. But something was changing inside of me. In a healing kind of way, I began to take personal responsibility for the situation I'd created.

Without words and without any kind of announcement, I made a decision to respect my husband and to begin to honor his position as leader of our family. I wanted more than anything to trust him wholly. I won't say it was easy. It was so out of character for me to even consider giving up control. I won't say I was instantly successful, but little by little things began to change. One hour at a time, a day, a month, and then year after year.

Though both Harold and I had made big mistakes, I was primarily the one who had brought us to the point of financial and emotional ruin. I knew what had to happen. I needed to start making major financial contributions to our marriage partnership. I had made far too many withdrawals. I went back to work.

Because I had a real estate license, I was able to combine property management with sales, providing a steady income plus commissions. It was a good thing too because Harold decided he needed to stay home for a while.

What an amazing turn of events. We immediately eliminated all day care costs. Two little boys got to spend huge amounts of time with their dad, who also took over many of the household tasks. It was awkward at first, but I adapted. Being scared witless was probably the best thing that could have happened to me. I was willing to try anything.

Slowly, we began to communicate. We began to know each other on a level we'd not known before. We had to hang on to each other. There was no one else who understood what we were going through. We were too embarrassed and ashamed to reach out.

At the same time, we had to learn frugality—a new concept for me. It didn't come naturally by any means. But we were shocked at how much we could cut back. The most amazing thing is that no one, including the kids, noticed our scaled-back standard of living. It just goes to show that others are not nearly as impressed by our artificial lifestyles as we think they are.

Gradually, we reversed our spending habits. We began to get out of debt, and our drastically reduced living requirements became our way of life. Things went so well that in 1985 we were able to go into business for ourselves in a more practical and sensible way. With backgrounds in banking and real estate, we opened our own industrial real estate company.

By that time, we had struggled through ten years of financial recovery. We didn't have a good master plan, but we had paid back the major portion of our debt, and things were going reasonably well. I was becoming impatient and began looking for a way to bring excitement into my life and at the same time make enough additional income to get rid of the debt once and for all.

My search ended when I got the wild idea to write and publish a subscription newsletter. I had the equipment, I had a modicum of computer knowledge, and I sure knew the subject matter. After a few months of planning and strategizing, Cheapskate Monthly was born in January 1992.

In the first issue, I gave an abbreviated version of my story, the mess I'd made, and the journey we were taking toward recovery. I had learned to refer to myself affectionately as a "cheapskate" because that was the best word I could come up with that defined the radical changes in my life. I redefined a cheapskate as a person who saves consistently, gives generously, and never spends more than he or she has.

Within a short time, I felt as if someone had turned on a faucet. Subscriptions began pouring in, the media started calling, and I had to get a bigger post office box to handle all the mail. Repeatedly, I would open a letter that would begin, "Dear Mary, I've never told anyone what I'm about to tell you . . ." and then the floodgates would open. With each issue of Cheapskate Monthly, I would open my heart further, which in turn would encourage readers to do the same. As I became accountable to thousands of people throughout the United States and Canada, my own personal recovery began to speed up.

I read everything I could get my hands on in preparation for writing a new issue each month, and I began to understand where I'd been, why I had done what I'd done, and how far I'd come. I found validation. Much of what we had done in order to get back on the right financial track was right. I also had moments of regret and sadness as I admitted that we'd blown it on more than one occasion.

One of the most remarkable things I learned was that many others shared what I'd considered my unique problem. I even discovered people in situations worse than mine. But the wonderful thing was the sense of fellowship. In time, I would receive so many letters that answering them became my number one challenge. I couldn't ignore them because these people needed me as much as I needed them. As I wrote reply after reply, I could feel myself becoming stronger. The more I shared of my own recovery struggle, the more easily I was able to reject the constant opportunities to return to my old ways.

In time, I began speaking publicly, telling my story and offering hope and encouragement to others. Soon I found myself living my recovery in fast-forward and in the public spotlight.

Since then, I have been privileged to watch thousands of people use simple principles to turn their lives around, to get out of debt, and to go on to live reasonably and within their means. I've seen divorces averted, marriages restored, and families preserved.

If all of this sounds too easy, understand this is the condensed version of my life. Nothing happened overnight. In fact, it took thirteen years to reverse twelve years of financial damage and to pay back the more than $100,000 in unsecured debt we'd amassed, including everything we borrowed to get into that "business." But we did. We paid back every single dime of interest, penalties, and principal.

Did developing financial harmony in our marriage promote a new kind of intimacy we'd never known before, or did the intimacy promote the harmony? Whichever way it happened, thank God it did. It wasn't easy in the beginning, but we did start talking about money and the kinds of issues that reside deep inside in that place we rarely allow anyone to enter. It was many, many years before I understood the relationship between my childhood dreams and my adulthood behaviors. But figuring that out and then choosing to confront the beliefs as false and unworthy to shape the way I live my life was a turning point for me.

In the past, the changes I made in my behavior were strictly external. They were put on to impress others or to get Harold off my back. Now I began to change from the inside out. It was only as God changed my heart and my desires that I experienced lasting and meaningful change.

The scars of financial recklessness and irresponsibility will be with us always. There's not a day that goes by that I am not in some way reminded of the wasted years, the lost opportunities. We will never be able to make up what we didn't save for retirement during the years that would have counted the most. We will always wonder what might have been. But one step at a time, we continue to make progress. And every day I offer my thanks for how far we've come and how much we've learned.

I know that who I am today is the sum total of all I've been in the past, all the things I've done and the experiences I've had. Every day I acknowledge how easily I could go back to my old ways, that my dignity and self-worth do not come from possessions, and that my value is not in the color and quantity of my credit cards.

When I prayed for God's forgiveness for the horrible mess I'd created and asked for help to rebuild my life, I never dreamed he would do all of that and so much more. I've been blessed beyond anything I could have ever imagined. And with that blessing comes a responsibility to share with others what I've learned.

2

A Stiff Dose of Reality

Money and Marriage

At the rate society is going with divorce, nobody is going to make 50 years of marriage. I think wedding anniversaries these days should be counted in dog years. One year together should count for seven. Seven regular years would translate to 49 marriage years. Throw in another year for sportsmanship and you've got yourself a Golden Anniversary.

Jim Shahin
American Way Magazine, September 1, 2001

Some years ago I flipped through the pages of *InStyle Weddings* while standing in the grocery checkout line. The cover promised details of celebrity weddings. Inside, the photos were beautiful. As I slipped the magazine back into the rack, I wondered how many copies the publisher would be hauling to the dump. By the time that issue had hit the newsstand, two of the couples had already filed for divorce.[1] As I paid the checker and dashed off to the car, I could only imagine that in all of the glitz and glamour of producing the posh weddings and photo shoots, somebody forgot to plan a marriage.

The State of Our Unions

According to the National Marriage Project, 40 to 50 percent of all first-time marriages in the United States end in divorce.[2] We've been hearing this statistic for so long that it's old news. But what about the other half—the 50 percent of marriages that don't end, the couples who don't split up? The results are only slightly more encouraging. More than half of those couples who don't divorce (60 percent to be exact) are admittedly not happy.[3] While every couple starts out believing they will be happily married for a lifetime, 80 percent of the time that doesn't happen. What a shocking commentary on marriage and the family in America.

As for second marriages, we might assume that when people remarry, they have learned from their mistakes and make better choices, but that is not so. The divorce rate for remarriages is even higher than for first marriages.[4]

Marriage is risky business, the most risky undertaking routinely taken on by the greatest number of people in our society.[5]

Even though we've heard that money is the leading cause of divorce in this country, there is no evidence to prove that is true. There is plenty of evidence, however, that the number one killer of marriages in the United States is unresolved conflicts.[6]

While all couples have disagreements, the problem arises when conflicts do not find resolution. Like dirty dishes in the sink, unresolved conflicts pile up higher and higher, and before you know it, the sink is full, the counters are stacked high, and there's not a clean dish in the place! It may be that nothing in the pile is serious enough on its own to topple the marriage; however, the cumulative effect increases the chances a marriage will turn unhappy and possibly end in divorce.

Think of the most happily married couple you know. If these people are human, and I am assuming they are (even though I did once see a wedding ceremony for two dogs on *The View*), from time to time even they have conflicts. They do! The secret to their happiness is that somehow they've learned how to resolve their conflicts efficiently . . . and (apparently) privately.

So what do couples argue about the most? If you've been married for any time at all, you are probably way ahead of me because you're thinking the thing you argue about most is money. Bingo! An impressive study published by the Center for Marital and Family Studies at the University of Denver reported how couples rated their problem areas over an extended period of time.[7] The study tracked couples from before they married to many years after. People before marriage, people after marriage, people with lots of money, people with little money—they all rated their number one area of conflict as money.

Couples who try to clean the slate of their miserable marriage with a divorce almost always discover, too late, that divorce is not a solution for their unresolved money issues. In fact, divorce only makes things worse. Spouses don't disappear after a divorce, and neither do the money problems. Nobody wins in a divorce. A divorce has ripple effects that touch not just the family involved but the entire society. Each divorce is like the death of a small civilization.

The damaging effects of a divorce on spouses and children are so immense they cannot be calculated. Children of divorce experience feelings of rejection, loneliness, anger, guilt, anxiety, fear of abandonment, and a deep yearning for the absent parent.[8] Five years after their parents divorced, 37 percent of the children studied were moderately to severely depressed.[9] Children of divorce have a risk of divorce that is two or three times greater than children from two-parent families.[10]

Dividing families through divorce is the leading cause of poverty in America, leaving many children in poor, single-parent homes. No amount of child support can change the basic math: it costs more to live separately than together. Typically, it's the mothers and children who experience large drops in their income and standard of living following a divorce. Clearly, there are no winners in a divorce.

What Makes Us Happy

Couples who play the divorce card often say the motivation is to be happy. Statistically speaking, the chances of that working out are about slim to none. Only 18 percent of divorced persons say they are happy.[11] The other 82 percent must have been shocked to discover divorce was not the gateway to happiness.

Ask any group of people what they think will improve their lives, and the overwhelming response will be "more money." Not only do most people say this, but they also believe it. But this matter of money versus happiness can be quite tricky. There is some truth to the belief that money can buy happiness. Experts with years of study and documentation under their belts put it this way: if you are living in poverty, having more money will likely make a huge, positive difference in your life. However, if your basic material needs in life are met, having more money might be nice, but it is not likely to make you happier. Beyond the survival point, your income level will probably have little to do with how happy you are in your marriage.[12]

Happiness is strongly affected by the quality of our relationships, especially marital and family relationships. Happiness in a marriage is the result of lasting love with your husband or wife. People gain tremendous advantages in life by having and investing in long-term love with one spouse.

Research shows it's not how much you love each other that predicts the success of your marriage but how you handle the problems that come along in life. Problem solving is the key to a good marriage. Happily married couples view problems as "us against the problem" not "us against each other." They identify themselves as a team.[13]

Improving an Unhappy Marriage

An unhappy marriage is not doomed to divorce. In fact, the likelihood of an unhappy marriage improving dramatically is quite high. Labeling a marriage a bad marriage is not a hard fact. It's a judgment by one person at one moment in time about a future that can change. All marriages go through difficult times, but things can, and often do, change.

Research shows that except in cases in which one of the spouses or the children are being abused and their safety is compromised, an unhappy marriage is better for all involved than a divorce.

How many unhappy couples turn their marriages around by simply choosing to stay together? In one study, 86 percent of unhappily married people who stuck it out found that five years later their marriage was happier. In fact, nearly three-fifths of those who said their marriage was unhappy and who stayed married rated this same marriage as either "very happy" or "quite happy" when reinterviewed. Surprisingly, the very worst marriages showed the most dramatic turnarounds.[14] If these people achieved those results by doing nothing more than not leaving, imagine what could happen if they made a concerted effort to learn how to resolve their conflicts and improve their communication?

Married people live happier and healthier lives than singles. But the good news doesn't stop there. Married people do better financially than singles, not because financially successful people get married but because married people who behave as true financial partners do better financially. A healthy marriage promotes financial success.[15]

There's a reason why despite all the gloom and depressing predictions about marriage people continue to walk down the wedding aisle, some for the second time. God created each of us with a deep longing for close relationship, first with him and then with another person. Then he gave us marriage and the wonder of family to meet our deepest needs. We can research and ponder this until we can ponder no more, but the fact remains that first-time, lifelong, monogamous marriage is the relationship that best provides for the most favorable exercise of human sexuality, the overall well-being of adults, and the proper socialization of children.[16]

When it comes to making us happy, marriage has no rival. The way to make any marriage happier and more fulfilling is to learn how to resolve conflicts effectively—especially the most difficult of all conflicts, those having to do with money.

3

Marriage Is like a Dirt Road

Money and the Stages of Marriage

The real voyage of discovery consists not in seeking new landscapes,
but in having new eyes.

Marcel Proust[1]

Having grown up a city girl, I've never liked outdoor adventure.
I'm not a big sports participant and shy away from activities
that include the word *extreme*. You might call me a pantywaist.

The adventures I have experienced, few in number though they
be, I owe to the persistence of my brother-in-law Lloyd. The mere
mention of his name takes me back to the longest day of my life,
on Engineer Pass.

It was a beautiful summer morning when we took off from Ouray
in southwest Colorado. Also known as the "Switzerland of America," this tiny picturesque town is tucked into the San Juan Mountains, the youngest, steepest, and most rugged range in the great

Rocky Mountains. Before day's end, we would find ourselves more than two-and-a-half miles closer to heaven, elevationally speaking. Lloyd, Marsha, and their kids led the way in their stately Jeep; we followed in our junior model. Destination: Lake City, Colorado.

As we turned off US Highway 550 (also known as the Million-Dollar Highway)[2] onto a gravel road, we bid farewell to level ground and all sense of equilibrium. A road sign directed the way to something that sounded very much like an amusement park ride: Alpine Loop. This should have been my first clue for what lay ahead.

Gravel soon gave way to a steep and rocky dirt road. We wove our way around fallen rocks almost as big as our Jeep. It was one steep switchback after another as the trail quickly ascended.

At one switchback, our tires spun, so we had to roll back down through the hairpin, switch to low gear, and try again. The road, if you could even call it that, was narrow with big drop-offs, which I might add were always on my side.

Meeting another vehicle coming the opposite way was nothing short of terrifying, since the road was not, from my viewpoint, wide enough for even one vehicle. Of course, our two boys thought this was the greatest fun ever. I, on the other hand, was certain none of us would get out alive.

For hours we crawled and clawed our way up the steep terrain until we were far above the tree line. The view was spectacular, but I know that only from the photos. My eyes were all but glued shut by fear.

Now if all of this wasn't scary enough, once we reached a certain elevation, our Jeep decided it couldn't handle thin air, high temperature, and low-octane fuel all at the same time. Every five minutes or so, it rebelled with a condition known as vapor lock. Of course, this never happened on a semi-level spot but always while we were hanging precariously from yet another steep embankment.

Eventually, we made it to Lake City but not without having a full five years shaved from my life expectancy. By the time I could relax, I was so grateful to be on level ground that I all but gave up my plan to have my brother-in-law taken down. In the years since, I've managed to get a lot of mileage from the story. I still love to give Lloyd a hard time about the day he tried to kill me on Engineer Pass.

What I've never told him until now is how much comfort I found in knowing he was driving the vehicle up ahead. I trusted him to know the way. He'd been there before. He knew about the ruts, the rocks, the steep switchbacks, and the other perils. While I did wonder if we'd get out alive, never once did I worry about getting lost. Lloyd was our guide. He knew how to get from here to there. Had we attempted this trip by ourselves, I know we would have given up because we would not have known where we were going. We would've thought for sure that not another soul had been that way and lived to tell about it.

In the same way that children go through predictable developmental stages, so do marriages. Marriage therapist Michele Weiner Davis says, "Everyone is familiar with the infancy stage of marriage—the infamous 'honeymoon period'—but what happens after that? Does marriage have its equivalent to the 'Terrible Twos' or the stormy teenage years? In fact, it does."[3]

Unlike our trip over Engineer Pass, where we had a knowledgeable guide to assure us that 24 percent grades were to be expected, most couples are unfamiliar with the emotional terrain, the normal hills and valleys of marriage. They take off on their honeymoon and assume they'll have interstate all the way.

They come to the gravel and conclude something's just not right. Maybe they're lost. Couples misunderstand the transition to the dirt road, the rocks, and the perilous climbs, so they react inappropriately. They fail to get guidance from those who've already been this way. They overcorrect and make radical, permanent decisions in response to temporary problems. The result is that half of them give up and choose divorce. Still, 50 percent don't. Happily or not, half stick it out through the perilous climbs of marriage and usually reach the sunset years with greater love and commitment. That's the good news. The bad news is that many arrive battle-scarred, debt-ridden, and ill-prepared to face retirement because at times the journey was so difficult.

What follows in this chapter is a marriage map drawn from the experiences of many couples. Of course, not everyone experiences these stages in exactly the same way. And there's always an occasional couple who insists they've enjoyed a lifetime of romantic bliss without a moment of disagreement or conflict. I say they're full of baloney. At any rate, this map of the emotional stages of marriage[4] is not for them; it's for the rest of us.

Some couples move through the stages quickly, others spend years, even decades, in a single stage, while some skip stages altogether. And not all go through the stages of marriage sequentially. Some backslide into a stage they thought they'd left. For sure all married couples, at some point between "I do" and "till death do us part," leave the smooth highway of premarital innocence only to discover that marriage really is very much like a dirt road.

Stage 1: Magnetic Attraction

Stage 1 begins long before the wedding, during courtship. You discover you have fallen in love with the most amazing person on the face of the earth. She is the woman of your dreams; he's everything you've waited for and so much more. You worship the ground she walks on; he's so smart. You are bowled over with fresh passion, raging hormones, and romantic love. Finally, you understand what "soul mate" really means. New love is exciting, overwhelming even. It makes your heart skip a beat. You know beyond any doubt there is nothing the two of you cannot overcome. Your love can and will conquer all.

You make the most exciting decision of your lives, to get married. And why not? You are quite a match. Every day you discover more reasons you are perfect together. You are the romantic equivalent of peanut butter and jelly or chips and salsa. Your happiness fills you with new energy, expectancy, and intense passion. Time ceases to exist when you are together. It drags on interminably when you are apart.

You think each other's thoughts, can finish each other's sentences. You spend hours talking about your dreams, goals, and future. Other than day-to-day spending, money doesn't really come up. It won't be a problem because two can live as cheaply as one. Anyone knows that. By getting married you will effectively double your income because your combined expenses will drop by half (just one example of stage 1 fuzzy math). If things get tight, you'll just get another job, or a better one, or both. Everything will be just fine. Besides, you don't care if you don't have much money as long as you have each other.

You plan the wedding of your dreams. The big day arrives. You say your vows and mean them. Without hesitation, you promise before God and the world to love and honor each other until you are separated by death. With that, you set off on your own Million-Dollar Highway, naively assuming the road will always be this smooth.

Stage 2: Reality's Rude Awakening

Most couples have an encounter with reality sometime after the honeymoon when all the intensity begins to wear off. For some, this happens very soon after; for others, the onset of reality comes weeks or months down the road.

Marriage is a complex relationship that does not reveal itself ahead of time, so most of us don't realize what we are getting into. Bliss fades under the bright light of reality as our shocking differences bubble to the surface. Who is this person I married? He changed! He's thoughtlessly silent; she's so picky—sometimes controlling. You may feel tricked, trapped, and scared. Secretly you ask, "What was I thinking? How did I miss that?"

A subtle but critical shift begins to take place from your stage 1 attitude of "All I want to do is meet your needs" to "What have you done lately to meet my needs?"

During stage 2, there are times of great doubt, confusion, sadness, and frustration as you attempt to regain your balance and adjust to this new life you've chosen with the person you thought you knew so well. It can get very rough. And scary.

You argue about money almost from the start. If it's not the ATM withdrawals, it's the credit card bills or the checkbook balance. You don't have nearly as much money each month as you planned and far more expenses. Rent, utility bills, car payments, groceries, friends' weddings, student loans, birthdays, anniversaries, baby showers, dinners out, Christmas, stuff for the apartment, clothes . . . there's not enough money to go around. You have no idea what to do. You can hardly run to your parents for help. All you know is that you need cash, and you need it now. More credit seems like the only answer.

So what went wrong? Stage 1, while wonderful, was hardly a good indicator of what marriage would be like. Both of you were on your best behavior during your courtship and honeymoon. You showcased yourself in the most favorable light. Stage 1 was one big emotionally charged megadate. As much as you believed you got to know each other, what you revealed was selective. That's not bad. In fact, it's perfectly normal. The problem is you did not know what to expect and how to prepare for the initial steep incline and sharp switchbacks of stage 2.

Stage 3: I Love You; Now Change!

Once the shock of stage 2 wears off, the Spouse Improvement Committee moves into action to fix the marriage and get things back on track. One spouse becomes committee chairperson and sets out to bring the errant spouse around to "my way," which, of course, is the right way. Blame, hurt, and resentment move in where care and respect once resided.

Ironically, it's during stage 3 that couples make important long-term life decisions: to have children, where to live, career decisions, who handles the finances, how the chores are divided. The financial impact during this stage can be enormous because while earning power has not yet peaked, expenses are sharply increasing as the family is in expansion mode.

This is the time many couples buy a home and a couple of SUVs, and feel the pressure to keep up. Add all those constant arguments about money, credit, and debt, and you often end up with one spouse throwing up his or her hands in despair and checking out from any involvement with the family finances. Even more anger, resentment, and blame result, and that only exacerbates an already difficult financial situation. All the conflicts push spouses apart rather than move them more closely together.

Some couples respond to all the difficulties of stage 3 by giving up. They can't take it anymore. Somewhere during this time, they conclude they made a mistake; they've fallen out of love ("I love you; I'm just not in love with you anymore") or cannot handle the conflicts and the horrible financial pressure another day. More than half of those who will eventually call it quits do so before their seventh anniversary.

Stage 4: Surrender and Acceptance

Couples who stick together no matter what, after fifteen or twenty years, eventually reach stage 4. They get tired of fighting and of everything resulting in a conflict. They are wounded and weary. They lay down their arms in a treaty-like manner and just give in. They accept and surrender.

Spouses in stage 4 come to accept the fact that they'll probably never see eye to eye on things. There's really no perfect relationship anyway. They default to accepting each other. Some spouses admit to being worn-out from so many years of nagging, begging, yelling, and trying to change each other. The children are getting older now; the nest is starting to empty. Life mellows, and a new awareness of the preciousness and brevity of life emerges. There is a deep sense that despite their differences they've learned to need each other. This settling down seems to create a climate in which compassion and understanding can begin to emerge.

Unfortunately, by this stage, many couples are reaping the consequences of decades of mismanaging their finances—years of living paycheck to paycheck, using credit to get by, cashing out home equity, spending secretly, and making poor financial choices. Stage 4 couples often find themselves deeply in debt despite decades of dual incomes. It's not unusual for spouses to have split the finances out of pure desperation, resulting in secret debt on one or both sides. Couples at this stage are often behind on preparing for retirement, clueless about where to start and what to do to catch up. Many are helping kids through college and at the same time caring for elderly parents. An undertone of regret mixed with panic best describes their financial situation.

Stage 5: Peace, Harmony, and Romantic Love

You know couples who have reached this final stage of marriage. They are older couples you see or know who are so cute, so devoted to each other. You assume they've been this way since the day they married. While that's a remote possibility, I seriously doubt it. The truth is they hung in through all the seasons of marriage.

Couples who make it to stage 5 often report that the romantic love of their stage 1 youth reappears. But now it is more mature and comes with a strong sense of caring that runs deep and strong due to the effect of time, commitment, and endurance.

That person with whom you fell so deeply in love way back when is the same person to whom you've been married all these years. Back in stage 2, you were sure he or she changed places with a stranger, but now you know differently. This is the person you loved from the start. You have a long, shared history woven from years of trials and pain, joys and successes. Perhaps you've raised a family, walked together through times of grief and despair, and now you have the wisdom that comes with living for many years. Despite your differences and the rough roads you've traveled, time binds you together. You are teammates for life. You have a unique connection. You've come full circle. Nothing short of death will tear you apart.

You Can Reach Stage 5

There you have my interpretation of the marriage map. Sure, it's general, perhaps dramatic. Still, it paints a very real picture of the journey we call marriage.

Now which would you like first . . . the good news or the bad? Let's get the bad out of the way: it's not unusual for couples to be married thirty years or longer before they finally make it to stage 5. Remember, more than half bail out long before they get there.

The good news: no couple has to sit back and just let marriage happen, no matter where they are on the marriage map. Even if you are still on your honeymoon (the mental picture of the two of you reading this while lying on the beach in Hawaii makes me laugh, but I guess anything is possible), you can opt for all the deep satisfaction and emotional connection of stage 5 starting right now.

Can you imagine how wonderful it would be to rear your children and make your major life decisions about where to live, where to work, and how to manage your money with all the joy and harmony of stage 5?

Would you, if you could, blow past the agony of feeling so alone and so isolated? Skip the financial angst and turmoil? Wouldn't you rather not waste so many years yearning for the close, romantic, and loving relationships that you observe and envy in couples you either know or watch from afar? Wouldn't you rather have the wonderful, gooey kind of love of stage 1? Well, guess what. You can have that, and you can have it starting now.

Financial harmony thrives in the environments of stages 1 and 5. That's not too difficult to figure out because it's in those stages that a husband and wife are not repelling each other. They're a team. They're not trying to change each other, they are not distanced by emotional barriers, and they're not fighting all the time. They feel safe and secure.

Those are the conditions under which a couple learns to resolve their money conflicts and move forward with financial harmony. I've seen couples with the most difficult of financial situations pull things out in record time because in spite of those difficulties they enjoyed an intimate relationship. They were already teammates with a single focus and a united commitment. What they lacked was good, logical, and easy-to-understand information about money management like you will find in the second half of this book.

I've also seen couples with substantial financial assets and solid personal finance knowledge fail horribly because they were so polarized emotionally that financial harmony didn't have a prayer.

Regardless of how long you've been married or where you are on the journey, you can get to stage 5 now. You don't have to wait thirty or forty years . . . or even two. You can head for stage 5 right now. You're not going to get a free pass; there will be a price to pay in terms of hard work. Successful, intimate marriage requires both spouses to become skilled in learning how to care for the person they promised to love and cherish for a lifetime. And even if you believe the love you once had has died, there's still hope. That love is still there. It may be barricaded behind walls of resentment, anger, failed trust, unfulfilled expectations, and unsevered ties from parents. I want to help you rediscover what you experienced in stage 1 so you can quickly find the joy and intense pleasure you once knew . . . and financial harmony in the process.

4

The Currency of Life

Why Money Is Hard for Couples

Get wisdom. Though it cost all you have, get understanding. . . .
Why should fools have money in hand to buy wisdom, when they
are not able to understand it?

Proverbs 4:7; 17:16

The phone rings. You pick it up and hear your husband say,
"Honey, do you know what day this is? Seven years ago to-
night we got engaged. Let's go out for dinner and a movie to
celebrate!"

Long ago, in what seems like another time and place, you
fell in love with this man because he was both spontaneous and
sentimental. Now when he asks you out for a date, the first words
out of your mouth are, "Are you crazy? We don't have money
for that!"

Of course, your calculator-like mind is whipping through the figures: $40 for a babysitter, assuming you can find one at this late hour; $100 for dinner because he'll insist on a "nice" restaurant; $35 for a movie if you share popcorn and a soda. That's $175 you don't have to spend right now.

All week long you scrimp and do without, but does he even notice? Or care? Apparently not. While he's off in the big adult world enjoying his job, you're at home with laundry, dirty dishes, kids, and bills. Doesn't he know the mortgage is due next week, the Visa bill is a month late, your daughter's birthday party is two weeks from Tuesday, and the washing machine is just one spin cycle away from a total meltdown? Sure, you have a few bucks in the bank, but you've been counting on that money for a weekend away with your girlfriends—something you haven't had a chance to tell him yet. With all the financial stress you're under, how can he think about dinner and a movie?

He's hurt because you come across as cold and distant. You're hurt because he is insensitive and uncaring. Both of you think this is about money. You believe with all your heart that if you won the lottery none of this would be a problem. And you are wrong. Money problems are rarely about money only. They are mixed up with issues of self-worth, fear, and power. And until the two of you learn how to manage these aspects of your relationship, more money will only mean bigger problems.

Money exposes the differences in our personalities, the ways we were brought up, our money beliefs, and our goals. The way we think about money and what we do with it reflect what we believe about it. But money issues are buried so deeply in our emotions that it is often difficult to know what we believe or where our money attitudes came from. And if you don't know a lot about yourself, it's likely you know even less about your spouse.

Of all the issues in your marriage, money has the greatest potential to ruin your relationship. That's the bad news. The good news is that knowledge is power, and learning why money is so difficult will help you make a huge leap toward financial harmony.

When you were single, you dealt with one set of values, beliefs, and life views: yours. You didn't have to discuss your financial situation, decisions, or mistakes with anyone. You were free to live in denial if you wanted to. You did what you wanted, the way you wanted, when you wanted. Your money situation, whether pathetic or prosperous, was your secret. But now you're part of a team. It's no longer my money, your money, your student loans, my debt. It's our income, our mortgage, our pension, our future. Everything—the assets and the liabilities, the good and the bad—is "ours" now.

You kissed the single life good-bye, but it's possible you've hung on to your old money ways and attitudes. To complicate matters, you married someone who is not like you and who may also be hanging on to a lifetime of money attitudes—managing methods, financial secrets, habits, goals, and beliefs. When you think about it in these terms, it's not difficult to understand why money causes problems for so many couples.

It would be foolish to say that money is a commodity of exchange and nothing more. Money is emotional, tangible, and useful. Money is indispensable. It is the currency of stuff, but it is also the currency of life.

Money determines where you live, what you drive, where your children grow up, and where they go to school. Money dictates how you spend your time. Money is God's protection on you and your family. Money puts a roof over your head. It protects you from hunger and says you don't have to walk around naked. Money is about the basics of life, and it is important. But it has its limits.

Money cannot heal a child with a terminal disease; it cannot fill an empty soul. Money cannot buy happiness or deep and lasting fulfillment. Money cannot fix a broken heart.

Why Is Money So Hard?

Why is money so hard? I've asked myself this question a lot. When I was single, I thought I knew the answer. Money was hard because I didn't have a husband to take care of it for me. I found the solution to my dilemma, but before we could celebrate our first wedding anniversary, I was back to asking the same question.

Over the years I've made some discoveries, communicated with countless couples, and researched what the experts have to say. Here are the most common reasons why money is so difficult for couples.

Personalities and Temperaments

Knowing your personality types can be helpful in understanding your individual behaviors. Much has been written and theorized about the subject as far back as 450 BC, when a fellow named Hippocrates observed four dispositions he called "temperaments": the popular and impulsive sanguine, the perfect and emotionally sensitive melancholic, the powerful and passionate choleric, and the peaceful and impersonal phlegmatic.

That all held pretty well until 1522, when Paracelsus came along and simplified things by describing the four temperaments as changeable, industrious, inspired, and curious. In 1947, Erich Fromm described the four temperaments as exploitative, hoarding, receptive, and marketing. One animal-loving, modern-day interpretation categorizes us as otters, lions, golden retrievers, and beavers.[1] If you become a serious student of personality/temperaments, you'll discover designations such as sensor-perceivers, intuitive-thinkers, sensor-judgers, and intuitive-feelers;[2] concrete-pragmatist, abstract-pragmatist, concrete-cooperator, and abstract-cooperator.[3] All of this can get very complicated and quite intimidating.

I find the differences in our money personalities to be far simpler. I boil them down to this two-part theory:

52

1. There are two money personalities: spenders and savers.
2. The typical marriage has one of each.

There. That's it. Clean and simple.

The designation of saver or spender refers primarily to a person's attitude about money. A saver doesn't necessarily have a big savings account, nor is a spender always shopping, although that would make both types very happy. Let me explain.

Savers are not generally eager to spend money. Given the choice of spending or saving, they are more likely to opt for the latter. Savers hesitate, drag their feet, and if they cannot avoid spending, look for the cheapest way out. Savers are aware of how much things cost, look for coupons, and reach for the store brand when they have a choice. Savers live with the possibility of a rainy day on their minds. Savers sleep best when they have money in the bank. The thought of overdrawing a bank account makes savers uneasy. Savers are reluctant to apply for credit and when they do are eager to pay the balance in full every month. For savers, the minimum payment option on a credit card balance is unacceptable. Savers see a sale as a way to spend less money. Savers tend to be somewhat pessimistic, so they tend to be cautious with money.

Spenders, on the other hand, are carefree with money. They are optimistic and daring. Because they assume there'll be more where this came from and everything will work out in the end, spenders believe it's okay to spend all they have now plus whatever they can get their hands on in terms of credit. Spenders are more fun loving when it comes to money. They operate on some version of the belief that if there are checks in the checkbook, there must be money in the bank. To spenders, available credit is the same as income. Spenders don't look at account balances. It's easier to assume that everything is okay. Spenders believe that if banks, stores, and credit card companies approve them for more credit, they must be able to afford it. Spenders don't usually worry much about how they will repay the debt. Somehow, they reason, it will all work out in the end. Spenders see a sale as a way to get more stuff, not as a way to spend less money. They justify purchases because they "save" so much money buying things on sale.

Spenders and savers come in varying degrees of intensity. In the extreme, a saver becomes a hoarder, going to ridiculous lengths to save not only money but also stuff. A hoarder builds big bank accounts while living like a pauper. Saving in the extreme indicates a mental or pathological disorder. Likewise, spending can be taken to the extreme where the spender cannot stop. Severe debt, embezzling, and theft are the spender's extremes, leading to the ruin of marriages, families, and lives.

In a healthy marriage, the saver-spender combination creates balance. Spouses keep each other from going to extremes. The spender husband is thankful every day that his saver wife is so good with money. She is diligent to see that they have money put away for the proverbial rainy day. He admires the way she can stretch the family income by using all kinds of cost-saving techniques. The saver wife knows that without her husband's optimism they'd probably not have the nice things she enjoys. He encourages her to enjoy their blessings and the income they have. He's more carefree, and that keeps her from going off the deep end.

But put a saver and a spender together in an unhealthy marriage, and watch the fireworks. The spender wife hates the saver husband's attitude about spending, so she spends in secret. He has his secret accounts and hopes she never finds out. It's an outright civil war every time the credit card statements show up in the mail. She uses the ATM like a slot machine and never records the transactions. Their opposite money personalities do nothing but push them farther apart. They argue about money all the time and blame their problems on the fact that they are so different, when the real problem is that neither one of them is getting from the other what they want so badly. Money becomes the scapegoat for all the hidden issues in their marriage.

Money Is Personal

Renee was so excited to tell me about her engagement. "He's wonderful," she bubbled. "But I'm concerned about money." She went on to tell me that she'd read several of my books and, using the principles and methods, was well on her way to becoming debt-free. How should she handle this issue of money once they were married?

I asked her to tell me more about their financial situations. How much does he earn? Have you traded credit reports? Does he have savings? Is he a giver? Does he have credit card debt? Student loans? She just kept repeating the same answer: "I don't know." Trying a different approach, I asked if he knew all those things about her. Sheepishly, she answered, "No."

She shared what she knew, and believe me, it wasn't much. She had, in fact, more concerns than information and indicated she had reason to believe he might have a checkered financial past. Perhaps a bankruptcy, possibly collections and charge-offs. The solution was clear to me: ask him! She said she just couldn't do that.

"Do you love this guy?"

"Oh yes! I'm certain this is the man for me. He's perfect."

"How's your communication?"

"The best! We talk about everything. We have so much in common. We plan to have kids. He wants me to be a stay-at-home mom . . ." The list went on and on.

In an attempt to clear things up for myself as well as hold up a mirror for her to take a look, I said, "So are you telling me that you are going to marry him, share your heart and soul, share his life, share his bed, bear his children, and grow old together?"

"Oh yes." She blushed. (I think I said "get naked" somewhere in there, thus the blush.)

I went on, "But you cannot ask to see his credit report, how much money he makes, and how much debt he has?"

"I could never do that," she replied. "That would be too personal."

I asked her if there was any other area of their lives too personal to share. She couldn't think of anything else, just this one subject: money.

I had only a few minutes with her, and I spent it helping her to see this matter as one of the most important to their future. Without opening the financial books and determining early on how they would manage their money together, they would be setting themselves up for a ride much rockier than it need be.

Like most couples, Renee and her fiancé, Jim, are quite opposite, thus their attraction. But unlike their other differences, the way they think about money has created a barrier in their communication. She's secretly worried that he's a spendthrift, that her financially irresponsible husband-to-be may destroy her good credit rating once they are married. She's worked so hard to pay off her debts and accumulate a savings account. Now there exists the possibility that she'll have to assume his debts and that he'll squander what she's worked hard to accumulate. She's terrified to find out the truth about his financial condition.

I gave her a quick rundown of what they needed to accomplish before their big day and a few suggestions for how she could break the ice. Number one on the list was to start talking. I left her with an ominous warning: if you don't tear down this barrier that stands between the two of you now, it will grow into a brick wall that will keep you from enjoying full intimacy in the future. I finished by telling her that this issue topples half of all marriages and most of them before the seventh anniversary.

As children, didn't we learn never to talk about money? It is rude, our parents explained, to ask how much things cost or how much money a grown-up has. Annual incomes are top secret information even within families. It's a cultural thing, I suppose—part of proper etiquette and good manners.

I can understand how Jim and Renee got this far in their relationship without talking about money. Perhaps Jim does have a lot of debt. Maybe he has a lousy-paying job. It's embarrassing. Maybe the guy's really wealthy and is the type to keep his private matters close to the vest. I think this expectation of our culture contributes to the difficulty many spouses have talking about money. So they avoid the subject, thinking it will come up later, after they are married and that happily-ever-after thing kicks in. I don't think Jim thought he was hiding anything from Renee. He just didn't know how to talk about it and perhaps believed he was expressing love by not bothering her with it.

Financial Ignorance

Amazingly, most adults are fairly ignorant of the basics of money management and personal finance. My experience has been that the typical adult in this country doesn't have a basic working knowledge of effective spending, saving, consumer credit, credit reports, and credit scores. Most cannot articulate sound principles for managing a paycheck, the type and amount of insurance to carry, how to get out of debt rapidly, the pros and cons of paying off a mortgage, and so on. Simply not knowing how to manage a family's income in this world of raging consumerism and easy credit can wreak havoc on a marriage and make things far more difficult than they should be.

Family History

The way your parents handled money during your childhood may have a lot to do with the way you think about money today. Some would even suggest your birth order plays a role. Since money management has never been a core subject in school, what most of us knew going into adulthood we learned from observation and emulation. And depending on other elements and influences, you might have unconsciously embraced what you saw or rebelled against it.

Let's say you grew up in a warm and loving home where your father handled all the money behind closed doors. You didn't actually see him pay bills, and you never understood much more than he went to work every day and complained from time to time that money didn't grow on trees. Your mom cooked great meals, kept a spotless house, and was always waiting for you after school with warm cookies and milk.

Now you are married. You assume you will work for a living and pay the bills, and your wife, like your mother, will see that everything runs smoothly at home. Your mom didn't work, so why should your wife? Your mom never got involved in the finances, so why should your wife? Your mom never complained about money, so why does your wife? Without something to jog your memory and prompt you to think through the way you grew up, you could easily live with a huge disconnect between assumption and reality.

This can go the other way too. Say you grew up in a very stressful single-parent home. Your father, an alcoholic, abandoned you when you were very young, leaving your mother with the entire burden of raising a family. She worked a couple jobs. You as the oldest child were forced into the role of a quasi-parent for the younger children. A lack of money played into every thought, every action, and every conversation. Every month when the bills came due, your mother would sit at the kitchen table ranting, raving, and weeping. You worried every day about going to foster care or the poor house, whatever that was. In the privacy of your own thoughts, you determined that when you grew up, you would never live like this. Your children would never know the pain of poverty.

You marry; you have children. Your childhood memories keep you forever moving in the opposite direction of your childhood so you won't fall into the same patterns. Every move you make with money and your marriage is a direct reaction to what you knew as a child.

Family history and childhood perceptions about money and finances are subjects that couples rarely, if ever, discuss prior to marriage. That's because we don't think much about them even though they are always there. The perceptions are stored away in our minds right along with memories of kindergarten and learning to ride a two-wheeler. Before we know it, our marriages are precariously based on faulty memories and preconceived notions.

Many of the couples I have interviewed over the years responded with a blank look when I asked, "What was your perception of the money management style of the home in which you grew up, and did you assume your role would mirror your father's/mother's when you married and had your own family?" After the blank look, the response was overwhelmingly the same: "I never really thought about it, but I wish I had."

While your parents might not have intentionally taught you about money, what you observed had a large influence on how you handle it. Your money memories influence your attitudes until at some point you choose to either confirm them as true and useful or replace them.

Money Myths

As useful and necessary as money is to our lives, there's another side to money—the side that lies and leads people into its ruinous and destructive traps.

Author Ray Linder says there are six fallacies that plague the thinking of many Americans:

1. Achievement: Money says that I do things well.
2. Freedom: Money says that I can have what I want when I want.
3. Respect: Money says that people like me.
4. Power: Money says that I am in charge of my life.

5. Security: Money says that I will always be safe.

6. Happiness: Money says that I enjoy myself.[4]

There is enough truth in these statements for them to be credible. We could easily find real-life examples of people who have achieved great things and have money to show for it. There are plenty of wealthy people who seem to have options in life that many of us do not. And I am sure that there are wealthy people who are authentically happy. Where myth plays into all these examples is that money does not play a primary role. There are just as many people who have all these things but do not have great sums of money.

Achievement

It is a common belief that success and wealth go together—that money proves achievement. And why not? Everywhere we turn the world confirms this misguided notion. We think wealthy people are happier and that somehow money is a reward for goodness. It is so easy to fall into the trap of equating poverty with evil and prosperity with good. Subconsciously, we see poor people as lazy and lacking intelligence.

If you believe that wealth proves success, you are going to run into real trouble if you go through a season of financial difficulty. You will have to deny, cover up, lie about, and hide the problem because having no money would surely mean you are lazy, unsuccessful, and undeserving of approval.

Freedom

If you've ever watched late-night-television get-rich-quick financial gurus and their infomercials, you've heard the promises of financial freedom. I'm not talking about freedom from debt. The "freedom" they peddle says that with enough money you will no longer have any limitations or restrictions in your life. This myth promises that money can fix any problem and therefore make your life perfect.

Respect

This money myth says that money can command or buy respect, love, and approval. The truth is that when we go on a never-ending quest to please others, trying to win their approval through buying and giving, we are reflecting our own feelings of unworthiness. We desperately want others to approve of and love us to fill up the huge void left by our inability to find approval within ourselves.

It's fascinating to follow the lives of people who have come into instant wealth via a lottery or some other kind of financial windfall. Newly found friends and loved ones come right out of the woodwork! And sure, in the beginning it appears that money can buy friendship and even love, but wait and see how many of these dear friends remain once the money is gone. Money cannot buy love, friendship, or respect. To believe otherwise is to believe a lie.

Power

This money myth says that money equals power, and if you have enough power, you can win every conflict because you will have control over people and circumstances. In truth, the way to have power is not to manipulate and control people but to serve them. "Money's greatest power is unleashed when we use it cooperatively not competitively," says Linder.[5]

Security

This myth, that money can make us secure, contains a great deal of truth. There is no doubt that we need to be prepared to handle future needs by building a nest egg or emergency fund. And there is a feeling of security to be found in certain types of insurance. But relying on money to fix all life's unknown and unexpected circumstances is foolish. In this life, there is pain and suffering. No matter how much money we have socked away, we cannot control our financial futures. That is why we need to have faith that God cares about our welfare and will take care of us through the good times and the bad.

Happiness

There is no doubt that money and the things it can buy give us moments and seasons of pleasure. And for those living below the poverty level, money can relieve a great deal of daily stress, such as being cold or hungry. But studies have proven that once our basic needs are met, more money does not result in more happiness. There is a point at which more money complicates life far more than it enhances it. Satisfying relationships, not more money, are what fulfill our needs and bring us lasting happiness.

Money has its place in our lives, and when used responsibly, it can certainly bring a great deal of satisfaction. That kind of satisfaction is much deeper than simple happiness, which comes and goes depending on how much money we have at any given time.

Barriers to Financial Harmony

Invisible forces can create barriers between spouses that make money a difficult—if not impossible—topic. These barriers are a lot like glue-laminated beams.

The next time you're in Sam's Club or Costco, look up. Those huge beams that span the width of the store hold up the roof and are known as glulams. A glulam is quite an ingenious invention. It is a series of thin pieces of wood glued together with industrial-grade wood glue. One of those layers alone is so weak it would be considered quite fragile in the world of industrial construction. However, the accumulation of many layers interspersed with glue results in a beam far stronger than any single piece of lumber of the same dimensions.

Unresolved conflicts are like the layers of a glulam beam. Just one of those conflicts may be fairly weak. However, when allowed to accumulate, these layers, held together by blame, resentment, and anger, can become a barrier of considerable proportion.

Barriers are the enemies of financial harmony because they come between spouses and prevent them from having the kind of open and honest relationship that is necessary for financial harmony to develop.

Issues of Entitlement

Something significant happened in America in the 1970s. The consumer credit industry exploded with the advent of bank cards and relaxed qualification standards for consumer credit. Americans were encouraged to ignore their limited incomes by assuming higher levels of installment (auto, furniture, appliances) and revolving (bank, retail credit card) debt. Consumption patterns changed as Mr. and Mrs. Mid-America discovered they were entitled to far more than they could afford on their measly incomes. Americans' attitudes went from surprise they could consume beyond their ability to pay to expecting that it should be so.

Some years ago PBS produced a documentary on this subject. The title: *Affluenza*. Through revealing personal stories, expert commentary, hilarious old film clips, dramatized vignettes, and anticommercial breaks, *Affluenza* examined the high cost of achieving the most extravagant lifestyle the world has ever seen.[6]

Overindulged children often bring their attitudes of entitlement into adulthood. Conversely, children who grow up feeling financially deprived can also arrive at the front door of marriage determined that now they can have it all and are entitled to it, especially if they believe their spouse is the ticket to having it all.

Unrealistic attitudes of entitlement contribute greatly to a couple's money issues. Invariably, the spender will jump on the opportunity to overspend, while the saver will balk. The pull of monetary entitlement can drive a huge wedge between spouses.

Infidelity

It's not what you're thinking, although being sexually unfaithful to your spouse could certainly create one industrial-strength barrier to financial harmony. I'm talking about financial infidelity, which is the subject of many letters I receive.

Dear Mary,

Is there any hope for my situation? I have run up more than $75,000 of unsecured debt. My husband doesn't know, and I will never be able to tell him. It takes my entire payroll just to make the payments on this debt, and it seems like I'm getting nowhere with it. What can I do? I don't want to file for bankruptcy, but I'm beginning to think this is my only way out. Please help me.

While not all financial infidelity is as serious as $75,000 of secret debt, money secrets between spouses can grow into barriers of serious proportion. Money secrets destroy trust.

My standard response to letters such as the one above is this:

Imagine for a moment that it's not you but your spouse who wrote to me. How do you want me to respond? Shall I tell him to just keep quiet and do the best he can so you never find out? Or would you want me to plead with him to confess with total remorse and a willingness to make things right?

No one has responded that they'd like me to advise their spouse to keep quiet. Just thinking about the situation in those terms helps the letter writer see what must be done.

Because financial infidelity is such a pervasive problem these days, I'm going to interject right here the steps I offer to anyone in this situation.

Acknowledge the offense for what it is: betrayal and deceit. Financial infidelity is not occasionally forgetting to record a check or an ATM transaction. Financial infidelity is consciously and deliberately lying to your spouse about money, credit, and/or debt. Tell it like it is, and don't argue, justify, or debate the issue.

Show remorse. Your spouse needs to know that you are truly, sincerely sorry for what you have done. You probably can't apologize often enough. Authentic remorse doesn't include "Yes, but . . ." or any other attempts to justify your actions. True remorse says, "I was wrong, and I am sorry."

Understand. Remorse, as necessary as it is, doesn't take away the pain, but it does put the recovery process in motion. Understand your spouse may need time to process.

Promise change. If you can honestly say you are now committed to total financial honesty, let your spouse know in no uncertain terms that this is your plan.

Share details. Your spouse has every right to know the full extent of your financial indiscretions as well as your specific plans for recovery.

Offer reassurance. Even though you have decided to reform, your spouse may still react for some time. This is normal, and you owe it to your partner and yourself to bend over backward to prove your trustworthiness. Your first reassurance needs to be that this activity has stopped. Then understand that the rebuilding of trust takes time.

Commit yourself fully. One of the keys to financial harmony is mutual respect and accountability. Let your spouse know that you are 100 percent committed to this program.

Consider counseling. There are times, although rare, that a spending problem signals something much deeper, such as addiction or serious depression. If you suspect this may be true, you should seek professional help from a qualified therapist who specializes in such disorders.

For many couples, the disclosure of money secrets serves as a wake-up call that moves them to begin to address the underlying issues in their marriage.

Unresolved Anger

Anger is not bad or evil. Anger is an emotion that is a mask for hurt or fear. It is a normal response to an unsatisfied hunger. We get angry when we feel threatened or when some value we hold dear is violated. Sometimes we throw a tantrum for selfish reasons, which is a terrible waste of energy and should be dealt with immediately. Other times we get angry because something good and right has been transgressed. Clearly, it's not the anger that is the problem but rather what we do with it. We have two choices.

Stuff it. Several years ago I was in San Francisco to appear on a local television show. The producer asked me to bring props to demonstrate some of the tips that appear in the Debt-Proof Living newsletter. I like to go for the dramatic, so I bought a ten-pound box of baking soda and a gallon of vinegar.

I arrived the night before and checked into one of San Francisco's historical hotels. Since the containers were just props, I decided to empty the contents of the box and bottle.

I dumped the baking soda into the toilet and flushed. I knew that wouldn't be a problem. It's a natural, biodegradable product. Then I poured the gallon of vinegar down the toilet.

Several hours later Old Faithful visited my room. A fountain of amazing proportion shot right out of the commode and into the air. Once it calmed down and gurgled to a stop, all the sewer gases from under the city of San Francisco came forth, driving me and other hotel guests into the hallways. The hotel engineer came to assess the situation. All he could say was that whatever had been clogging the hotel drains for quite some time had finally let loose. Ironically, and to my total chagrin, one of the tips I would share the following day was how to clear a sluggish drain with none other than baking soda, vinegar, and boiling water. Had I known they were having plumbing problems, I could've come sooner! And while I had to believe the engineer was grateful, I was far too embarrassed to take any credit.

Anger is like the stuff I flushed down the toilet. You think that once you've stuffed it so far away you cannot see it, it's gone, over, done. But pushing anger down is the worst possible thing you can do with it. You don't know what other stuffed angers it will team up with. Repressed anger has the potential to do terrible damage to your health (physical and mental), your marriage, and your family. It's like ten pounds of baking soda and a gallon of vinegar collaborating somewhere in the plumbing of that hotel. You might not be able to see it or feel it, but it is active nonetheless. Unresolved anger can cause illness and bitterness. It can grow and multiply, and it can destroy marriages. Therapists' offices are filled with people whose stuffed anger turned to toxic waste and bubbled to the surface.

Ventilate it. Talking things out, praying, and confronting the issues behind the anger are the ways to dissolve it. It takes a lot of restraint and skill to have a constructive angry talk—not a fight—to disarm anger. If you understand that most anger comes from trying to change another person and that you cannot change anyone but yourself, you can use your anger as a catalyst to submit yourself for change.

Not all unresolved anger is new or fresh. You may be hauling a load of unresolved anger that goes way back, possibly premarriage, even preadulthood. I am not a therapist and certainly not qualified to counsel you beyond suggesting there is help available to assist you in identifying and dealing with unresolved anger.

Unrealistic Expectations

People come to marriage with illusions of what things will be like. I had illusions of remarkable wealth. Illusions unrealized can quickly turn to disillusions and then to barriers. Here are some examples.

Just like mom and dad. It's not unusual for couples to come to marriage assuming their mates will fulfill all the good things they saw in their parents. A husband, for example, may assume that since his mother cooked and cleaned all day, his wife will do the same thing. Or if the wife's dad handled all the finances and never wanted her mom to worry about a thing, she may have those kinds of expectations about how her marriage will work. When these illusions turn to disillusions, barriers go up and spouses have a difficult time forgiving the other for not being their parent.

Married singles. I hear from so many people who've made the assumption that they can keep their financial lives separate and still have an intimate marriage. It all starts with a prenuptial agreement, then the decision to maintain separate checking accounts while sharing expenses. That's an illusion that lasts about as long as it takes one spouse to lose a job or run into some other financial snag. Resentment begins to build (it's not fair that I have to pay half the rent when he makes twice the salary!), and soon a barrier grows. A healthy marriage provides for the pooling of all resources, has a system of checks and balances, and provides security for long-term investment.

Dual-income lifestyle, one-income family. Many couples enter marriage with the expectation of the wife staying at home once the children come along. In the meantime, they gear up their lives with the big house, the furniture, the cars, and all the trappings of a modern-day have-it-all family. Baby number one shows up about the same time reality sets in that a single paycheck cannot possibly support this lifestyle.

Broken Trust

In their book *The Case for Marriage*, authors Linda J. Waite and Maggie Gallagher say, "Every kind of partnership fosters opportunities for specialization and exchange, economies of scale and even social support. But the marriage partnership is even more productive than most because it is fueled by a magic ingredient: trust."[7]

Spouses expect to trust each other—financially, sexually, and emotionally. Stealing and dishonesty are things they need to watch for in the outside world but certainly not within this intimate arrangement known as marriage.

Whenever this trust account is violated (one or the other spouse makes a "withdrawal"), the choice is to either resolve the issue or let it begin to grow into a major barrier. Layer upon layer of broken trust can push spouses far apart and do terrible damage to their marriage.

No matter the barrier, if it is standing in the way of your having an open and deeply honest marriage, it needs to be identified. And then it's time to schedule a demolition party. But how do you do that? Ah, my dear friend, read on!

5

News Flash:
You Are Different

His Needs Are Not Her Needs

Marriage is more a process of learning the dance rather than finding the right dancer.

Paul Pearsall, *The Heart's Code*

Brace yourself; this may come as a huge shock: you are different. Yes, one of you is a woman, the other a man. Right there are enough differences to prompt one well-known expert to suggest that you not only don't speak the same language but also don't come from the same planet!

It always makes me laugh to read a study that turns up yet more evidence that indeed men are different from women. Do we really need more evidence? Men and women are different by the design of the Creator. It was God's plan to make us different from the moment he imagined us. God created man, and because he saw how incomplete and lonely he was, he created a woman to fulfill man's basic human need for intimacy and relationship.

Take our brains, for example. The male brain is on average approximately 10 percent larger than the female brain.[1] But the female brain has more nerve cells. This means that unlike our husbands, who use only one side of their brains at a time, we ladies are able to use both the right and the left sides simultaneously.[2] I know that's a trivial bit of information, but I happen to like it a lot.

Not to be outdone by the medical research community, automobile researchers have determined that men are more aggressive than women when they drive sports cars and light trucks, whereas women are more aggressive than men when they drive SUVs and luxury cars.[3] Go figure.

Men, on average, are willing to take greater financial risks than women.[4] Within relationships, women resolve the day-to-day issues, while men settle the life-changing disputes.[5]

Women typically express their feelings and thoughts better than men and are often irritated by their husbands' reticence. Dr. James Dobson says that God may have given a wife 50,000 words per day and her husband only 25,000. He comes home with 24,976 used and merely grunts his way through the evening. He may descend into *Monday Night Football*, while his wife is dying to expend her remaining 25,000 words.[6]

Women ask more questions—no surprise there. What may surprise you, however, is that men make more than three-fourths of interruptions in conversations.[7]

Authors Bill and Pam Farrel summarize the gender differences this way: Men are like waffles; women are like spaghetti.[8] A waffle, they explain, is a collection of boxes separated by walls. The boxes are all separate holding places. That is typically how a man processes life—one box for one issue and one issue at a time. One aspect of his life goes in one box, another in the next box, and so on. Issues do not intersect or relate. When a man is at work, he's at work. When he is in the garage tinkering, he's in the garage tinkering. When he is watching television, he's watching television. That's why a man can ignore everything going on around him. He's not choosing to be annoying in that way; it's the way he was created. One box at a time. Social scientists call this compartmentalizing—putting life and responsibilities into different compartments.

This makes men problem solvers by nature. They enter the box, size up the situation, and come up with a solution. The Farrels conclude that men feel best about themselves when they are solving problems. This is why men spend most of their time doing what they are best at, while they attempt to ignore the things that cause them to feel deficient.

Spaghetti, on the other hand, is a lot of individual noodles that all touch one another. When it is piled on a plate, not a single strand stands alone. Each noodle intersects with a lot of other noodles. If you were to follow one, you could switch to another noodle quite seamlessly. That's how women face life. Every thought and issue is connected to every other thought and issue in some way. Life is much more of a process for women than it is for men. This is why women can do lots of things at the same time. Speaking for myself, I find it perfectly normal to talk on the phone, fold laundry, and keep an eye on dinner all at the same time. The Farrels say that because all their thoughts, emotions, and convictions are connected, women are able to process more information and keep track of more activities. And why not? We have the ability to engage both sides of our brains at the same time.

While our personalities and temperaments color who we are as individuals, gender plays a much larger role in making money difficult for couples. We reason differently, and we have different genetically based methods for solving problems and looking at situations.

Three Distinct Parts

Every man and woman has by design of our Creator three distinct parts, each of which has its own distinct need for fulfillment: emotional, spiritual, and physical. If we ignore any one of these, or attempt to satisfy them inappropriately, we become confused and needy and forever search for fulfillment. For example, you can feed your emotional needs with hot fudge sundaes all day long, but you will never find emotional satisfaction. Nor will working out five hours a day, six days a week ever satisfy your deep spiritual needs.

Emotional

Every person has an inborn need for loving relationships. Research has shown that happiness and contentment in life are strongly affected by the quality of our relationships, especially marital and family relationships. Based on ten years of research that went into their book *The Case for Marriage*, Linda J. Waite and Maggie Gallagher concluded that, on average, people gain tremendous advantages and happiness by having and investing in long-term relationships. All the money in the world cannot take the place of meaningful, personal relationships.

Spiritual

Every one of us is created with what some have characterized as a "God-shaped hole" in our hearts that only he can fill. I believe that the God of the universe, in an incredible act of love and a desire to relate personally to the people he created, told us all about himself in the Bible. He is perfect in character and nature and the source of all that is true. If you are attempting to fill your spiritual needs with human relationships or with money, you will be left feeling empty, unsatisfied, and unfulfilled. Those things will never fit, and you will be left with a gaping void that cries out to be filled. God's love, which fills our spiritual needs perfectly, is proactive. He pursues us and offers us what is best for us—self-worth, peace, joy, and contentment. Money promises to give us worth and meaning but leaves us empty and spiritually unsatisfied.

Physical

Just as we have emotional and spiritual needs, we have physical needs too. This is where money comes in—to fulfill our needs for shelter, food, and comfort. I'm the first to admit that I thoroughly enjoy working hard to earn a living, and I enjoy spending money like most anybody else. Wealth is good. Financial security is crucial. We should not be opposed to work or money. But money needs to have its proper place in our lives.

Our Deep Emotional Needs

While I'm sure you know that you and your spouse both have deep emotional needs, you may be unaware just how different those needs are.

If you are a man, you were born with all kinds of male characteristics. They're in your genes. Some of them are physical characteristics that affirm you are male; others are emotional. Had you arrived on this earth with an instruction manual, high on the list of "Things I Need Most to Meet My Deep Emotional Needs" would have been a single word: *respect*.

I wouldn't be surprised if you've never thought about that in such specific terms until right now. I know without a doubt that because you are a man, it makes you feel good when someone you care about lets you know they respect and admire you. Trusting you enough to leave you alone and not remind, nag, or otherwise check up on you is one of the best ways a person can show you respect.

If you are a woman, you were born with all kinds of female characteristics. Some are physical, others emotional. And I can guarantee that leaving you alone as a way of expressing respect doesn't even make it into the manual, let alone on the list of "Things I Need Most." High on your list is affection, which for a woman means any nonsexual expression of love that says you are important to me; I will care for you and protect you.

So far, so good. But it's at this point that things start to go sideways. A woman, unaware that her husband's emotional needs are not the same as her needs, instinctively gives her husband what she wants, while he gives her what men want, emotionally speaking. Both mistakenly assume that the other has the same needs and desires. So when his needs go unmet because she is giving him what she wants, and her needs go unmet because he is giving her what he wants, both find themselves dissatisfied, resentful, and frustrated.

At first, the results are minor and completely unintentional. But as these needs continually go unmet, conflicts arise and accumulate. Spouses begin to repel rather than attract. They begin to move apart.

I was anxious to do for my husband what I wanted him to do for me. I didn't have a clue that what I wanted most from him was not the same thing he wanted from me. I thought I was being loving when I asked a lot of caring questions and expressed concern for all the details of his life because that's what I wanted so badly from him. For example, I was very generous with my expert driving instructions and pointed out potential hazards, believing with all my heart this was a loving and kind thing to do. Now I know that I might as well have been continually poking him in the eye with a sharp stick because my actions were screaming to him how much I didn't respect, admire, or trust him to get me to our destination.

So how was he responding to my needs? He was not asking lots of caring questions and expressing concern for all the details of my life. I know now that he thought he was being loving by offering to me the thing he wanted most—no questions. It's like we were both stumbling around in the dark, each of us without a clue how to care for the one we promised to love and cherish throughout life.

Perhaps you've seen a creature called a sea anemone. I think every dentist's office has at least one in its waiting room aquarium. When the conditions are favorable, the anemone opens and shows its beautiful, brightly colored flowerlike form. Gorgeous! But when something pricks it, even in a seemingly insignificant way, it gets all annoyed and closes tightly into something that looks like a lump of jelly. That's a picture of how quickly and effectively we can close our spouse's spirit. And I have to admit it comes much more naturally for me to push my husband's close-up buttons than to make sure I'm creating conditions that make him happy, open, and approachable.

Conflict between Spouses

Marital conflict is created in one of two ways: (1) we fail to make each other happy, or (2) we make each other unhappy.[9]

The first way is passive—we don't consciously meet our spouse's emotional needs because it's just easier not to or, more likely, we don't know how. The second is aggressive—we make a conscious decision to irritate, annoy, and otherwise push our spouse to turn away and shut down emotionally.

What does all this have to do with creating financial harmony and debt-proofing your marriage? Effective money management requires teamwork. It takes two individuals who are ready, willing, and able to participate harmoniously. If spouses are repelling each other, there is little hope they will find the common ground and appropriate atmosphere necessary to make harmony happen. Financial harmony exists when a couple is growing together, not growing apart. Financial harmony occurs when spouses are pulling together toward a common goal, not when they are heading in opposite directions, doing all they can to make each other unhappy.

I know this may sound overly simplistic, but what I am about to tell you is absolutely true. If you are serious about creating financial harmony in your marriage, you must be emotionally open to each other. You may already know what that means, but then again you may not.

The "I" Word

Every person has an emotional center, a very private place that is deep within. It's where our most private thoughts are kept, our most vulnerable feelings, all those things that are deeply personal. To allow your spouse access to that place and vice versa is to experience intimacy, and I'm not talking about sex or even physical attraction. Intimacy is a deep emotional connection to this person you promised to love forever. Intimacy is the advanced version of what you felt and experienced back in stage 1, and it's critical for the development of financial harmony in your marriage.

Intimacy is the freedom and confidence two people enjoy when they are completely vulnerable and exposed in both psyche and spirit without any fear of rejection and without being ashamed. Intimacy is an emotional safety zone. Spouses need to know they have a place in their relationship where it is safe to talk about everyday disagreements as well as deeper, more sensitive issues or expectations. Intimacy is love between two mutually weak and emotionally needy people.

Intimacy is insurance for all the stages of marriage and the promise of safe passage through the storms of life. Of course, there's always the chance that if you stay together long enough you will eventually make this kind of intimate connection (remember stage 5). But why wait? Why run the risk of your marriage not making it by keeping your relationship at a surface level? The way I look at it, you choose either emotional distance or intimacy. There is no neutral zone.

North Meets South

Imagine two magnets. One represents you and the other your spouse. Let me explain what happens based on one of my favorite books, *The Way Things Work*,[10] a great big book with lots of pictures and just as much humor.

A magnet is a seemingly ordinary piece of metal surrounded by an invisible field of force that affects any magnetic material within it. All magnets have two poles. When magnets are brought together, a north pole always attracts a south pole, while pairs of like poles repel each other.

The two of you are like magnets. You have the power both to attract and to repel. The force field is everything that connects you. It's the chemistry, the spark, that special thing that turned into love, plus all that you've shared since the first time you laid eyes on each other.

Now picture your magnets inside a container. It represents your marriage. When positioned in such a way that the lines of force extend from the north pole of one magnet to the south pole of the other, the magnets are pulled together by this force that I'll call commitment and love. All it takes is for one of the magnets to rotate even a bit and the fields begin to repel. The strength that pushes them apart is as strong as what brings them together. If you've ever played with magnets, you know exactly what I'm talking about. You cannot see the force, but it is real and powerful.

Within the strong boundaries of a committed marriage, magnets that are repelling cannot go beyond the walls of the container. But they can certainly turn from each other and hug opposing edges tightly.

This object lesson illustrates an important fact about marriage. Spouses are either in attracting mode or repelling mode. They are either together in body, mind, and spirit, or they are repelling.

Unresolved conflicts are the powerful invisible forces that move spouses into repelling mode. In every relationship, there is bound to be conflict. But conflict alone does not twist a relationship so that the partners begin to repel each other. Failing to deal with the conflict and find a resolution is what closes down communication.

Unresolved conflicts can accumulate like piles of laundry, dirty dishes, or the city dump. Allowed to accumulate, they become barriers that grow into walls that divide spouses. The more unresolved conflicts, the more barriers. The more barriers, the more difficult it is to get back to attracting mode.

Here's the most important thing you need to take from this chapter: it will be nearly impossible for you to find financial harmony while in repelling mode. In fact, I don't know of a single situation in which spouses found financial peace in their marriage while they were in opposition to each other. But attracting mode? That's a completely different story because in that mode intimacy thrives. That's what happens when a husband and wife are committed to intimacy by choosing to satisfy the other's deepest emotional needs.

Intimacy is like good, fertile soil. That's where we are going to create financial harmony. If the soil isn't ready, the seeds are not going to grow. It would be like throwing sweet pea seeds on my concrete driveway. There's nothing wrong with the seeds, and the climate is certainly favorable, but I'm not going to get a single bloom.

A Shortcut to Intimacy

The way to move toward authentic intimacy is to begin to meet your spouse's emotional needs. Today. Right now.

It's as simple as that. It doesn't matter if you are reading this book together, while nodding your heads in complete agreement, or the two of you are not even speaking. Either way or something in between, I believe you can get out of the repelling mode. Even if you are so far apart you believe love has died, even if you believe there are too many barriers between you, even if your spouse is unwilling to participate or cooperate, I believe you can do this.

The only thing that matters right now is that you have a desire to become skilled at fulfilling the emotional needs of the one you promised to love throughout life. Your spouse stood up before God and everyone in the audience the day you were married and made a public proclamation that gave you exclusive access to care for his or her deepest needs. As battered and battle worn as that gift might be at the moment, it is still as precious as it was on your wedding day.

Spouses who find their needs unmet often become thoughtless and inconsiderate. When that happens, marriages turn ugly and destructive, often leading to unbearable pain and, ultimately, to divorce.[11]

Discovering what your spouse needs and cannot live without and then, by an act of your will, choosing to meet those needs is an act of giving. It's an outward expression of a heart's desire to love, honor, and respect.

In the likely event you are not quite sure what your spouse's deep emotional needs are, I've listed the most essential ones below. They are based on the ten emotional needs for husbands and wives that Willard F. Harley Jr. identified in *His Needs, Her Needs*. For now, I believe you will find this list to be right on target and sufficient to get started.

What a woman needs from her husband and cannot live without:

1. *Affection*. For a woman, affection is any nonsexual expression of love that says you are important to me, I will care for you and protect you.

2. *Conversation*. Every wife needs meaningful, intimate conversation from her husband delivered with his undivided attention. Women have lots of conversations with many people, but those are superficial. This is different; it's the kind of conversation she wants to have with only one person—her husband.

3. *Total trust*. A woman has a deep need for radical honesty. She needs honest and open communication and the assurance

that she can trust her husband totally—that he is hiding nothing. She needs a clear and unobstructed view into the mind of her husband. It makes her feel safe and secure.

4. *Financial support.* A woman has a deep emotional need for financial support. She needs assurance that there is enough money to pay the bills and to live without fear of want.

5. *A good father for her children.* A woman wants her husband to have a profound influence on their children and for him to be a strong and godly role model in their lives.

What a man needs from his wife and cannot live without:

1. *Sexual fulfillment.* A man's need for sex is much different from a woman's need for affection.

2. *Respect and admiration.* A man is empowered when a woman genuinely approves of and admires him. He needs unconditional respect for his intelligence, ideas, and suggestions.

3. *An attractive wife.* A man, with this deep emotional need, feels good whenever he looks at his attractive wife.

4. *Peace and quiet.* He needs to have a place and time when and where he can steal away from everything domestic to be alone, enjoy solitude, and not have to talk, even if for just a short time each day.

5. *Recreational companionship.* This need rolls two needs into one: the need to participate in recreational activities and the need to have a companion or playmate.

The Love Bank

Harley says that every person has a Love Bank, figuratively speaking. It contains many accounts, one for each person we know. Each person in our lives either makes deposits or withdrawals whenever we interact with him or her. The number one account in your Love

Bank has your spouse's name on it. Pleasurable interactions result in deposits in the form of "love units," and painful interactions cause withdrawals.[12] The important thing to remember is that our Love Banks never close and our needs keep score with relentless precision.

You invest love units in your marriage and build intimacy every time you satisfy one of your spouse's deep emotional needs in a way that conveys love to him or her—even if you don't understand why it is pleasurable or would not want the same thing in return. If you ever wondered how to define "hard work" in marriage, this is it.

Conversely, withdrawals are all the ways we hurt our partners, whether intentionally (choosing to make each other unhappy) or by neglect (failing to make one another happy).

Let me sum this up by stating the obvious. If you are making withdrawals at a greater rate than you are making deposits into your spouse's Love Bank, you're overdrawn. That means you are in debt, and that's not a good way to live, whether we're talking about love or money. Building a strong balance in your respective Love Banks is the way to invest in your marriage. It is also the path to intimacy.

If you start meeting your spouse's basic emotional needs, the benefits will be immediate, and amazing things will begin to happen. You will start to enjoy intimacy, which makes for the most ideal conditions for developing financial harmony in your marriage.

6

For Wives Only

Real Men Don't Ask for Directions

It's better to stay outside on the roof of your house than to live inside with a nagging wife.

Proverbs 21:9 CEV

Imagine that you and your husband are having a nice evening out and for some strange reason you want to end it by making him angry. Can you think of anything you could say or do to effect that kind of change? You know what I'm talking about, right? All I would have to do is tell my husband how to drive or suggest that if he'd bothered to ask for directions we would have been on time. I know how to make him furious. I have a feeling you know how to push your husband's buttons too.

Pay careful attention to what I'm about to say because it may be the most important thing you will take away from this chapter: if you know how to push his buttons to effect a negative response, you have the power to push his buttons to produce a positive result. You can stop doing things that make him unhappy. You can ignore his faults and choose to meet his needs by giving him what is important to him whether you understand it or not.

On your wedding day, your husband made a promise to "forsake all others." That meant he gave you the exclusive right to meet his deep emotional needs. I'm not sure many of us knew what all that meant when we took our vows. Forsaking all others sounded to me like it referred to sex, that our marriage would be monogamous. I'm older and wiser now and understand it meant that, but it also meant meeting all my husband's other deep emotional needs too.

Your husband, like mine, has a longing for your respect and admiration. It is one of his most essential emotional needs. How do I know this about your husband? Because he is a man. Your husband needs your deep and authentic respect for who he is, for his ideas, and for his solutions. He needs you to listen to his thinking. If a man doesn't feel respected, often he'll get angry. If the anger doesn't work, he'll withdraw and begin to move away from you emotionally. Worse, he may look elsewhere for the respect he craves.

I'm going to devote the rest of this chapter to encouraging you to stop trying to manage your husband and shift all that effort toward respecting and admiring him—not because he always deserves your respect but for the sole reason that he needs it. If your husband is not compromising your safety or physically abusing you or your children, I believe he is capable of loving and cherishing you even more than he ever did during the glorious days of stage 1. And isn't that what you really want more than anything?

Perhaps you've seen the bumper sticker that reads, "I've got just one nerve left . . . and you're on it!" I don't know of a woman who hasn't had that thought at least once in her life. As long as we are imperfect women, people are going to get on our nerves. And no one does that quite as effectively as our husbands. That's because they, like us, are mere mortals and are imperfect.

Women are born caretakers. It's in our genes because we were created to bear and nurture children. We are genetically programmed to know how to take charge, run a household, and get the job done. We are intuitive, observant, and if I do say so myself, quite capable. Take all these qualities and put them next to an imperfect husband, and it's easy for us to start seeing him as a project in need of improvement.

You deposit love units when you respect him by choosing to refrain from doing things that may come naturally to you but rub him raw. Read: keep your mouth shut when you are just aching to correct or criticize. You deposit love units when you say or do things that convey your respect and admiration. You make withdrawals from your account in his Love Bank whenever you do things that convey disrespect.

How Wives Show Disrespect for Their Husbands

Based on the thousands of letters I have received from a vast cross section of people over the past decades, I think most women are pretty sure their lives would fall apart if they stopped controlling their husbands.

If you are unfamiliar with this concept, let me list for you the ways a wife exercises control over her husband: by correcting and criticizing him (double withdrawal if this is performed in public); by nagging, bossing, and questioning his actions and decisions; by giving him unsolicited advice and burying him in lists of chores; by attempting to take over every situation; by directing him, managing him, supervising him, coaching him, and reminding him; by checking up on him and otherwise treating him like a child; and by questioning his ability to be a good provider. Of course, most women who engage in these kinds of activities would justify them as loving attempts to make him an even better man.

I am sure you have remarkable abilities to manage, direct, supervise, and coach. Those are highly desired skills in the workplace or on the soccer field but terribly demeaning when exercised on your husband. When you criticize, correct, or direct your husband, you become his mother. Picture that. Regardless of what a lovely woman she is, trust me when I say your husband is not attracted to his mother. The last thing you want is to step into her role.

The truth is there's not one controlling behavior that will do anything to change your husband. More likely these behaviors will repel him and push him away so that he withdraws emotionally. And that will leave both of you lonely, unfulfilled, and frustrated.

How Wives Show Respect for Their Husbands

You show respect for the man you married when you listen to him and hold his ideas, thoughts, and suggestions in high regard with delight and approval. You let him know you are amazed by his unique characteristics. You accept his choices even if you don't agree with them. You treat him as an intelligent adult, not an irresponsible child. You give up control over his actions and trust him to be the leader he was designed to be. You leave all theories of equality (whatever that is) at the workplace, opting to assume the feminine role in your marriage.

I'll say this again as my way of underlining such an important truth: wives get love units for what they don't do—for not volunteering to help, for not offering suggestions, for not reminding, for not following up. Just between you and me, I don't think I will ever fully understand that. However, I choose to believe it because as wrong as it feels, I know it is true. Just by "not doing" in these ways, I'll bet I average twenty to thirty love units a day.

Here are some specific examples of how you can make deposits into your husband's Love Bank:

1. He makes a mistake; you choose to say nothing, not a word of advice or even an "I told you so." The bigger the mistake, the larger the deposit. Two bonus units for not rolling your eyes.

2. He forgets something; your only response, "That's okay."

3. You accept his gift—any gift—with unrestrained gratitude, even if you don't need it and would never have thought of it in a million years.

4. He says something that hurts your feelings; you don't scream at him or complain. You say a silent "Ouch!" by leaving a quiet space so he can face the ugliness of hurting the person he loves the most.

5. You avoid trying to guess what he is thinking or drawing conclusions before you hear what he has to say.

6. You don't say anything with a negative expectation. Example: "Why don't you just call an electrician?" which he hears as, "You can't fix it yourself!"

7. You thank him for what he does: being a capable, loyal, hard-working, dependable man.

8. You praise him for who he is: his strength, wisdom, intelligence, choices, courage, leadership, skills.

9. You don't make demands, issue orders, or give ultimatums.

10. When desperate to criticize, contradict, or in some other way steer your husband's actions, you bite your tongue and, if necessary, hold your breath until the urge passes.

11. You let him solve some of your problems.

12. You listen to what he's really saying. When he says, "No matter what I do, nothing ever pleases you!" he's really saying, "Please notice and appreciate me."

13. You don't admonish, beg, manipulate, or cajole him.

14. When you slip back to disrespecting him, you make a heartfelt and specific apology.

If you are a controlling wife by nature, making a choice to start respecting your husband is going to be quite a challenge. And you are going to make lots of mistakes. Still, choosing to fill your husband's Love Bank with respect and admiration will change your life and his too.

As your husband receives your respect and admiration, you'll find him responding in ways you might have given up as impossible. As you become more willing to stop speaking up about everything, you may begin to hear your husband expressing his views and desires and be amazed to discover that he's not filled with apathy after all. Perhaps you just couldn't hear him over your constant chatter.

I believe with all my heart that as you honor your husband by meeting his deep emotional need to be respected and admired, you are going to discover that, more than anything, he really does want to love, cherish, and care for you exactly the way you long to be by him. Eventually, you will regain his trust as you make more and more deposits into his Love Bank. Where he used to withdraw emotionally, he will move closer. This remarkable exchange will result in the two of you becoming of one mind, and together you'll be ready, willing, and able to resolve your conflicts in mutually acceptable and effective ways. As a bonus, you will begin to create a climate that is conducive to developing financial harmony.

Respecting your husband is not about subservience. It's about working hard to build a relationship that brings out the best in both of you—the kind of relationship you have dreamed about since the day you said, "I do." Respecting your husband is appointing yourself as the president of his fan club.

Your husband feels loved when he knows you trust him. You feel loved when he cares for you. As you give up control in favor of respect and admiration, he is going to feel trusted and loved. And his response will be to love and care for you more than ever before. You will be amazed.

7

For Husbands Only

You Can Have What You Want

They do not love who do not show their love.

William Shakespeare[1]

Did the subtitle of this chapter pique your interest? Good. There are a couple of very important things I need to tell you.

On your wedding day, your wife, the love of your life, made a promise to "forsake all others" and keep herself only unto you. I don't know what you thought when you heard those words, but I know that when I answered with "I will," I thought the minister was referring to sex—a promise to be monogamous. Many years and lots of experience later, I know that our vows were about more than that—a lot more. So were yours.

All of us, both men and women, have deep emotional needs. Prior to marriage, those needs were met through relationships, friendships, activities, etc. But marriage changes all that. I'll use myself and my husband as examples. When I told Harold that from that day on I would forsake all others, I gave him exclusive access to my deep emotional needs. I promised to make that area of my life off-limits to anyone but him. And as the caretaker of my needs, he promised to take full responsibility for meeting them. And then the minister asked him if he was willing to "forsake all others," and he too said, "I will." That was and continues to be a very big deal, much larger than either of us fully understood at the time.

I want to talk to you about just one of your wife's deep emotional needs: affection. She has others, of course, but I have chosen to concentrate on just this one in preparation for creating financial harmony in your marriage. When you are regularly fulfilling her need for deep emotional affection, her response will be to trust, respect, and admire you, which will be the key to the two of you becoming equal financial partners.

Within the genetic code of every human female is a need for affection. It's as great a need as her need for food and water. This need is evident from the time of her birth and continues until the day she dies. Women are just wired that way. When your wife agreed to marry you, she promised to find you, her husband, as her exclusive source for meeting her deep need for affection. When you are affectionate with her, it brings her intense pleasure, and for a time, the need is fulfilled.

Perhaps you recall the Old Testament account of manna, a type of bread and God's provision for the Israelites as they spent years wandering in the wilderness. The amazing thing was that no matter how much they received, even if it was more than they could possibly consume, it would last for only one day. That put them in the position of having to trust God to meet their needs one day at a time.

Your affection is like manna. It's fresh, warm, and satisfying. But it lasts only for a short time. As unfair and ridiculous as that might seem to you, it is true. You might believe that once you have fulfilled your wife's need for affection, she should know from then on that she is loved. But it doesn't work that way. Your wife needs expressions of your affection every day because her need starts over every day. Your best bet is to believe this even though you might not understand it. Then determine that no matter what, as an act of your will and in response to the second most important decision you've ever made in your life (to marry her), you will give her the affection she needs every day.

If she stops receiving that affection from you, she's going to get frustrated. She'll see it as proof that you no longer value her. She may begin to withdraw. As she looks elsewhere for affection (remember she cannot live without it), she may turn away and begin to repel rather than attract you.

The kind of affection she needs from you is not at all sexual. And it is not the same as the affection she might derive from a friend's hug or a birthday card from her father. Every day she needs words, gestures, and actions from you that convey these kinds of messages:

- I'll take care of you and protect you.
- You are more important to me than any other person on earth.
- I don't want anything bad to happen to you.
- I'm concerned about the problems you face.
- I think you've done a good job.
- I am so proud of you.

You, like many men, may find it difficult to verbalize those kinds of messages. That is because you do not have the same need, and you may not understand how important it is for her to get these kinds of messages. You have to believe me; it doesn't matter if this comes naturally for you or not. Saying you are quiet or an introvert is no excuse. You promised to meet her needs; now you need to deliver. And often.

This next part may be difficult for you to take, so consider this fair warning: you need to give her affection even if she's completely undeserving and behaving in a way that is repelling you at the moment. And you need to do it without expecting anything in return. There may be times when the last thing you feel like doing is being affectionate with this woman. Meeting her needs when she is the least deserving is a true act of love. It might help if you remember that it's easier to act your way into a feeling than to feel your way into an action.

Now I'm going to let you in on a little secret: while you must not expect anything in return, something remarkable is going to happen when you begin to regularly give this kind of affection to your wife. She is going to start feeling that she is number one in your life, and then she will not be able to stop herself from responding with admiration and respect for you. The more affection you give her, the more respect she'll give you. But that's not all. She'll stop trying to control you.

Your affection can be verbal or nonverbal. It can be expressed as an action, a gesture, a gift, a phone call—how doesn't matter as much as how often you give it. A big birthday gift with a mushy card is nice, but that's not going to do it for the entire year. She needs affection from you every day of her life.

Let's say you'll be home late. You know your wife wants you to call to let her know. It's a simple gesture but one you've never really understood because you would not expect her to check in with you if she was going to be late. But knowing that a simple call tells her she is important to you and will score you at least a one-unit deposit in her Love Bank, you make the call.

You walk into the house, and before you do anything else, you make a point to find her and give her a hug. Another love unit. Just about then you look around the house and ask, "What in the world did you do all day?" In the time it takes you to say those nine little words, you've just withdrawn three love units, and you, my friend, are now overdrawn. Your words cost you both the call and the hug—not because she's moody, unreasonable, or ungrateful but because she is a woman.

Of course, the Love Bank is not intended to be a mathematically accurate concept, but it does illustrate how we affect each other emotionally. You have a Love Bank too. Your wife makes deposits and withdrawals but in very different ways.

Let's say your wife wants to let you know how much she misses you when you're gone all day. She greets you at the door with a simple bouquet of tulips and lilies of the valley tied with a bow. Does she score? Not exactly. You assume she's on her way out to visit someone in the hospital.

But if you arrive home with the same bouquet, hand them to her, and say, "I missed you so much today," I can guarantee you at least a five-unit deposit. You made her feel special and adored. Excellent!

After dinner you head for the dryer, fold a stack of towels, and put them away because you know she's had a rough day. Another score because she felt your appreciation and support. I hope you are beginning to see that what constitutes a deposit for your wife wouldn't even make it to the bank for you. For women, it's the little things that make a big difference. Offering your wife your affection in many small ways will keep your account in her Love Bank in the black with her interest compounding.

If you truly don't know what actions your wife translates as affection, start paying attention. Experiment. Make notes. You will soon discover that it takes so little to make points with a woman.

Here are a few examples of things you can do to make deposits in your wife's Love Bank:

1. Hugs. At least four a day.
2. Ask her something specific about her day. This shows her you care about what's going on in her life.

3. Instead of trying to solve her problem, empathize. Many wives feel their husbands don't listen or understand their hearts.

4. Give her your undivided attention for at least fifteen minutes (turn off all electronics and set the timer if necessary).

5. Compliment her on something specific (Say, "You look great in those pants," not "New pants?").

6. Listen and ask her questions.

7. Give her flowers.

8. Bring her little presents for no particular reason.

9. Open the door for her.

10. Touch her with your hand when you talk to her.

11. Say thank you when she does things for you.

12. Take her for a walk without the children.

13. Put the toilet seat in the down position. Every time.

When you maintain a balance in your wife's Love Bank, she knows that you love her, and that makes her trust and respect you in return. And as a bonus, she won't be able to help herself from making deposits in your Love Bank.

8

Getting It Together

Honey, Let's Talk about Our Relationship

> Couples can discuss difficult topics, even when they disagree. The key
> is to show respect for your partner's thoughts, feelings, and opinions.
>
> Natalie H. Jenkins, *You Paid How Much for That?*

Emotional intimacy is the key to a healthy marriage and a precondition for financial harmony. And the secret for creating emotional intimacy in your marriage is for each of you to meet the needs that are most important to the other. Emotional intimacy is the key because it produces authentic trust and respect—the two ingredients that act like superglue to keep a husband and wife happily married. In almost a self-perpetuating cycle, emotional intimacy produces trust and respect, which in turn promote greater intimacy. And that's a cycle you want to begin operating in your marriage as soon as possible.

I know that it's been difficult for you to communicate in the past, particularly about money issues. And I also know that once you take your eyes off yourself and your needs and begin to concentrate on meeting the needs of your spouse—even if you do not feel like it—wonderful things are going to happen. At first, it will be barely noticeable. But slowly, as you choose to fulfill your spouse's needs, your heart will change. Your spouse will not be able to resist your efforts because his or her needs cry out to be met. And that cannot help but affect your relationship in ways you never dreamed possible.

Financial Partners

The first step in reaching financial harmony is to make a commitment to each other to become equal financial partners in your marriage. This can be a verbal or written commitment, whichever suits you best. For some spouses, this step of commitment will mean giving up control. For others, it will require them to get involved.

Studies show that married people who behave as true financial partners tend to do better financially and emotionally.[1] Begin thinking of the financial aspects of your marriage as a business rather than an extension of your relationship. As business partners, you:

- have trust in and respect for each other's unique abilities, knowledge, and skills
- bring individual strengths and abilities to the partnership
- have no secrets; each of you is fully aware of the other's activities and the state of their business
- do not make independent decisions, and when there is a disagreement or conflict, you negotiate and compromise until you reach a solution that both of you can agree to enthusiastically
- make decisions with the best interest of the partnership in mind and are fully committed to the success of the partnership

Switching Hats

Think of all the different hats you wear in your daily life. You are a wife or husband, a parent, perhaps a committee chairperson, and an employee. You're someone's daughter or son; you may have responsibilities in your community or church. All these roles require you to wear different hats. You don't respond to your fellow board members, for example, in the same way you respond to your children. One of the most important things you can learn is to wear different hats within your marriage as well. You need to know when to put on your financial partner hat, which signals that it's time to put the emotions and feelings on the shelf and shift into money management mode.

As a way of illustrating how a business partnership works, let's say that you and a friend decide to go into business to run a coffee shop. You are a marvelous cook; your friend has terrific business skills. It's only natural that you divide the responsibilities of the partnership according to your strengths and abilities. You cook; she runs the front. You order supplies; she pays the bills. The reason you need each other in this coffee shop scenario is because where you are weak, she's strong and vice versa. Still, you are both fully aware of everything going on in the business; you have no secrets. Both of you show up every day and carry your load. You share the good times and the bad. You work out the procedures and negotiate each business decision and refuse to move forward on any decision until both of you are in enthusiastic agreement. This is a model you can follow as equal financial partners in your marriage.

I suggest that in the beginning you schedule weekly business meetings, at which time you wear your money management hats. We'll get into this more in the following chapters.

Time to Talk

The idea of one-on-one meaningful conversation with all electronic devices turned off and the door closed can be threatening for some couples, particularly if money issues have turned into barriers. Some spouses are reluctant to converse on an emotional level. That may be due in part to personality traits, but more likely it's the result of fear—fear of being known, fear of opening up, fear of being found out. Some spouses just don't know what to say to each other when the weather, the office, and the kids are off-limits. By opening the door to the most private place in your heart and soul.and taking the risk of letting your spouse in, you will be taking a huge step toward the kind of intimacy that promotes financial harmony.

You need routine, daily, planned conversations that do not include the weather, the kids, or your finances. A reasonable starting place would be to set aside at least fifteen minutes every day for meaningful conversation, with both of you offering your undivided attention to the other. As you will recall from chapter 5, this is a basic and deep emotional need that at least one of you cannot live without. Now would be a good time to shuffle back through your mental notes from the first day in Communication 101 and remember the three fundamentals of effective communication: good eye contact (affirms your spouse's value and also keeps your attention focused), one speaker, one listener.

Talk without Fighting

If you are having difficulty talking without arguing, here's a method that will help you slow down and gain clarity.

The speaker is the first to hold the floor. As hokey as it might seem, it is helpful if you designate a symbol to represent the "floor," such as the television remote, a pen, a spoon, or anything that makes it clear who's speaking. The speaker talks, and when he or she is finished (it's not polite to hog the floor), the listener paraphrases back to the speaker (without comment or question) what he or she understood the speaker to say. If that isn't what the speaker intended to say, the speaker retains the floor and tries again. Once the listener is sure he or she heard what the speaker said, the speaker gives the floor to the listener, and they trade roles.

I'll admit this is a slow and tedious way to have a conversation, but if you can discipline yourself to adhere to the guidelines, it will stop the arguing and misunderstandings. And the more you do it, the better you'll get at framing your thoughts and speaking them in a way your spouse hears and understands.

Set an Agenda

The idea of setting an agenda may seem too formal or intimidating, but as one who hates surprises, I can tell you that knowing what we're going to talk about gives me a certain level of calm and comfort. I like to know what's ahead. When you set an agenda, you simply figure out what you're going to focus on. The more specific, the better your chances of coming out with a reasonable and satisfying solution.

Brainstorm

I love brainstorming if for no other reason than the visual image it brings to my mind. Brainstorming, not a new term by any means, was refined by NASA during the early years of the United States space program when eager scientists were pushing the limits to achieve what many thought to be impossible.

To brainstorm means to contribute any idea no matter how far-fetched. Get creative and say whatever comes to mind. This works best if someone can quickly jot down all the offerings without response, suggestions, comments, or judgment. This is a remarkable conflict resolution tool because it gets the juices flowing and helps to break down barriers. Because brainstorming has an aspect of fun, it is also disarming when the topic is otherwise tense.

Compromise and Reach a Settlement

The Internal Revenue Service (IRS) coined the phrase "compromise and settlement," which refers to working out a deal for a taxpayer who for some reason has a troublesome relationship with the IRS. After much negotiation and settlement of terms, a deal is struck and the taxpayer makes the agreed-upon payment. But there's more. Once the IRS accepts the payment, the problem is over and done—at least that's the way it's supposed to work. While there are not many times I would consider using the IRS as a model for right living, I find this an excellent model for spouses struggling to put a difficult issue to rest. Of course, compromising and reaching a settlement are greatly simplified when the parties have a deep emotional and intimate relationship.

Tear Down Barriers

In chapter 4, we discussed barriers of unresolved anger, unrealistic expectations, and broken trust. If these exist in your relationship, you must take the bold step to begin tearing them down. I know no other way than to approach them with complete honesty and remorse. I'm not saying this will be easy, but it is necessary. If you need a professional to help you get through the really tough issues, don't hesitate for one moment to find one.

My experience leads me to believe that most conflicts in marriage are resolved by the spouses simply talking about them. Communication is the secret. Of course, there will be conflicts from time to time that do not have a simple resolution. These will require a lot of grace, wisdom, and understanding. For conflicts of an emotional or spiritual nature, I am confident that as your emotional intimacy deepens, your ability to resolve these conflicts quickly will increase. And as business partners, you will be able to negotiate conflicts of a financial nature once you have the tools for debt-proofing your marriage.

Never forget the value of time. Time heals wounds, and time has a way of resolving conflicts. Decisions made in haste are often filled with regret.

Part 2

How to Debt-Proof
Your Marriage

9

Debt-Proof Living

An Overview

We make our plans, and then our plans turn around and make us.

F. W. Boreham, *Mushrooms on the Moor*

I have great news for you. It will not take a fortune to achieve financial harmony in your marriage. You won't have to participate in any get-rich-quick schemes or gimmicks. You can debt-proof your marriage without winning the lottery or receiving a big inheritance. You can get out of debt, prepare for the future, and live within your means—all on your current income and with your current resources.

You may be expecting me to say this is going to be so easy you won't believe it, something you can achieve overnight. Uh, no. But that should not surprise you. In your heart, you know that nothing of lasting value comes without some measure of hard work. And you didn't get where you are overnight. So you can't expect to fix everything overnight either. But if you follow the steps and do the work, I promise you great results.

Debt-proof living is a principle-based system of money management. That is the opposite of an emotionally based system in which financial decisions are made impulsively, based strictly on feelings and desires. You may know something about those kinds of decisions. I could easily fill several books with my own examples along with the painful consequences. I won't because I'm sure you have a few of your own real-life illustrations.

Let's say you are twenty-five and your family income is the United States median, last reported to be $67,019 for a family of four.[1] Further, let's make a somewhat unrealistic assumption that in your earning lifetime you will not receive a single raise. Still, by the time you are sixty-five years old, $2,680,760 will have passed through your fingers. Wow.

Now let's say that you stay in that same job for forty years and your salary increases by a paltry 3 percent a year, only somewhat more reasonable. In your working lifetime, you will earn nearly $5 million before you retire. If you land a promotion, you'll rake in even more. So how are you doing so far with managing your millions?

Most people dream of having a lot of money and believe that once they become millionaires they'll automatically know how to manage it even though they are failing miserably at managing much smaller amounts. The truth is that you are becoming a millionaire right now. You are receiving your wealth in installments, a portion every payday.

It doesn't matter if you are managing $50,000 a year or $50,000,000. Unless you have a specific plan that is based on values and principles you believe in and a method to keep all of it from leaking away, you will always be in a financial mess. All you have to do to remind yourself of this is to look at the pro athletes, celebrities, and lottery winners who wound up bankrupt. Debt-proof living is all about learning reasonable and effective principles to help you plug the leaks and hang on to more of the money that flows through your life.

Debt-proof living is a systematic way to manage your money so that you are consistently able to pay as you go and are preparing for the future without relying on credit or incurring debt. To debt-proof your marriage means to live within your means so that your income is greater than your outgo. It requires that you become responsible stewards of all the resources you have now and those that will be entrusted to you in the future.

In a poll taken on my website, DebtProofLiving.com, I asked this question: What grade would you give your high school for how well it prepared you to manage your personal finances? Of the more than one thousand people who responded, 19 percent gave their educators a D and 67 percent flunked them. Surprised? Not me. I didn't learn a thing about personal finance in any of my years of education. Oh, there was that story problem in fifth grade math about buying apples and oranges at the market, but that was about it. I took years of home economics, but not once did I learn how to put together a grocery budget. I learned a lot about making cinnamon toast and sewing a skirt but nothing about how to manage a paycheck. And I didn't get it at home either. My family didn't talk about money.

Most of us arrived at marriage without a clue how to manage our money. So we did what felt good and came naturally. We spent it as fast as we could earn it (sometimes faster). "Buy now, pay later" became sweet words to our ears. Now it's later.

Debt-proof living is not only a plan for getting out of debt. It's also a plan for staying out of debt and going on to live in such a way that debt is no longer an issue. It's an attitude that makes living beyond our ability to pay no longer attractive. Debt-proof living is a set of principles, directives, checks, and balances. It's a plan that is logical and simple to implement.

In the same way you would insist on a sturdy, well-built foundation under your dream house, you need a strong foundation on which to build your financial life. Debt-proof living will provide that foundation in your marriage. Don't be surprised if at first you find some of this information overwhelming. Remember, the process takes time.

As you get your debts and spending under control and as you learn specific strategies and let go of the hit-and-miss method of money management, you are going to discover a new sense of oneness and well-being. There's a lot to learn and a lot to do even if your finances are in fairly good order. You won't be able to do everything at once, so relax and learn all you can. Take it one step at a time, and you will find that you can begin immediately to improve your financial picture and your relationship. Everything will not change overnight, but as you take the first steps and commit to steady progress, you will be well on your way to achieving the financial harmony you desire.

Why You Need to Debt-Proof Your Marriage

Here are reasons why you need to debt-proof your marriage.

To insure your relationship. I'm sure I don't have to repeat it again, but I'm going to just for good measure: financial problems can put your marriage at risk. Finding a workable solution for those problems is like taking out marriage insurance. Removing the problems opens the way for you to love and be loved in the way you desire.

To survive lean times. Living paycheck to paycheck has little to do with the size of the paycheck. I hear from people all the time who make impressive six-figure annual incomes yet are so overextended they are one paycheck away from being homeless. That is a scary way to live! After all, who has any guarantees on the next paycheck? One of the major tenets of debt-proof living is being prepared for the future—good times and bad. Let me give you an important piece of advice: you are going to experience lean times in the future. I can guarantee it. Even though you think that's the craziest thing you've ever heard because you know you will never lose your job or will never experience a medical emergency, I say you are wrong. It's going to happen, so the best thing you can do is to begin now to prepare for it.

To reduce your stress. Do you have trouble sleeping because of your money worries? Do you find yourself short of breath at the thought of paying bills this month? Do you fudge the truth with your spouse, creditors, or kids because you just cannot face another outburst or lecture? Then you know stress. It's no secret that stress takes a terrible toll on our health. When we are under stress, we are less immune to disease and illness. Our bodies bear the consequences of the heavy loads our minds carry when we place our lives in financial jeopardy. Debt-proofing your marriage will turn stress to joy, rest, and peace of mind.

To teach your children. If your kids read magazines, go to school, watch television, listen to the radio, know what a fast-food restaurant is, or have ever been inside a store or supermarket, they already know something about entitlement and instant gratification. Right under your nose, they are developing into world-class consumers. They may be well on their way to becoming future debtors of America too. If you do nothing to intervene, statistics indicate your kids are headed for a life that will be severely and negatively impacted by consumer debt. By debt-proofing your life, you will affect your children's lives as well because families reproduce themselves. Kids learn through observation and imitation, and when all the smoke clears, they usually turn out like their parents.

To allow God to care for you. It's not easy to let go of depending on credit to bridge the gap between what you have and what you want. It takes faith to stop looking to Visa and MasterCard to be your financial rescue team and depend on God for all your needs, your emergencies, even your wants.

Debt-Proof Living Principles

While I've never seen them, I've seen pictures of the cables. The people I know who have climbed Half Dome in Yosemite National Park tell me the final ascent up the sheer granite surface of that landmass is by far the most challenging. The cables are there to make sure the climbers reach the top safely and with a modicum of ease. However, I understand that "ease" in this context is terribly relative.

The principles for debt-proof living are a lot like those cables on Half Dome. You install them by writing them on your heart, memorizing them, and reviewing them often. You put them there because you know you'll need them. They'll be there for you to hang on to and will protect you from your human fears and self-defeating attitudes during times of financial challenge and blessing, when you have a lot and when there is little.

The principles that follow are intellectually based, not founded on feelings and emotions. It is so important that you understand the difference. Your emotions are fickle. That is why you dare not base your methods of money management on how you feel. It is unlikely that the two of you will feel exactly the same on any given day. So right there is one huge problem.

Basing your money management program on principles means you are building a system that is strong and enduring. When your feelings take a nosedive, you can hang on to the principles. They represent truth and a standard that is not going to change. You can count on them even when you don't feel like it. These are the cables that will remain strong and that you can use to pull yourself through the journey ahead and up to the top, where you will enjoy the spectacular results.

Principle 1: God Is the Source

Your employer, your spouse, your investments, your trust account, your parents, or any other financial entity is not the source of your money. You may think these are sources, but they are merely delivery systems, the conduits through which God delivers his care and protection of your life in the form of money.

You might argue that you, not God, are the source of your money because you put in the hours and devote your brainpower and talents, which then are turned into cash on payday. As interesting as that argument might be, it is faulty. You cannot take credit for your talents and abilities. They are God-given. Every good thing comes from God, and this is the first principle of debt-proof living: God is the source. The conduit and delivery system may change, and the flow of income may not be an even and steady stream. That's because God is not limited to our monthly calendar system. His provisions don't always come evenly spaced in weekly or monthly installments. Still, God is the source.

What great news! This means you don't have to worry about the loss of a job or the fluctuations of the stock market. The ebb and flow of real estate values should not send you into a tailspin. All those things could change, even fail, and they probably will. Still, God is the source. As you have faith and relax in this truth, you will understand that your role in this is to manage well what you receive and not to worry that the source will disappear.

Principle 2: Money Is Not for Spending

Hang on to your hat because I'm going to tell you something that may be hard to swallow. Money is not for spending. It took me the longest time to understand this. Money is for managing first and then for spending. This truth profoundly changed my attitude about money. Once I understood it, I began to change from the inside out. I understood my role as a steward, or caretaker, of

God's provision in my life. As I became a more trustworthy and obedient steward, I was given more to take care of.

It is foolish and unsatisfying to spend money that has not been managed. It's like eating raw eggs, flour, butter, and cocoa and believing you just had a piece of cake. You need to do something with those ingredients first—like follow the steps in a recipe and exercise a little patience while the cake bakes and cools. In the same way, you need a plan by which to process your money before you disperse, appropriate, and spend it.

Trying to hold on to unmanaged money is like trying to hang on to a handful of water. No matter how tight your grip, it leaks away. Money that is not managed has a way of disappearing.

Principle 3: Never Keep It All

The first thing you must do when money comes into your life is give some of it away. No strings attached, no expectation of anything in return. Giving away some of what is very precious is the way you offer gratitude. It's a thank-you note, an acknowledgment that while you may not have it all, you do have enough. To keep it all is to invite greed and discontent into your life. Giving pulls the plug on greed. Giving proves the condition of your heart. Giving forces you to step out in faith. And the result? It releases supernatural intervention in your finances.

Principle 4: Never Spend It All

After you give some back, you must pay yourself. That means you always put some aside for the future, and you do this before you pay anyone else. If you've ever felt a hollow feeling of failure and defeat knowing your paycheck is completely spoken for before you even receive it, you are going to love living by this principle.

Principle 5: No More New Debt

Unsecured debt is like cancer. At first, it's not life threatening. It's small and hardly noticeable. But it never stays that way. It begins to multiply and grow to the point it takes over. The only way to stop it from growing and to reverse the process back to financial health is to begin living according to this principle: no more new unsecured debt.

Principle 6: More Money Is Not the Solution

Of all the debt-proof living principles, this may be the most difficult because it does not require an action. It is rather an attitude—and a difficult one to accept. Everyone struggles with this at least occasionally. I've come a long way in this regard. However, I used to believe that if I had more money, everything would be fine. Then we'd get a raise or a tax refund that was larger than expected. Was everything okay? No. That's because money became a qualifier, the down payment on whatever it was I decided we needed that cost more than the money we actually had. And that made things worse than ever because we managed to turn more money into new debt.

Managing money is a learned discipline and requires a conscious effort. It is not difficult; you just have to learn how to do it exactly—step by step. Anything in life—whether driving a car or operating a computer—would be difficult if you didn't have an instruction manual, not even an example to follow.

So here you are, financial partners jointly responsible for the money that flows into your marriage, responsible to each other for what it does, where it goes, and how it performs. You are the co-bosses. You can watch it drift away out of your control, or you can manage it according to a formula, a plan, a specific recipe you have developed that is a part of who you are. The key to all this is that you have to know ahead of time how you will manage your money—regular paycheck(s), irregular income, that unexpected inheritance, even the $2 rebate check.

When you introduce sanity and reason to the management of your income, feelings of dissatisfaction, worry, and hopelessness seem to settle down. Anxiety begins to quiet. Over and over again my readers tell me these principles work for them. They worked for me. You need a system through which to process every dime that enters your life. I have developed such a system, which I call debt-proof living. It is logical and simple to implement. Most of all, it works.

In the chapters that follow, I'm going to help you figure out where you are. Then I'm going to teach you a key formula, followed by the four basic elements of debt-proof living. Think of each of these as an important piece in a puzzle. One piece standing all alone may not make much sense to you. However, once we have the pieces, we'll put the puzzle together. At that point, I believe you will see the big picture of how all this works together to get you headed in the right direction. Soon you will be taking care of the present, cleaning up the past, and preparing for the future.

10

Till Debt Do Us Part

The Trouble with Debt

Debt, it seems, is a lot like a grease stain. When you finally notice it, it looks terrible, and in hindsight, you could have prevented it. Now there's no quick way to make it disappear.

M. P. Dunleavey, *A 24-Hour Debt-Reduction Plan*

There was a time, and not so long ago, when I would have told you that if you are an adult with an income, the consumer credit industry is after you. They are falling all over themselves to give you credit card accounts without regard for whether you can actually afford the debt. Their design is that you agree to a life of perma-debt. Yes, it used to be that you had to be an adult and prove you had an income to be the object of their "affections." But things have changed. You can forget that adult part and drop the necessity of having an income, as millions of college students can now attest.

Consumer credit is readily available to anyone with a pulse without regard for income, age, or apparently species. A few years ago I read about a dog named Spark who received a preapproved credit card offer with a limit of $30,000 and a 5.99 percent rate guaranteed for three years. His owner said she would have loved to have returned Spark's paw print signature, but sadly, Spark had died more than ten years before. The company apologized for its mistake, but that doesn't negate the ease with which credit is offered these days.[1]

As far out of control as the credit card industry seems to have gotten, it is important to understand that not all debts are created equal, nor is every type of loan hazardous to your wealth. Even I am willing to concede that some debts are helpful, at times advisable.

There is a world of difference between a home mortgage and a revolving credit card balance. Both are legally binding liabilities. However, beyond that one similarity, the two types of consumer debt have little in common. A home mortgage is what I call intelligent borrowing. Credit card debt, on the other hand, should be called exactly what it is: mindlessly ignorant.

Intelligent Borrowing

I characterize secured debt as intelligent borrowing because there is a level of safety involved; there is limited risk for both the borrower and the lender. For a loan to be an intelligent decision, it should meet the five basic characteristics of intelligent borrowing.

1. The loan provides a way out for both the borrower and the lender. Both have a safety valve—a legally and morally sound way to get out of the obligation. In the case of a home loan, if the borrower can't handle the payments or wants to get

out for any reason, he can sell the property to pay off the loan. If the lender wants out, he can sell his position in the deal to another investor.

2. The debt is secured. The lender holds something that is at least as valuable as the debt. Collateral acts as a security deposit to guarantee the borrower's faithful performance. If the borrower fails to perform, the lender can sell the collateral as payment for the outstanding loan. In the case of a mortgage, the title to the property is the security.

3. The loan is for something that has a reasonable life expectancy of more than three years.

4. The loan is for something that has the likelihood of increasing in value over time.

5. The interest rate is reasonable.

Toxic Debt

The opposite of secured debt is, of course, unsecured debt, or as I would rather have you call it, toxic debt. Take each one of the characteristics of intelligent borrowing and insert "not." Now you have a picture of toxic debt.

The first clue about the danger of unsecured debt is how ridiculously easy it is to get. Remember Spike? This is the kind of debt you agree to and use on a whim, impulsively, when your emotions are high and your brain is napping.

The most common way to rack up toxic debt is with a credit card. There's no qualifying process to speak of to get a credit card. In fact, some would say that the less qualified people are, the higher the credit limit they can achieve. Plastic rules. Just swipe that baby, sign your name, and presto! You've made a long-term commitment for money you haven't even earned yet. And then there's all that compounding interest when you opt for the low minimum monthly payments.

"Toxic" pretty well characterizes the activity of paying two or three times for things that may be gone and forgotten long before the bill even arrives. Turning restaurant meals, travel, groceries, utility bills, movie tickets, vacations, gifts, gasoline, and school clothes into debt, and then choosing minimum payments over many years and at rates that effectively double the original costs, brings new meaning to the term *ridiculous*. Here's an example. You find a gorgeous skirt on sale for $50. It's a bargain you can't pass up. You opt for the easy payment method by paying for it with your credit card, which carries an APR (annual percentage rate) of 18.99. Your minimum monthly payments start at $1 (2 percent of the outstanding balance). If you stick with the minimum required, you will pay for that skirt for 102 months, or 8.5 years. In the end, you are going to pay $101.02 for a $50 skirt that you might wear for a couple of years. But just to be fair, let's compare this debt to intelligent borrowing.

1. Does the borrower have a way out? With unsecured consumer debt, such as a credit card balance, the borrower has no way out but to pay it back—including all the interest. There is nothing to repossess. If you don't pay as agreed, Visa won't come after your skirt. No, they'll come after you, but only after they've zinged you with fees, increased your interest rate significantly, and made your life fairly miserable.

2. Is the debt collateralized? Nope. The credit card company holds nothing of value to guarantee your faithful performance except your good name and credit report. The company doesn't care about what you bought and sure doesn't care about you. All they want is their money.

3. Does this purchase have a reasonable life expectancy of at least three years? In other words, will it last long enough and retain enough value so you could sell it to pay off your debt? Clearly, no.

4. Will it appreciate in value? You'd be lucky to get ten cents on the dollar at a garage sale.

5. Is the interest rate reasonable? Hardly. As of this writing, the average credit card annual interest rate is 17.8 percent,[2] while a thirty-year fixed-rate mortgage is 3.98 percent.[3]

But that's not all. Credit card issuers have become so aggressive and so competitive in the last several years that the consumer has taken a bigger hit than ever. It's called punitive efforts: late fees, over-limit fees, inactivity fees, shortened grace periods, and the list goes on and on. Credit card issuers now derive approximately 30 percent of their profits from these fees, which pile up on top of high interest rates. It has been estimated that, with fees, some consumers pay an effective rate of 35 to 40 percent interest. Toxic debt for sure.

The Real Lowdown

Let's say you have a $2,500 balance on a revolving credit card account with an annual interest rate of 17.8 percent. The terms of your debt are that you will pay 2.5 percent of the outstanding balance each month. You have stopped using the card, so you are adding no new purchases. You make your minimum payment every month without fail, and you are never late. Still (and I hope you are sitting down for what follows), it will take twenty years and one month to reach $0. You read that right: 241 months. But wait! There's more. Of course, you will repay the $2,500 you borrowed, but you will also pay $3,275 in interest for a total repayment of $5,775. What makes things even worse is that the chances you will own any of the things you purchased on that credit card by the time you pay it back are slim to none. And, worse still, the chances you will pay faithfully for 241 months and never add another dime to the card are also quite slim. Your best bet is to pay the entire balance now and then get rid of that card altogether if there's the slightest chance you will ever again roll a balance from one month to the next.

Perhaps you see more clearly now why credit card companies are so eager to sign up new customers and to increase the credit limits of their current customers. It's not that they have a particular fondness for you or want to make your life easier. In fact, they are quite happy when you pay late or go over your limit. And they love it when they can resort to the fine print on the application you signed to increase your interest rate to the highest allowed in your state.

Semi-Toxic or Somewhat Intelligent?

Not all debt situations are as black-and-white as the mortgage loan versus the credit card balance. There's the automobile loan and the home equity line of credit. And who can forget the ever-popular student loan? Would those debts fall under intelligent borrowing or toxic debt?

Automobile Loans

Technically, this is a secured loan because the lender retains ownership of the car until it is paid for in full. If you have an auto loan, a bank or finance company is listed as the "lien holder." Only when the loan is paid in full do you receive the title with full ownership transferred to your name.

An auto loan is an intelligent debt for as long as the vehicle has a market value greater than the amount of the loan. In some situations, that lasts about twenty minutes after driving it off the showroom floor. Some experts say a new car loses 20 percent of its purchase price the first time around the block. If you have a substantial down payment, you may be okay, with the loan remaining less than the value. However, it is far too common for an automobile loan to turn "upside down," where the debt is

120

greater than the car's value. At that moment, the auto loan slips into toxic territory.

Student Loans

If ever there was a gray area in this matter of debt, it has to be the troublesome student loan.

Some argue that a student loan qualifies as intelligent borrowing because one's education will appreciate over time and will more than pay for itself in future income. That argument, in my opinion, makes some bold assumptions: first, that you will actually finish school; second, that you will be well suited for the field in which you are getting your degree; and third, that the field will welcome you. It is sobering to think that 73 percent of college graduates do not end up working in their major field of study.[4] That is understandable. I recall changing my mind many times at that young age. The problem arises when that young person is compelled to drag heavy, often debilitating student loans through life with none of the safety valves associated with intelligent borrowing. It is a harsh consequence and one that has the potential of severely altering the course of one's life.

I've lost count of how many letters I've received from people who believe they've had to settle for second best because their student loans have prevented them from following what they believe to be the call of God on their lives. They are compelled to remain chained to a job they loathe because to go to the mission field or join a cause that is dear to their hearts would not pay enough to service a lifetime of student debt repayment.

Home Equity Loans

A home equity loan, appropriately referred to in the industry as HEL, is a second mortgage secured by the equity in your home. It does have all the earmarks of intelligent borrowing in that it is a mortgage. But the nature of a HEL makes it risky. If you borrow against your equity to clean up your credit card debt and then run up your credit cards all over again, you will have twice the debt—the HEL and the credit card debt. It is not intelligent to use an appreciating asset (home equity) to pay for depreciating goods and services (credit card balances).

Another HEL risk is that, together with the first mortgage, your mortgages exceed the market value of your home. Some lenders will finance the full value of a home; some will even exceed it up to 125 percent. At that point, selling the property ceases to be a way out because more is owed than could be realized from a sale.

That's what happened in 2007 to set off what has come to be known as the Great Recession. Happy homeowners discovered they could mortgage their homes for more than market value by simply taking out big HELs. When market values plummeted, they found themselves "underwater," owing more on their homes than the properties were worth. That's a very simplified synopsis of a very complicated economic situation, but it should serve as a warning for why it is dangerous, if not foolish, to use a HEL to tap into a home's equity.

If it were not for the home loan industry in this country, few of us would be able to buy a home. However, I am hardly a fan of unsecured consumer debt. From now on, when I refer to "debt," I am speaking of unsecured consumer debt, unless otherwise noted. In your desire to debt-proof your marriage, your mission is to rid your life and your future of all toxic debt, to borrow money only when it cannot be avoided (buying a house, for instance), and then to do so as intelligently as possible.

11

You Are Here

Discovering Your Worth

If you live for having it all, what you have is never enough.

Joe Dominquez, *Your Money or Your Life*

Years ago I read the book *Your Money or Your Life*.[1] For the first time I understood the correlation between income and expenses. I had assumed the money we received was ours to spend. And spend I did—all that we received and a lot more. As far as I was concerned, our income qualified us for certain things. Our income determined how nice of a house we could live in, what kind of cars we could drive, and how much credit we could get. Naively, I figured that magically somehow in the end everything would just work out. That flawed thinking meant I had to learn some very difficult lessons.

The truth is it doesn't matter how much money you earn. What counts is what you do with it and how much of it you keep.

Take a look at this simple illustration of your household income over your earnings lifetime (fig. 1). Your income starts low and increases over time. Simple concept.

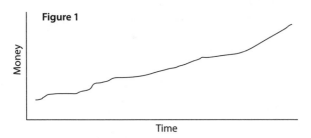

Now let's chart your spending by contrast. If you spend what you earn, no more and no less, your money life looks like figure 2. You have as much left at the end of your earning years as you had at the beginning: none. That's because you spent every dollar you earned. You enter retirement broke, hoping Social Security and any pensions you've qualified for along the way will see you through your sunset years.

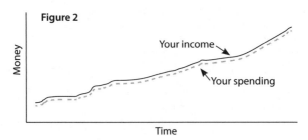

As pathetic as figure 2 may appear, your situation could be even worse, as shown in figure 3.

In this scenario, you start out fine. Your earnings are slim, but you manage to keep your spending in check. Soon you are spending all you earn. Then you discover the "magic" of credit. You can spend money you haven't earned yet. You buy things now and pay for them at the end of the month. Then things get tight

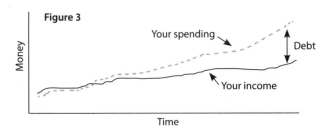

because you start overspending. You discover the minimum monthly payment option and decide to accept the credit card company's kind offer to let you carry over your balance to the next month (how generous). Before you know it, you have several cards, and you are carrying several balances. Your card companies love you so much that they increase your credit limits to give you more "spending power." Spending more than you earn becomes a way of life. It would not be unlikely, given this very common set of circumstances, for you to arrive at retirement deeply in debt, with your retirement income not coming close to meeting your financial obligations.

Thankfully, there is a better way. In the scenario illustrated in figure 4, you start out spending beneath your means even though your income is meager. As your income increases, you find ways to keep a lid on your spending. You live frugally. You spend less than you earn as a rule of life. You are careful to find every way possible to live well and still limit your outgo.

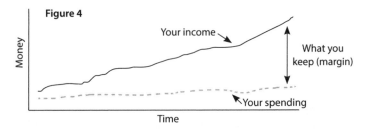

Your expenses do not increase at the same rate as your income. What you are not spending goes to work for you. Each month you sock it away, exposing it to compounding interest. You accumulate wealth on a limited income while living a life that is free from financial stress. As life hits you with seasons of unemployment, medical emergencies, and other financial challenges, you don't panic. You are prepared to handle the events of life because you live beneath your means and have created a nice margin. Figure 4 illustrates a debt-proof life.

For their book *The Millionaire Next Door: The Surprising Secrets of America's Wealthy*, the authors followed self-made millionaires for many years to discover what it was about their lifestyles and money management styles that allowed them to amass large sums of money.[2] What they discovered is fascinating. It's not that these people made so much money. What set them apart was their willingness to live simply, to drive used cars, to live in homes that were well beneath what they could qualify for—basically to live frugally so they could put the difference between what they earned and what they spent to work for them.

If you find yourself living a lifestyle that resembles figure 3 more than figure 4, don't be discouraged. The good news is that you can rechart your course. You can make a U-turn on the road to financial devastation. You can do some repair work. You can't start over, but you can start now. You can determine that you will do whatever it takes to get back on track, to spend less than you earn. Will it be difficult? That depends on how far off course you are. I'm not going to say it won't be hard work. And it's going to take some sacrifice for the short term at least. There are decisions you may have to make regarding your feelings of entitlement to drive fancy leased cars or to continue living in a home you cannot afford.

As you gain a clearer understanding of the big picture, as you begin to see the value of a warm, open, and honest relationship that is filled with respect and trust (not angst and despair), you will discover that material things are not all that important. A car is just a tool to get you from here to there. It does not define who you are. Contrary to a popular ad campaign several years ago, you are not what you drive! All the stuff that fills your life is just stuff.

How to Begin

Imagine you are lost in the forest. You've been wandering around for some time unable to get your bearings. You are confused, disoriented, and beginning to panic. But then you come upon a sign with a map and a big red arrow pointing to "You Are Here." No matter how far off course you've wandered, figuring out where you are in relation to where you want to be is empowering. Knowing where you are gives you a new sense of confidence and hope. Now you can figure your way out.

Seeing the big picture allows you to understand how you got lost and where you made a wrong move. And how you can find your way out. In a way, just getting your bearings and pointing yourself in the right direction is a kind of rescue even though you are in the same place you were before coming upon the sign.

You may be feeling that same kind of desperation when you think about your financial situation. You feel confused, disoriented, and hopelessly lost. Or it may only feel that way when, in fact, you could be much closer to where you want to be at this point in your life than you realize. But until you discover where you are, the confusion and fear will only escalate.

As scary and difficult as the process might seem to you right now, believe me when I tell you that just knowing where you are is going to give you that important starting point from which you will begin to measure your progress. You have to know where you are before you can plan to get where you want to be.

The way to pinpoint your exact location is with a balance sheet that lists everything you own and all that you owe. The purpose of a balance sheet is to determine your net worth. Your net worth is not determined by your income but rather by how much of your income you keep. The way you keep income is either by saving it or parlaying it into assets.

Before you can find out exactly where you are, you need to get organized. Knowing how different the two of you are, I have a feeling organization might come more naturally to one of you than the other. One of you may be a filer, the other a piler. Or it could be both of you are meticulous with your personal records or you're a couple of hopeless slobs. No matter which category you fall into, the two of you need to come up with a system for keeping things organized well enough to get the job done.

As financial partners, you both need to have a working knowledge of where your important papers are, what information is contained in those important papers, and the division of labor that will be required to maintain your financial routines. Your ideal situation might not be the exact system I suggest or even one anyone has ever heard of before. If it works for you, then it's the right system for you. But for now, it's important that you learn my system well. Once you've gotten it down, you'll be ready to customize things to fit you and your lifestyle.

You want a simple system. Your financial documents should be in a location that is accessible and convenient so the two of you can use the information on a regular basis without wasting a lot of time trying to find it. It needs to be a system that both of you like and are willing to use. Both of you.

If you're worried this is going to be a huge time commitment, relax. It really is a misconception that it takes a lot of time to manage your finances well. It can, but it shouldn't—unless, of course, you find this kind of thing enjoyable, in which case you might have just discovered a new hobby you can do together. One to two hours per month spent on money matters should do it. That leaves lots of time to work on your relationship and enjoy your lives.

At the end of this chapter, you will find guidelines on which documents you need to keep and for how long as well as those you can get rid of. You will need some of the information in those important papers to prepare your balance sheet.

A Balance Sheet

If you have kids, you probably remember those trips to the doctor during the first year. At each visit, you were so eager to see how much that precious little bundle weighed. You knew to the ounce how much he or she had gained, even wrote it down in a book. As our boys got older, we devoted a special wall to recording their growth. At least once a year, they stood up to the wall, and we placed a mark indicating their current heights to see how much they'd grown.

A balance sheet, sometimes called a statement of net worth, is like a growth chart. It is a snapshot of your financial situation at a certain point in time. Simply put, it shows you on paper how much money you would have left if everything you own was converted into cash and used to pay off all that you owe. A balance sheet shows what the two of you own (assets), all that together you owe to creditors (liabilities), and the net value or difference between what you owe and what you own (net worth).

Your balance sheet is an important tool for debt-proofing your marriage because it helps you:

- check and measure your financial progress and how you are doing with reaching your financial goals
- make decisions about acquiring assets and taking on liabilities in the future
- estimate how well-off your family would be if you were suddenly taken from them
- determine your need for life and property insurance

129

- make adjustments in your insurance coverage
- estimate what your income will be during your retirement

I don't want to underestimate or minimize how difficult this process may be for one or both of you, and I'm not talking about figuring out the math. I'm thinking of the emotional impact. Some of us find more comfort in not knowing this kind of thing because as long as we don't know, there's always a chance things aren't so bad (can you say, "Denial"?). I can identify with that kind of thinking. I really understand. Still, it is not a good excuse. You must do this. I'll hold your hand, and we'll walk through this together.

Your best approach is to talk first. Work toward sharing your fears. Try to figure out why you are so fearful to learn the truth about your financial situation. Even if you are sweating bullets, I encourage you to proceed with this task. Don't dawdle or hesitate. That will not make it any easier. Instead, write down your fears. Put into words what you are feeling and why it makes you uneasy. Ask your spouse to read what you wrote, and you should read what he or she wrote.

Preparing your balance sheet may be the first time you are brutally honest with each other about any money secrets you've been hiding. If you have no secrets, it may still be the first time you come face-to-face with the enormity of your debts. Perhaps you've been naively lulling yourself into a false sense of security because you have checks in the checkbook and the ATM card still does its magic. Your financial situation could be many times better than you ever dreamed or far worse. But you'll never know and you'll never get started improving it and developing financial harmony until you sit down and do this very difficult thing.

Below is a sample balance sheet you can follow as an example. You could spend money to buy a preprinted balance sheet or net worth statement form at a store, but why spend money when you can do this yourself? Notebook paper will do just fine. If one of you is handy on the computer, you'll whip out a perfect form before you finish this chapter.

Bob and Sally's Balance Sheet

	Amount in 2013	Amount in 2015
Wealth-Building Assets		
Cash	1,500	1,500
Contingency fund	0	10,000
Stocks, bonds, and other investments	0	3,500
401(k)/IRA	12,500	35,800
House, current market value	120,000	165,000
Other Assets		
Car 1, current market value	6,000	2,000
Car 2, current market value	18,000	10,000
Personal property	5,000	8,000
Furniture	5,000	4,000
Total Assets	168,000	239,800
Liabilities		
Home mortgage	85,000	65,000
Home equity loan	12,000	0
Car 1 loan balance	5,000	0
Car 2 loan balance	16,000	9,000
Student loans	45,000	41,500
Credit card balances (all of them)	14,500	3,500
Miscellaneous	2,000	0
Total Liabilities	179,500	119,000
Net Worth	($11,500)	$120,800

What made the difference in Bob and Sally's net worth between 2013 and 2015? They didn't win the lottery or get an inheritance. Their income didn't increase significantly. What changed was their attitude toward debt, spending, and building wealth. They decided to buckle down and debt-proof their marriage. Just imagine where they'll be five or ten years from now!

Assets

Your assets are divided into two categories: wealth-building assets and other assets.

A wealth-building asset is a possession that generally increases in value over time. Examples would be a house, a savings account, a retirement plan, stocks and bonds, and some collectibles. On your balance sheet, list each of your wealth-building assets with a corresponding value. For example, if your home is worth $200,000 on today's market and you have a $100,000 mortgage, list it as $200,000 under your wealth-building assets.

Use actual cash figures for cash on hand and in checking and savings accounts. If your savings account shows $1,273 today, enter that amount exactly. Include money owed to you only if you are certain of repayment. For example, if you lent $1,000 to a friend at 8 percent interest and he has already repaid $300, enter this as $700 under wealth-building assets. Do not value potential interest you will earn. To find the current value of your investments, check market quotes in a current newspaper or online by simply typing the ticker symbol into your search engine. If you don't know the symbol, you can look it up at a site such as www.finance.yahoo .com.

Possessions such as your car, big screen television, boat, clothes, jewelry, and household goods are "other assets" because while they have value, they are depreciating or becoming less valuable with time. Unless your car is a rare collector's item, it is worth less today than it was yesterday. In fact, if you bought it new, it was worth 20 percent less the day after you bought it due to depreciation.

It is customary to group assets into categories such as "real estate" or "personal property," which would include your clothes and household goods. Some experts suggest an estimate of $10,000 current market value for the personal property, including furniture, of a typical two-adult household. You may wish to use that figure or determine your own. If you have a lot of valuable furniture or collectibles, you can list them separately. It's up to you because this is, after all, your balance sheet.

If you have many personal assets, you may want to start with a household inventory on another sheet of paper, assigning market value (not replacement value) for each item and then organizing them into groups. (Keep that document in the event of a major loss in the future.) When it comes to assigning current dollar values, estimate conservatively. To get an estimate of the current value of things you own, check ebay.com to see what similar items have sold for recently. For special personal property such as jewelry or antiques, you might want to consider getting an appraisal by a credentialed expert, although that is certainly not necessary. Vehicle valuations can be found in the Kelly Blue Book, available at the library, automobile dealers, financial institutions, or online (kbb.com). Don't hesitate to get the help of an expert in estimating the value of your home or other real estate if you do not have an idea of what those possessions are worth.

Okay, add it up. You should have an accurate picture of the value of your assets. Wouldn't it be nice if you could just stop there? Perhaps one day you'll be able to do that, but until then you must take into account your debts.

Liabilities

List everything you owe, including credit card balances, medical bills, personal loans, overdraft protection account balances, student loans, mortgages, home equity loans and lines of credit, loans from your retirement accounts, auto loans and leases, taxes if you have an unpaid balance due—everything you have a legal and moral obligation to repay. You can find current balances on payment stubs, monthly statements, or by checking with lenders. Start listing your current outstanding balances, and don't stop until you have accounted for every debt. Total your liabilities.

How to Debt-Proof Your Marriage

Net Worth

Now for the decisive moment. Subtract the liabilities from the assets. Take a deep breath, hold hands, cry, laugh . . . whatever it takes to get through the moment. The result is your net worth as of this date. Yes, it is possible to have a negative net worth even though you have a great-paying job, a beautiful home, and money in the bank. If, God forbid, you do have a negative net worth, consider this a wake-up call and determine right now that you're going to do whatever it takes to change it.

If you are in the red—a term that comes from the days when negative entries were written in red ink—you are living beyond your means thanks to the generosity of the consumer credit industry. You have more debt than you have assets. You are asset challenged, overextended. You are beholden, in bondage, and at the mercy of creditors who don't care one whit about you or your future. Do you know what you are to them? An asset! Your names are all over the top half of their balance sheets. Surely King Solomon had this very thing in mind when he wrote, "The rich ruleth over the poor, and the borrower is servant to the lender" (Prov. 22:7 KJV). I know what that feels like—to know that MasterCard and Visa (and so many more) owned a piece of me.

Please pay special attention to this very important fact: it doesn't matter how much money you earn. Your balance sheet is so unconcerned about your income that there is not even a place to record it. So if you've been patting yourself on the back because you make six figures, get over it.

What matters is how much of that income you hang on to. Your net worth tells the story. It doesn't lie; it doesn't deceive. What matters is the last number—the bottom line—which reveals how much of your income you've managed to keep. If it is a negative number, you've spent more than you've earned and have relied on credit to fill in the gap.

What you see on your balance sheet is your financial condition today. If you are discouraged, let me encourage you. As helpless or as hopeless as you may feel right now, you have control over this situation. This is a picture you can change starting now. Look at your balance sheet again. Focus on one of your debts, like a credit card debt. Imagine that you reduce that balance by $5 when you send a check tomorrow. That will immediately increase your net worth by—you guessed it!—$5. Five dollars here, $10 there . . . one step at a time—that's the way you're going to debt-proof your marriage.

Whatever your financial situation, you have to see your balance sheet as a summary of all the financial decisions and choices you have made in the past. Whether it was a decision that resulted in a big student loan balance or a great pair of shoes, it comes home to roost eventually.

You can continue to run and hide and pretend it doesn't matter how much you spend or what you do with your money. You can continue to assume that the only thing that matters is whether you can keep the bills current or how much more credit you can amass. Or you can face the truth, get real about the way money is leaking out of your life, and make a decision right now to do something about it.

Basic Resources for Organizing Your Financial Life

To keep track of your financial life, you need certain financial documents. Some financial documents are important to keep indefinitely, some should be kept for only a while, and others are just clutter and should be purged regularly.

To stay organized, at the very least you need:

- file box, file drawer, or cabinet
- file folders

- paper shredder
- small fireproof box or safe

Your passports, mortgage, wills, trusts, birth certificates, marriage certificate, and other significant documents should be kept in a locked, fireproof and heat-proof safe or a safe-deposit box at your bank. Just remember that in many states in the event that one of you dies, a jointly held safe-deposit box cannot be opened without a court order unless you have power of attorney for each other (which you should).

How long should you keep your important papers and legal documents?

Keep the following records indefinitely:

- deeds
- trusts, wills
- original cost, value, and purchase date of all investments or other property that could be sold or transferred
- dated receipts and explanations of home improvements
- income tax returns used in divorce or estate settlements
- education and employment records
- family health and medical records
- pension and Social Security information
- insurance and accident reports and claims
- identification cards
- blood types
- driver's license information
- emergency information
- living wills, organ donor authorizations, power of attorney
- birth certificates, marriage certificates, divorce decrees
- passports
- personal property inventory

- location of important papers
- a list of jewelry, antiques, collectibles
- location of legal documents
- safe-deposit box contents and location
- military service records

Keep the following records for seven years:

- tax returns
- all records pertaining to income or deductions on your tax returns
- moving expenses
- business or employee expense records
- appraisals
- charitable contributions
- medical expenses
- depreciation inventory

Keep the following records as long as the situation is active:

- legal documents and contracts
- membership records
- insurance policies
- credit card numbers, addresses, and account information
- installment and mortgage records
- receipts and records of bills paid
- savings and investment documents and records
- vehicle records
- owner's manuals and warranties

In general, you do not need to keep:

- bank statements for closed accounts
- expired warranties

- canceled checks for minor items that are not proof of purchases or income tax related
- grocery store receipts
- instructions for appliances or equipment you have sold or discarded

Once you have designated the location for your important papers, decide on the categories you will need. Each category should have its own file folder or section.

1. personal papers
   - birth certificates
   - marriage certificate
   - medical records
   - divorce settlements (if any)
   - wills
   - power of attorney

2. insurance policies
   - health
   - life
   - auto
   - homeowners
   - disability
   - long-term care

3. banking
   - account statements
   - canceled checks (if you still receive them)
   - certificates of deposit (CDs)
   - savings bonds
   - negotiable notes and certificates

4. bills to be paid
   - telephone
   - gas
   - electric
   - cable
   - internet
   - other
5. credit cards, mortgages, and other loans
   - original terms and copies of all signed documents (one folder for each creditor)
6. financial records
   - pay stubs (keep one year's worth and then discard)
   - balance sheets
   - rapid debt-repayment plan
   - freedom account
7. investment records
   - IRA and other retirement account records
   - brokerage and investment records
8. major appliances
   - receipts
   - warranties
   - owner's manuals
9. taxes
   - returns
   - receipts and documentation
   - donation records

Are your assets more than your liabilities? Great! Good work. We'll talk about how to make your good situation even better. Was the balance sheet your wake-up call for action? In the same way your past financial choices brought you to this moment, you can make the choice right now to change things. Together you can effect change in the way you manage and care for your income. No matter what your balance sheet reveals, you can improve it, and you can begin today. I'm going to show you exactly how.

12

Getting Where You Want to Be

The Basic Elements of Your Financial Plan

We all want progress, but if you're on the wrong road, progress means doing an about-turn and walking back to the right road; in that case, the man who turns back soonest is the most progressive.

C. S. Lewis[1]

Houses come in all sizes and varieties, from the Biltmore Estate at one extreme to, well, my house on the other. You'd know what a range that represents if you saw my house. Don't get me wrong. I love our home, but it's no Biltmore.

As dissimilar as these two dwellings are, I can guarantee my house has several things in common with the Biltmore. Both have a foundation, structural framing, an electrical conduit, and a plumbing system. In fact, most houses share these elements of basic infrastructure. Once the basic elements are in place, houses take on their uniqueness, so eventually no two are exactly alike. Some may look very much the same from the outside, but once a family moves in, each takes on unique characteristics that reflect the lifestyle, personalities, and tastes of the people who turn that house into a home. Still, the basic elements remain vitally important to the very existence of that home.

In the same way no two homes are exactly alike, no two financial situations are the same either. That means that the money management system Harold and I have devised over the years to fit our situation and lifestyle probably would not work well for yours. That's because we have taken basic, standard financial management elements (the ones I am going to teach to you) and customized them to fit us.

Creating your unique money management plan will be a lot like building a house. I will give you the basic elements for your management system and then show you how to put them together so that each one supports the others. But here's the best news: once you have them in place, you're good to go, and not just for the foreseeable future but for the rest of your lives. You won't have to dump the system in favor of something more sophisticated as your earning power, your net worth, and your options increase. As your financial picture changes, your management system will adjust and change right alongside it. And once the basic elements are in place and you are comfortable with the way they work, you'll be ready to customize the system to reflect your situation, your personalities, and your marriage—perfectly.

The debt-proof living plan consists of a formula and four tangible elements that you will be able to hold in your hands.

The Formula

The formula of the debt-proof living plan says that for every dollar you receive, you will give away 10 percent, save 10 percent, and then adjust your lifestyle to fit within 80 percent of your income. No matter how your financial situation fluctuates, this is an unchanging financial principle that will guide you for the rest of your life.

In the interest of full disclosure, I must tell you that in the past I would have encouraged you to apply the 10-10-80 formula to your gross income, thus treating your payroll taxes and other withholding as regular expenses. Practically speaking, doing so is complicated and confusing beyond reason. Dealing with net income, or take-home pay—the amount you receive in your hand—is more doable. You can always adjust in the future if you decide you'd rather work with your gross income, which is the full amount you are paid before any withholding for taxes, Social Security, and so forth.

The Contingency Fund

The contingency fund is a pool of money that will keep your financial boat floating in the event you and your income part company for some unknown period of time. There will come a time when, for one reason or another, your income stream will be cut off, and if you have not prepared, you could find yourself in big trouble. The contingency fund is an emergency nest egg. Your top priority will be to keep it safe.

The Spending Plan

How many of you have tried making a budget in the past and concluded it just doesn't work? Come on, let's see those hands. Okay, that's just about everybody. I'll be the first to say that budgets don't work. Just the word sounds like a diet, and that means deprivation. So you can relax. No budgets in this book. A spending plan is different. It's just a plan for how you will spend your money—a plan you design and customize to fit your exact situation. Once you get past the shock of what you learn in the process, I believe you will find a spending plan to be empowering. You're going to get a sense of relief as you find yourself gaining control of all the money that has a way of leaking out of your life.

The Freedom Account

The freedom account is a separate bank account in which you set aside money to cover irregular, unexpected, and intermittent expenses. Think back to the times you were caught off guard with a big expense for which you were not prepared. How did you respond? If you ran to a credit card or some other kind of credit, you're certainly not alone! We've been conditioned to believe that's what credit cards are for—to cover all life's little emergencies. But that's wrong, and the freedom account is going to be your emancipation.

The Rapid Debt-Repayment Plan

Here is the best way I know to describe my rapid debt-repayment plan (RDRP): amazing. You are going to be amazed to see not only that you can get out of debt but also that you can do it methodically and rapidly. And you're going to do it using your current minimum monthly payments. Even if you can pay no more each month than you are right now, you are going to get out of debt! My RDRP fits all the criteria of a good plan. I will tell you exactly (1) how to start, (2) what to do, (3) how to measure your progress, and (4) the exact month and year you will reach your goal. In fact, I'm going to help you reduce your entire debt mess to a simple, logical payment schedule you can print and hang on your refrigerator. That's so you can look at it every day and know exactly where you are in relation to where you're going.

13

A Life-Changing Formula

The 80 Percent Solution

Without frugality, none can be rich and with it, none can be poor.

Samuel Johnson[1]

You may be thinking that the only way you could live on 80 percent of your income would be if you stopped eating and moved the family into a tent down by the river.

If you can't make it on 100 percent, what kind of a fool would suggest you could do better on even less? The truth of the matter is this: if you're carrying a load of debt, you are probably living on something closer to 125 percent of your income. Worse, you probably don't know for sure where all your money goes or how much your current lifestyle is actually costing. That's a real problem. And I believe I have the solution. The 10-10-80 formula is brilliant in its simplicity. Wish I'd thought of it. Some say the concept can be traced to ancient Babylon.

145

The 10-10-80 formula offers structure, form, and discipline to any financial situation. It eliminates the guesswork. This formula completely changed my life and my marriage, and I've seen the same thing happen for countless others. I know it can work for you too.

Give Away 10 Percent

Take a look at the formula again and notice the order. It's not 80-10-10 or 10-80-10. The correct sequence is 10-10-80. You give first, you pay yourself second, and with the 80 percent that remains, you pay your creditors and you live life to its fullest. Is that just about opposite of the way you've been handling your money? If you are like most people, you pay your bills and your creditors first, and if there's anything left—which there is rarely—you put some in savings and tell God, sorry, maybe next month.

I'm going to assume, based on the fact that you're reading this book, that your method is not working out for you. And I'm not surprised. You're doing everything backward when you fund your lifestyle first and assume by some miracle that you'll be able to put on the brakes, not spend all your income, and have some money left for your future and for God. Most of us just aren't that disciplined. This is why it is so important that you give before you pay yourself or anyone else.

Why Give

Giving is the antidote for greed, selfishness, and attitudes of entitlement. It's like an antibiotic for a terrible disease. Giving is the purest form of gratitude because it is the tangible way we can say thanks. When we give, we acknowledge that while we cannot have it all, we do have enough.

Giving is the solution to what's wrong with our attitude toward money because it changes our hearts. Giving helps us see the bigger picture so we can set priorities and make necessary sacrifices. Giving is the best treatment for envy, covetousness, and peer pressure.

But giving does more than that for us. It connects us to the world and helps us see past ourselves. Giving allows us to see the world through eyes of compassion. Giving develops our faith and pulls the plug on our greed and compulsive money behaviors. Giving calms down that thing that lives inside some of us that says, "I want more and more and more!" It quiets our insatiable desires because it helps us take our eyes off ourselves and, as a bonus, brings much-needed balance to an otherwise out-of-control financial situation.

Where to Give

As you turn your eyes outward, you will begin to see all the needs. I have a feeling something or someone is going to come to mind. What issues are you compassionate about? Are you involved in a church? Think about your community. What needs tug at your heart?

Once you've made your decision about where to give, do it with no strings attached. Write the check, give online, or deliver the cash. Giving in its purest form is done with a heart that says we wish it were more and we expect nothing in return.

There are no rules here, only a few guidelines and suggestions. As long as you are giving with no strings attached and no expectations of anything in return, you can make just about anything or anyone the object of your giving. However, keep a couple of things in mind. When giving to charitable organizations, including ministries and churches, you have a responsibility to know what that organization does, how it operates, and how the leaders use their money. You can ask for financial statements if you are not already familiar with the organization. If the group is recognized by the IRS as a nonprofit corporation, you will receive a receipt for your donations, the total of which you may deduct from your gross income when you itemize your income tax return. There are websites where you can check up on charitable nonprofit organizations to see how much they spend on administration, salaries, and other expenses and how much of the money they receive actually makes it to the cause for which they are in operation. Charity Navigator (charitynavigator.org) is the largest independent charity evaluator, providing free ratings of the financial health, accountability, and transparency of thousands of charities. Another site, guidestar.org, offers access to many nonprofits' form 990, which is filed with the IRS and offers insight into the organization's management.

How to Give

The easiest way to get started with consistent giving is to treat it like a regular bill. Make up envelopes and your own payment coupons and keep them in the front of your bills folder. Treat your giving with the same level of commitment you do your rent or mortgage payment and other essential expenses.

If this idea of giving is something new for you, 10 percent may seem like a high hurdle. Please don't let that number appear to be so large that you convince yourself to give nothing. If you can't agree on 10 percent, negotiate until you find an amount you can agree on. Like 2 percent. Then next month talk about it. Consider 3 percent. Ask God to increase your faith and your willingness to trust him. I want you to start giving because I know how this is going to turn out. What giving will do to your relationship and your financial situation will be amazing. I believe that giving exposes our financial situations to God's supernatural intervention. I don't want you to miss out on that.

Your willingness and commitment to give back some of what is so precious to you proves the condition of your heart. More than anything else, God is concerned about the condition of your heart.

Save 10 Percent

The second 10 percent in the 10-10-80 formula refers to the 10 percent of your income you are going to pay to yourself right after you give away 10 percent and before you pay anyone else. Before the mortgage, before MasterCard or Visa, before anyone else takes a bite out of your income, 10 percent is to be put away in a safe place and for a specific purpose.

When I say "put away," I mean put it away! We're talking about serious saving for the long term—not money to buy a new sofa or to go on a vacation. It's not a casual or haphazard activity.

While saving a set percentage of all income is not a new concept, it is something I'd never considered until I read a fascinating book called *The Richest Man in Babylon,* written by George S. Clason and first published in 1926. Clason writes:

> Say to yourself, "A part of all I earn is mine to keep." Say it in the morning when you first arise. Say it at noon. Say it at night. Say it each hour of every day. Say it to yourself until the words stand out like letters of fire across the sky. Impress yourself with the idea. Fill yourself with the thought. Then take whatever portion seems wise. Let it be not less than one-tenth and lay it by. Arrange your other expenditures to do this if necessary. But lay by that portion first. Soon you will realize what a rich feeling it is to own a treasure upon which you alone have claim. As it grows it will stimulate you. A new joy of life will thrill you. Greater efforts will come to you to earn more. For of your increased earnings will not the same percentage be also yours to keep?[2]

If you are deeply in debt or find it difficult to keep things together because money is so tight, you may be thinking that it would be wrong to keep some of your money for yourself when you owe so much to so many.

Paying yourself first is going to do more than build a nest egg. Caring for yourself in this way is a reasonable way to acknowledge your self-worth. It will also allow you to prepare for the unexpected, to repair the damage that debt has done in your life more quickly, and to prepare for retirement. It is also going to contribute enormously to your relationship and collective peace of mind.

You may be deeply in debt and believe with all your heart that you do not have enough to save. Even if you believe your financial situation is hopeless, I am going to make a bold statement: seeing yourself as worthy enough to keep some of the money you have been given the responsibility to manage is going to be key in fixing your money ills. Saving money is going to change your attitude and give you the courage and the strength to face the challenges that lie ahead. Saving money is one of the best attitude adjusters you will ever know. And since debt-proofing your marriage is going to be 10 percent about money and 90 percent about your attitude, you cannot get started soon enough.

Think of saving 10 percent of your income in the same way you think about wearing your seat belt. You wouldn't dream of driving without wearing your seat belt (you wouldn't, right?). It's a safety thing, a lot like insurance. You have it but hope you won't need it. It's there to protect you in case something broadsides you without warning. Soon you will see saving 10 percent of your income as a kind of shock absorber against the harshness and uncertainty of life. And just like belting up before taking off in the car has become a habit, paying yourself first will become a habit too. A comforting and joyful habit. The time will come, and not too far from now, when you'll be as uncomfortable not saving as you are not wearing your seat belt.

If you've ever experienced something called shopper's high, you and I have something in common. I used to depend on that rush of adrenaline as an antidepressant. If I had a bad day or felt particularly anxious, I could count on a quick trip to the mall to make me feel better. I'm sure we could analyze ourselves to death, but suffice it to say the sense of buying something without having to pay for it (that's what it feels like to a credit card junkie) gave me a buzz, a momentary rush. It didn't really matter what I bought. If it was clothing or shoes, I'd rarely try them on, telling myself I'd just return them if they didn't fit. If it was something for my boys or husband, I rationalized that I was being a good mother or wife. I loved the thrill of the bargain, the act of acquisition. And it really did the trick. If I could spend money, it felt as if I had money. It made me feel better. For a moment—two at the most.

I have discovered the most amazing thing. Giving and saving give me the same sense of satisfaction I used to get from spending with plastic, with one exception: it doesn't wear off. More than that, giving and saving help me clear my head so I can see the big picture. It's not all about me and my stuff and my house and my kids and my car and my furniture and how much I don't have compared to others. Giving to others and saving for the future put things into proper perspective, and that's when I find contentment. I understand that I am not in charge of my life, that I am a steward, a caretaker to whom God has entrusted a portion of his abundance. And when he sees that he can trust me with those gifts, I believe that pleases him, and then he can trust me with more.

Since we began to give and save with commitment and consistency, I've experienced contentment and patience in a way I'd not known before. I can truly say that Harold and I gave and saved our way out of debt and then on to financial health. Perhaps that doesn't make sense to you right now, but I tell you it is the absolute truth. Soon you will experience this for yourself. Then you will understand.

Live on 80 Percent

Getting in control of your money has little to do with your income. In your heart, you may still be convinced that if you just had more money everything would be peachy. Trust me. Whatever your present situation, it would only escalate if you had more money. If you're in debt now, more money would only increase the debt. If you have difficulty saving now, more money would make it that much more difficult. Getting in control of your finances depends much more on your spending habits than the size of your paycheck.

It is going to be challenging to adjust your living expenses so that your debt repayment and current bills do not exceed 80 percent of your take-home pay. It will get easier in time, you can count on that. What's more, I believe you are going to find a sense of relief in setting specific financial boundaries and then operating within them. Until now it's possible your spending has had a "floating" limit determined by how much credit you could stir up or when the ATM machine refused to cough up any more cash.

Reducing your living expenses so they fit within 80 percent of your net income will require you to scrutinize every expense and then find the best way to reduce it. By reducing everything a little bit, you may be able to avoid eliminating any spending categories. But I'll warn you now: this is going to require creativity and discipline. Thankfully, you have each other to share the requirement and the responsibility.

Frugality

Frugal, thrifty, cheap. Those words used to be so repulsive to me. I couldn't think of anything more insulting than to be called cheap. I equated frugality with digging through dumpsters in search of food and who knows what else. To me, cheap people skipped out without leaving a tip. I couldn't bear the thought of living that way, and to make sure I would never be mistaken for someone who did, I charged my way through life bent on proving to the world (and to myself) that I was not cheap.

All that is to say if you're feeling a little squeamish about the word *frugality*, I understand. You'll get over it. Frugality is doing whatever it takes to live within your means, which you now understand is 80 percent of your net income. The rightness and the joy that kind of living brings overcome all misgivings about what others might think about this matter of frugality.

Frugality is not about stuffing everyone into the same mold so we all spend the same amount of money on things like food or housing. Frugality is about restraint, discipline, finding the best value, and not being wasteful. It's about making choices and understanding that if you say yes to one thing, you may need to say no to something else.

Pulling in the reins on your lifestyle is going to require significant changes in the ways you think about and spend money. You didn't get where you are overnight, so to expect an instantaneous reversal would be unrealistic. If you just keep going one step at a time and determine that you will never give up no matter what, you'll make it—probably much sooner than you ever dreamed possible.

14

Knowledge Is a Powerful Thing

The Spending Record

Money is always on its way somewhere. What we do with it while it's in our keeping says much about us.

Rosalie Maggio[1]

For me, the word *budget* is like fingernails on a chalkboard. It screeches confinement, deprivation. Like a straitjacket. Or worse, a diet!

A plan, on the other hand, is a detailed strategy designed to accomplish a specific goal. Psychologically, there's a huge difference between a budget and a spending plan. Budgets confine; spending plans liberate. Budgets are fixed; spending plans are flexible. Budgets are absolute; spending plans are guidelines.

If a budget were an article of clothing, it would be ready-made, off-the-rack, with a one-size-fits-all label. In contrast, a spending plan is like fine fabric and exact measurements in the hands of an expert tailor.

In the same way an architect "builds" a house on paper long before the actual construction begins, a spending plan is a design on paper for how you plan to distribute your income. A spending plan directs a family's income the way a conductor directs an orchestra. And you are the co-composers. Together, the two of you are going to write the score.

If you've ever attempted to create a budget in the past (who hasn't?), you probably took out a sheet of paper, wrote down your expenses, and ran a total. Then you jotted down your income, deducted your expenses, and remarked, while scratching your head, "So what's the problem?" That's because most couples look great on paper. In most cases, however, that reflection is nowhere close to reality.

Perhaps you've met with a counselor or taken a class on money management with a single purpose: to get on a budget! You wrestled with pie charts and bar graphs, trying to cram yourself into a rigid framework that had "Budget" plastered across the top. As with a pair of jeans one size too small, with a lot of struggle you finally got that budget on, but you couldn't move. You tried to "wear" that budget for a while, but you gave up because it just didn't fit. So much for budgets.

Maybe it's a problem with semantics, but for whatever reason, my experience is that budgets just don't work. So let's forget the "b" word. Instead, I am going to teach you how to create your own custom spending plan—a system that will fit you and your situation perfectly. But more than that, it will remain flexible and fluid to move and grow in the same ways you will change and develop in the coming years.

Think of developing your spending plan as a five-chapter process. In this chapter, you will learn how to establish your spending baseline with a spending record. In chapters 15, 16, and 17, you will develop the infrastructure of your spending plan with your contingency fund, freedom account, and rapid debt-repayment plan. These elements, beginning with the spending record, are pieces to a puzzle, which you will put together in chapter 18.

Your spending plan will be a one- or two-page document that will be simple to decipher and more user-friendly than you ever dreamed possible. You will think of it as a road map or a cheat sheet because it will hold all the secrets for how you are going to manage your money so you can get out of debt, live financially prepared, even for the unexpected, and be on your way to financial freedom.

First, a Spending Record

Before you can create your spending plan, you need an accurate record of your spending. There are two critical pieces of information you need to create a spending record:

1. your average monthly net income
2. a detailed record of where that income goes

This information will form a baseline. It is crucial that your baseline reflect your expenses, your lifestyle, your desires, and your values.

If you don't have this information readily available, join the crowd. Most couples do not know their average monthly net income, nor do they know with certainty where all their money goes. In fact, most of us would just as soon not have to deal with this information. On the scale of terrifying things, facing the details of our financial situations comes in high. In fact, it wouldn't surprise me at all to know that your stomach is beginning to churn, your palms are getting sweaty, and you're concerned about what follows on the next few pages. Do me a favor . . . give this a chance. I can almost guarantee that your anticipatory fear is greater than what is warranted. And even if your situation is bad, nothing could be worse than continuing in the same direction you've been going.

The spending record is going to take some time and commitment from both of you, but this information is absolutely critical to the process.

How Much Do You Make a Month?

Most spouses have a fairly accurate idea of their annual income. I'm basing that on the people I've communicated with over the years. But here's an interesting fact: most of us express income as an annual gross figure ("We make $80,000 a year") rather than a monthly figure ("We average $4,398 a month").

I've concluded that it's human nature to use the more impressive number because it is, well, more impressive. (In contrast, most people don't express their expenses in annual terms but in the smallest terms possible, as in, "I spend $3 a day on cappuccino.")

Your first order of business is to determine your average monthly net income. This is what you actually bring home after all the deductions (whether mandated by law or done by choice, as in the case of a retirement plan) have been made. Your net income is what you can count on every month.

Regardless of your payroll schedule or the frequency with which you receive other sources of income, you must come up with your average monthly income. If you are self-employed, don't assume this does not apply to you. As an employee of yourself, you need to put you the employee on a strict salary (more about that later).

Determining your average monthly income can get a little tricky depending on whether you have one or more incomes between you, how often you are paid, and if you have additional sources of income you can count on. If you have more than one income between you and you are paid on different schedules, calculate them separately and then add the numbers together to come up with one figure.

Here's a formula to help you determine your average monthly income if you receive it other than once a month:

Weekly: Multiply your weekly net income by 4.333
Biweekly: Multiply your biweekly net income by 2.167
Semimonthly: Multiply your semimonthly net income by 2
Quarterly: Divide your quarterly net income by 3
Annually: Divide your annual net income by 12

When you get that number, take a moment to be either shocked or delighted, but stay as nonemotional as possible. Remember, right now you are business partners, wearing your business hats, with your business-meeting attitudes and mind-sets. You have set your emotions aside for the time, and you are dealing with facts and principles.

Once you determine your average monthly income, write it down. Begin now to replace your prior idea of your household income (that more impressive annual gross figure) with this more realistic monthly figure.

Where Does Your Money Go?

Determining your average monthly income is a cinch compared to your next task. I'm not going to sugarcoat this step. It will be tedious at times, emotionally threatening, and basically a pain in the neck. But I know that you are up to the task. I have more faith in you than you could possibly imagine. I base my confidence on the fact that you've come this far in the book and appear to have every intention of going the distance.

The goal is to be able to account for every cent that comes into your life from today forward. I know that sounds radical and nothing close to the way you may now define "financial freedom." That's because we have a way of equating financial freedom with not having to think about the money we spend. That is an unrealistic and unreasonable expectation. The truth is that not thinking about where the money goes is the fast lane to financial doom. Anyone who enjoys financial freedom will tell you that the only way to achieve it is to know what happens to every dollar and to be very reluctant to see it go. We want to live the fantasy "money is no object." But financial bondage is the result of spending without limitation. Submitting to reasonable boundaries is the key to freedom—freedom from both want and worry.

If there were any way possible for you to reconstruct your spending over the past few months so you could see where all your money went, that's exactly what I would ask you to do. But if you haven't been keeping track all along, it will be impossible. Sure, you can come up with the big amounts like mortgage payments, car loans, and other items for which you have a paper trail of canceled checks and account statements. But as big and important as those expenses are, they alone do not give an accurate account of what happened to your money. The only way to find out is to begin tracking now.

Right now you are in a financial fog. You have no idea where all your money goes. You're going to lift this fog by creating your spending record, not to be confused with a spending plan. For the next thirty days, you are going to record every single expenditure, no matter how small or seemingly insignificant. The goal is to see in black-and-white where every bit of your monthly income goes. To the penny. The purpose is to get a realistic picture of your current spending situation and habits. The more detailed and specific you can be, the more prepared you will be when you move to the next step.

While you can start doing this at any time, you need to track for at least one full calendar month. In the debt-proof living method, every month is the same without regard to the days of the week. Days one through seven are always week 1. Days eight through fourteen are always week 2. Days fifteen through twenty-one are always week 3. Days twenty-two to the end of the month are always week 4. You can see that week 4 will have anywhere from seven to ten days depending on which month it is, but that's okay. Always treat every month the same with the four weeks as stated above.

The debt-proof living method also deals with your income on a monthly basis, even though it is quite possible you receive your income on some other schedule. I have found that biweekly or semimonthly seems to be more common. However, for most of us, our expenses are billed and paid monthly (i.e., mortgage payment, credit card payments, utilities, and so on). Therefore, using a monthly time frame makes the most sense. Of course, you can make adjustments after you become more familiar with the process. For now, however, we will use monthly figures for both income and expenses.

We're not talking about changes in your spending habits yet. The purpose of this tracking exercise is to take a snapshot of your spending habits and to figure out exactly where all your money goes.

You may be thinking, "I hate this!" I can identify. It may feel for you, as it did for me, like being called to the principal's office or getting a letter from the IRS. Believe me, I know how this feels, and at first it feels horrible. But I also know it's not going to be as bad as you may be thinking at this point. It's like going to the doctor or the dentist. The anticipation is worse than the reality. What you are going to learn by shining a light on your spending and by sharing that information with your spouse and working together as partners, not adversaries, is going to set the stage for some amazing changes and the progress to come. This chapter is about research and observation. And it couldn't be simpler. Really. You're going to be amazed.

Getting Started

You will each need a notebook, index cards, or (my favorite) business cards that are blank on one side. You probably have something

161

like this already. Use what you have; don't run out and spend money on something. The point is to come up with a way you can conveniently and discreetly record your spending.

Every day each of you will start out with a fresh page or card. Put the date at the top. Throughout the day, as you spend cash, swipe plastic, or write a check, jot down two small details of that transaction: what for and how much. That's it. If you buy coffee that costs $1.50, record: coffee: $1.50. When you buy gasoline, write down: gasoline: $22.59. Regardless of the method of payment, write down the dollar amount. One page or card per day, every day. No days off, no endless details, and no daily totals. Just specific entries as illustrated below.

Sally's Daily Spending Record

Monday, January 1

Coffee	1.50
Gasoline	22.59
Pharmacy	5.79
Lunch with tip	16.45
Groceries	147.97
School field trip	8.00

(Note: Recording your spending in the manner outlined above will not take the place of recording your checks and ATM activities in your checkbook register. Your spending record is in addition to the way you've been managing your bank accounts in the past.)

Designate a place (a drawer works well) for your daily records. This should be a convenient place where both of you can deposit your daily spending records at the end of each day.

Let me predict some things that are going to happen, if not in the first week for sure in the weeks that follow.

1. The first two to three days of recording your expenses will be awkward at best, challenging at worst. You may feel like you've regressed to childhood and are under the authority of a stern parent.

You'll look for shortcuts, such as not writing down purchases at the time you make them but intending to write them down later when you get home. That's a shortcut that will sabotage your effort. Trust me, you won't do it—not out of rebellion as much as out of forgetfulness. How do I know this? Because I've been exactly where you are, remember? Believe me when I say you need to record each transaction as it happens—as you stand at the checkout and before you put away your wallet or purse and walk back to the car. You need to take five seconds to write down the amount the moment the money leaves your possession. This is why a five-inch-thick three-ring binder is not the best thing for keeping track of your spending. Anything the size of Nebraska is too cumbersome and embarrassing to haul around. Keep it simple and you'll improve your chances of sticking with the program.

2. You will be tempted to cheat. At first, you'll cheat by omission—simply forgetting to record transactions. You will consider more serious transgressions too, as in, "I shouldn't have to write down how I spend money my spouse doesn't know I have." Wrong. You must record every expenditure regardless of the source. You will be tempted not to record embarrassing or "personal" expenses, like three runs through McDonald's or enough coffee lattes to float a small ship. You'll want to hide those eBay auctions you won that you pay for through PayPal or any number of other things only you know about. Cheating in any of these ways by either of you is only going to delay and prevent financial harmony in your marriage. Both of you must come clean with the way you spend the money, whether cash, credit, or debit. The success of your money management is rooted in complete honesty with yourself and your spouse.

3. You are going to be more interested in your spouse's daily records than in your own. You will be tempted to not only review but also comment on, criticize, and question what your spouse has recorded. Do not do this. There will be a review time soon

enough. Extend to your spouse the same courtesy and respect you want to receive. Treat your spouse as your business partner. Don't question; don't nag. For now, just keep recording.

4. After a few days, something amazing is going to happen. You will begin to wake from your "spending coma" to see all the ways money leaks from your life. That might feel great or somewhat painful. And don't be surprised if you change your mind about buying something because it's just too much trouble to write it down or too embarrassing to own up to it in writing. While I don't want you to change your spending patterns in anticipation of creating your spending record (we're looking for a realistic picture of your money situation), rethinking in this way is a good thing . . . and you should see it as the first sign of progress.

First Week Review

At the end of week 1 (seven full days of recording), schedule a review meeting. Take your fourteen individual records (seven from each of you) and merge them into your week 1 spending record by combining like expenses. For example, if you went to the grocery store twice and your spouse went once, add together those three amounts to come up with one figure for groceries. If you have entries for two payments to two credit card companies, combine them under one category called credit card payments.

Combine your spending entries into categories until each entry has made it from the daily spending records to the week 1 spending record. Depending on the week, this could be quite simple or quite complicated. That's okay. Just take it one step at a time, avoiding the temptation to combine many things into that famous catchall category miscellaneous. For now, you want to be as detailed as practical. Once you have everything on one sheet of paper, calculate a total.

Bob and Sally's Weekly Spending Record

Week 1, January 1–7

Groceries	237.50
Fast Food	$74.75
Restaurant Meals w/ Tips	265.56
Kids' School Expenses	15.00
Gasoline	144.00
Auto Insurance	72.50
Cell Phone (2 bills—December)	178.00
Cable TV	145.00
Parts for Dishwasher	23.98
Newspaper	1.50
Dry Cleaning	25.00
School Lunches	18.50
Gifts (2 birthdays)	39.52
Housekeeper—December	90.00
Beauty Salon—Sally and Marta	75.00
Barber Shop—Bob	22.00
Walmart—Clothing	116.87
Pharmacy	35.79
Miscellaneous	92.00
Total for Week One	$1672.47

Now would be a good time to review the week and discuss the spending that took place—without criticism or hysteria. Remember that as much as humanly possible, you are doing this unemotionally. Review the situation before you as you would review a business if you were a paid consultant. Do you find the total amount spent in the week shockingly high or surprisingly low? If high, what are the areas of concern?

Do all you can not to let this meeting escalate into a fight. You are going through a season of discovery. You are committed to integrity with your business partner, who also happens to be your spouse. These first few steps on your journey to financial harmony are going to be among the most difficult. The more intimacy you create in the other hours of your marriage, the safer you will feel to reveal the role money plays in your life and what you do with it on a daily basis. As your spouse is increasingly willing to share his or her life at that level, a new level of understanding and empathy will emerge.

Make sure your weekly record includes everything both of you spent in that week, including checks written, cash spent, purchases made with plastic, gift certificates redeemed. If you took $200 from the ATM machine, you would not enter $200 on your daily spending record. Instead, you would enter exactly how you spent the cash at the time you spent it. Once you are satisfied that the week 1 spending record reflects the truest picture possible, toss the individual records and put the week 1 spending record in the drawer. You will need it later.

Continue with your daily spending record keeping, and at the end of day fourteen, meet again. Using the fourteen records from week 2 (seven from each of you), create a week 2 spending record in the same way you created the record for week 1. Once all the daily spending is transferred, run a total so you have one figure for week 2. Your week 2 spending record may look much different from that of week 1, and that's okay. When you are done, discard the daily records and put your week 2 spending record in the drawer with your week 1 spending record. Make sure that somewhere in all this you have recorded your regular monthly expenditures, such as mortgage or rent payment, car payment, utilities, and so forth. Remember, no matter how you make the payment (auto bill pay, paper check, or other), it must be recorded on someone's daily spending record at some point during the month so that it shows up on one of the four weekly spending records.

Continue in the same manner for week 3 and week 4.

Monthly Spending Record

Once you have all four weekly records, you have the ingredients for your first complete monthly spending record. You are not going to merge the weekly records but rather list them side by side according to categories. You may need to combine categories at this point if you were too detailed back in the earlier weeks.

You will create totals for individual categories in the right-hand column, transfer the totals for each week from the weekly spending records to the bottom of each column, and then come up with one grand total for the entire month. And now for the question we've

Bob and Sally's Monthly Spending Record
Month 1

Category	Week 1	Week 2	Week 3	Week 4	Total
Groceries	237.50	150.78	83.00		471.28
Fast food	74.75	35.50	42.00	24.00	176.25
School lunches	18.50	18.50	18.50	18.50	74.00
Restaurant meals	265.56	52.00	34.79	114.75	467.10
School expenses	15.00				15.00
Credit card payments		115.00	90.00	225.00	430.00
Gasoline	144.00	40.00	42.35	44.68	271.03
Auto maintenance/ repairs	72.50			53.00	125.50
Cell phones	178.00				178.00
Cable TV/internet	145.00				145.00
Newspaper	1.50	1.50	1.50	1.50	6.00
Pharmacy	35.79			25.00	60.79
Gifts	39.52			25.00	64.52
Housekeeper	90.00		90.00		180.00
Beauty shop and barber	97.00			27.50	124.50
Clothing and dry cleaning	141.87		45.88		187.75
Utilities (gas, electricity, water, refuse)		117.00	27.50	84.00	228.50
Mortgage payment				975.00	975.00
Home maintenance/ repairs	23.98		78.00		101.98
Car payment			273.00		273.00
Miscellaneous	92.00	232.00	108.00	248.00	680.00
Totals	1,762.47	762.28	934.52	1,865.93	5,235.20

Average monthly income: $5,114.00
Less total spent this month: $5,235.20
Amount <overspent> or underspent: <$121.20>

167

all been waiting to ask: how does your spending look compared to your average monthly income? I will not be terribly surprised if spending exceeds income, as is illustrated below. The only way that can happen is if you've been putting some of your spending on credit cards, an activity you've been programmed to do.

You should find your first monthly spending record quite revealing, although it is not an altogether accurate picture. Undoubtedly, you have expenses that don't show up here because they do not occur regularly each month in the same way your mortgage payment and cell phone bills do—expenses like vacations and Christmas. Or how about clothing? That's not a fixed amount every month in the same way your car payment is always the same. You have many irregular, unexpected, and intermittent expenses. It's possible you had a big unexpected expense during this first month of your recording that made this month appear unusually expensive. A single monthly spending record is a wonderful first step, but there is no way it will give you a true overall picture.

In the chapters that follow, we're going to take care of this problem. There is a way to make every month more realistic.

Money Leaks

As you study your first monthly spending record, look for leaks— places where money is pouring out of your life. The first place, not surprisingly, is probably in the area of food. This is why I have broken down food into several categories in the illustrations. Perhaps you're seeing categories such as fast food, school lunches, and restaurant meals taking a big chunk out of your disposable income. I've seen spending records where "hemorrhage" would be a better description for fast-food purchases.

Your assignment now is to identify all the places where money is leaking and to talk about ways you can plug those leaks in the coming month. As you look at the totals for various categories, mark those that can be reduced significantly. In the same way all those small expenditures add up, reducing lots of areas a small amount will also add up to something significant.

Money Laundering

Many spouses have a closely guarded secret. They launder money. I know how this works, both from personal experience (something I'm not proud to admit) as well as from years of communicating with husbands and wives.

Money launderers participate in this clandestine activity to avoid arguments over money. It's easier to skim than to face the hassle. She writes a check for more than the grocery bill and receives cash back. That's cash her husband cannot trace. As far as he is concerned, the checkbook says the groceries came to $112.08. In truth, the tab was $82.08, and she pocketed $30 to cover the cost of a pedicure, an expenditure her husband does not understand. She believes it just saves a big hassle to do it this way. She gets her pedicure, and he's none the wiser. Of course, this example works the other way as well.

He drops by the supermarket to pick up milk, bread, and a few other things they need for the house. He swipes his debit card and requests $30 cash back. As far as the bank record shows, he spent $58.30 at the grocery store when in truth he spent $28.30 and pocketed the $30 for pocket money that will simply evaporate.

Here is another popular way spouses launder money. She lunches with colleagues, puts the entire tab on the credit card, and collects cash from the rest of the party. The money goes into her wallet, and the charge washes out in the credit card statement, where it's buried along with the names of several other restaurants. He's none the wiser, and she has a pocketful of secret spending money.

So you might ask, is laundering money (also known in business circles as skimming) wrong if the reason behind it is to eliminate arguments and keep the peace? Let me ask you this: if your business partner was sneaking money out of the business with the sole purpose of deceiving you, would that be wrong? This is pretty simple: laundering is lying, so yes, it is wrong.

More than that, laundering money will build walls between the two of you and eventually sabotage emotional intimacy. If you don't have trust, what's left? So the bottom line is that if laundering is going on in your marriage, it is a problem. It needs to stop.

Now before you begin to worry that you will never again have any money to call your own, relax. That's coming! I think it is very important that both of you have money that is yours to do with as you please.

Your monthly spending record will eventually become the foundation for your monthly spending plan. But there are three important elements you must learn about before you'll be ready to move on to your first monthly spending plan: contingency fund, freedom account, and rapid debt-repayment plan. We'll address them in the next three chapters and put all the pieces together in chapter 18.

So readjust your seat belts, and let's keep going.

15

You Want Security?
I'll Show You Security!

The Contingency Fund

> Annual income twenty pounds, annual expenditure nineteen pounds
> nineteen and six, result happiness. Annual income twenty pounds,
> annual expenditure twenty pounds nought and six, result misery.
>
> Charles Dickens, *David Copperfield*

If you've ever driven California's scenic Pacific Coast Highway 1,
you've seen some beautiful, albeit steep and terribly jagged,
cliffs. At one point, you can pull off the highway, walk right up to
the edge, and look down. I can describe how I feel in a single word:
terrified. Even the guardrails cannot neutralize my fear of being
that close to the edge. As breathtaking as that view is, there's not
a single home at the top of that treacherous point. No one in their
right mind would choose to live that close to the edge.

If you are living from paycheck to paycheck, saddled by a mountain of debt, saving nothing for the future, and spending more than you earn, you, my friend, are living on the edge—the financial edge.

The edge is a terrible place to live. I know. You live with a constant fear that the slightest shift in your financial situation will fling you into the darkness below. And when it happens, you hope and pray that your credit cards, equity loans, consolidation loans—any source of credit—will come to your rescue. And just when you think things couldn't possibly get any scarier, a pink slip announces you are now unemployed. Or the transmission decides to stop transmissioning. You wring your hands, hold your head, and conclude you have no choice but to run to the credit cards for yet another bailout.

Emergencies. Credit cards. You've been led to believe they go together. Besides, what choice do you have? None, you conclude as you take up permanent residency on the edge.

The way to stop this vicious cycle is to make a bold decision to pick up and move. One step at a time, you can step away from the edge. You do that every time you pay yourself consistently and methodically. You must do this even if you are deeply in debt, which may seem illogical to you.

It is absolutely the right thing to do and the very thing that is going to enable you to get out of debt and to make things right with all those to whom you owe money. Saving money is one of the two catalysts (the other, giving) that will turn your money situation around.

The Contingency Fund

One of the four elements of debt-proof living is the contingency fund. This is a pool of money with a specific purpose: to replace your income during seasons of unemployment and to bridge the gap in the event of a financial emergency. (This may come as a shock to you, but a new sofa or a family vacation does not constitute a financial emergency. But take heart, sofas and family vacations are part of a chapter to come.)

You are going to build your contingency fund by contributing a set percentage of your net take-home pay until it contains the amount of money you would need to pay all your living expenses for at least three months (six months is preferable, but we'll work on three for now).

You already discovered how much you spent during the one month in which you created your spending record. Multiply that figure by three, and you'll have an idea of where this is going. However, for the sake of simplicity, let's agree that you need a minimum of $10,000 in your contingency fund. If that's a number that astounds you, relax. If you think of the entire sum, coming up with it will seem impossible. But how astounding is it that $4 for your coffee fix each day adds up to $1,460 a year? If you think of saving this much as eating the proverbial elephant, doing so will seem impossible. But when you approach this task one bite at a time, it's doable.

How to Fund It

The 10 percent of your net income that you pay to yourself (the second 10 in the 10-10-80 debt-proof formula) will be directed into your contingency fund starting now and until it is fully funded. That is your number one savings priority—a fully funded contingency fund. The freedom account and rapid debt-repayment plan are both funded from the 80 percent of that formula. You will build your contingency fund and fund both your freedom account and RDRP simultaneously. It is not one element at a time but rather all three of them at the same time.

If you currently have a savings account, you can get a jump start by designating it as your contingency fund and adding to it.

As tempting as it may be, do not cash in any retirement accounts to fund your contingency fund. That would undoubtedly create penalties and a taxable event, making such a move highly inadvisable. Your retirement accounts should be seen as out of your reach for now.

If, however, you have other savings accounts or sources of cash that you could steer into your contingency fund to build it more quickly, by all means consider doing that. Getting your contingency fund fully funded as quickly as possible should be your top priority.

The Big Three Considerations

While your contingency fund is an excellent way to "invest" in your marriage, it is not an investment account in the traditional sense of the word. This fact influences where you decide to park it. You want a guarantee that every cent will be available in the event you need it for the purpose the fund was created. Think of your contingency fund as debt insurance. Like all insurance, you hope you won't need it.

The big three considerations in managing your contingency fund are safety, availability, and growth.

Safety. You want this money in a place where the principal is not at risk. That rules out the stock market and any other number of at-risk situations. You also want it to be safe from you, so that rules out the sugar bowl or between the mattress and box spring. You need to be able to get it conveniently, but it should be farther than arm's reach. With as little as $50, you can open a savings account at a bank or credit union.

Availability. Because of the nature of emergencies (they don't usually come with a thirty-day notice), this money needs to be liquid, meaning you could get your hands on at least part of it in twenty-four to seventy-two hours without having to sell something or make any kind of arrangement.

Growth. You will be maintaining your contingency fund for many years. Before long, this will be a substantial amount of money, so as a good steward, you will want to expose it to the best compounding interest available provided you are not violating the safety and availability requirements. Clearly, your contingency fund is not going to make you wealthy, but that is not its purpose. Since growth is your third priority, the interest you earn in a simple passbook account or the like will be appropriate.

In the past decade in the United States, we've seen interest rates drop to unprecedented lows. In fact, ZIRP has become a fairly commonplace acronym for "zero interest rate policy," brought to us by the Federal Reserve, or the Fed for short. In an effort to stimulate the economy, the Fed has kept interest rates at rock bottom. If you have secured a new mortgage or refinanced your mortgage in the past few years, you've benefited greatly from this policy. But if you are one to count on earning interest in a savings or other kind of growth bank account, you've suffered terribly with interest rates at and even below 1 percent. Do not assume this situation will remain permanently. In fact, by the time you read this, the Fed may well have increased rates. The principle remains that you should park your contingency fund where it will be safe while earning the best rate of interest available to you.

Your contingency fund is an amazing tool and will do great things for your marriage. Knowing you are prepared for life's greatest financial challenges, should they come, is huge. Every time you make a deposit into your contingency fund, you are making deposits into your spouse's Love Bank. To your wife it says, "I love you and will take care of you." To your husband it says, "I respect and admire you for planning ahead for the unexpected." Even a partially funded contingency fund is going to give you a sense of calm that will help you to relax, think more clearly, and best of all, sleep well.

Where to Fund It

Credit Unions versus Banks

Here's a quick lesson in the difference between credit unions and banks. Banks are for-profit corporations with profits going to enrich the stockholders, while credit unions are nonprofit organizations that exist for the benefit of their members.

When a credit union generates a surplus, it is paid out to account holders in the form of either a small dividend or a rebate of loan interest at the end of the fiscal year. Typically, credit union fees are lower, while the interest rates they pay to depositors are a bit higher. If you are eligible to join a credit union, it is an excellent place to park your contingency fund. Deposits in banks are federally insured up to $250,000 (if the bank goes bankrupt, you'll be covered). Deposits in most credit unions are also federally insured, which is a feature you want and something you need to verify.

At both a bank and a credit union, you'll be given a choice of accounts for your contingency fund that may include the following.

Passbook savings account. This is at the bottom of the savings ladder but a good place for new depositors. You can expect to earn low interest, but the minimum requirements will also be minimal.

NOW account. You might consider this interest-bearing checking account once you have accumulated the minimum balance requirement. Just make sure any checks they issue are put away in an inconvenient yet safe place. You don't want to think this is a checking account from which you can start making withdrawals. You will find the interest rate a bit higher than with a passbook savings account, but expect that you will need to maintain a minimum balance of $1,500.

SuperNOW account. This account is similar to the NOW account with better interest rates and a greater minimum deposit of $2,000 to $2,500.

Bank money market account. Do not confuse this with money market *funds* that are offered not by banks but by mutual fund companies. While bank money market accounts carry the same federal insurance provision as other bank deposits, they typically pay lower interest than a money market fund.

Certificate of Deposit. This is similar to a passbook savings account in that you deposit money and are paid a set rate of interest. The difference is that in exchange for your promise to leave the money for a set period of time (90 days, 180 days, 1 year, etc.), you are guaranteed a higher rate of interest. If you take a short-term CD, you will receive slightly less interest. But keep this in mind: if you need your contingency fund quickly, you will have to request an early withdrawal, which will result in a penalty that will affect the interest you earn. The penalty will not diminish your principal.

Non-bank Options

United States treasuries. You can lend your money to the US government in the form of treasury bills (short-term government bonds), but I would not recommend it. However, if this sounds like a place you'd like to park your contingency fund, you need to do a little homework at www.publicdebt.treas.gov/whatwedo/retail.htm.

The minimum investment required is $1,000. Government securities are sold at auction, and there is a process you will need to learn to become an active participant.

Here again, getting your hands on your funds in the event you need them can take time—up to three weeks. So keep this in mind before you park your entire contingency fund here.

Money market funds. A money market fund (not to be confused with a money market account at a bank) is a large pool of money managed by professionals and invested in safe and stable securities, including commercial paper (short-term IOUs of large US corporations), treasury bills, and large bank CDs. Money market funds are an attractive place to grow a contingency fund because of:

1. *Safety.* Even though not guaranteed by the federal government, this type of fund is regulated by the Securities and Exchange Commission.
2. *Liquidity.* Deposits are not tied to any time frame, which means your funds are available at any time and in any amount. You can take out only the amount you need.
3. *Higher rates of interest.* The return on money market funds is typically 1 to 1.5 percentage points higher than for bank or credit union accounts.
4. *Check writing privileges.* This is a feature that allows you access to the funds without going through phone calls and wire transfers. Yet you cannot think of this as a checking account, and that's good. Money market funds have restrictions against writing checks for small amounts, say less than $200. Typically, there are no fees imposed or restrictions on the number of checks you can write in a month.

If your funds are parked in a money market fund, you don't have to worry about maturity dates, the possibility of early withdrawal penalties, or getting in before the auction closes. The interest effective yield (interest rate) moves with the general state of the economy.

While most money market funds require a minimum deposit of at least $2,500, some waive that requirement if you authorize automatic deposits of at least $50 a month.

There are literally hundreds of money market funds from which to choose if you decide this is a good place for your contingency fund. Before opening any account, you need to call for and read a prospectus so you fully understand the rules and risks involved. With the prospectus you will receive an application that looks daunting but is actually quite simple to complete. If you have any questions, you can always call the toll-free customer service number. Here are some reputable money market funds to consider.

Fund Name	Minimum to Open	Website
American Century Money Market	$2,500.00	americancentury .com[1]
Vanguard Prime Portfolio	$3,000.00	investor.vanguard .com
USAA Money Market	$3,000.00*	usaa.com[2]

*The minimum deposit is waived if you authorize automatic monthly deposits of at least $50.

Automatic Deposit Authorization

I am a huge fan of automatic deposits, especially when it comes to building your contingency fund.

With our busy lifestyle and my tendency to put things off, I know my husband and I would forget or find some reason to skip savings deposits from time to time. Authorizing our account manager to reach into our checking account on a specified day every month to take out the amount we authorize is one way we simplify our lives. It's like hiring a staff person to handle the saving and depositing we've committed to.

If you have any tendencies toward procrastination and feel better when things are taken care of for you, I suggest you think seriously about arranging for automatic deposits into your contingency fund. Even more important perhaps is the principle that if the money is gone before you see it, you won't miss it. In the beginning, you might feel the pinch of having your savings automatically deducted from your regular checking account and deposited into your contingency fund. But before you know it, this will become routine, and you won't have to worry about remembering to make that transfer of funds. I've proven this for myself and have had it confirmed over and over again by Debt-Proof Living readers and followers of my blog, EverydayCheapskate.com.

It's possible that your employer offers this service as a payroll deduction plan. You simply fill out an authorization form. Then your pay stub will indicate the money has been deposited automatically. Of course, you can change your automatic deposit authorization at any time. You can increase the amount, change the date, or even change your mind.

16

You Want Freedom?
I'll Show You Freedom!

The Freedom Account

The only thing money gives you is the freedom of not worrying about money.

Johnny Carson[1]

Like most couples, I'm sure you look good. That too, but I mean you look good on paper. When you write down your monthly income and take away your monthly expenses, things look okay. Ends should meet with plenty of room to spare. Right? So why don't they?

I'm no doctor, but I can diagnose this problem. You have a case of selective amnesia, also known as failure to anticipate. This affliction attacks couples and individuals in the irregular, intermittent, and unexpected expenses region of their brains.

181

Your predictable monthly bills are not a problem because they are, well, monthly. You're never shocked that the electricity bill shows up—the amount might be shocking but not the fact that you get the bill. And the rent or mortgage payment, are you ever surprised that you have to pay that? Of course not. Every month somehow the rent and utilities get paid, and the family gets fed. Some months it's tight, but somehow you do it.

Failure to anticipate lets us forget that every day we're wearing out our cars, that our kids' clothes are getting too small, that accidents happen, that our appliances are getting older, and that we're inching closer to Christmas and vacation. We assume that if there's money left at the end of the month, it must be a surplus. It's available to do with as we please. We assume that the expenses we have right now—this month—are our necessary expenses. Everything else is optional. When unexpected expenses hit, we collapse into a pitiful heap and bemoan the fact that once again we've been broadsided by an emergency.

And where do we run for aid and comfort? To the credit cards, of course!

Before the introduction of easy credit, people had no choice but to anticipate the unexpected. Failure to anticipate meant certain doom. Our grandparents called it a rainy day, and they were forever putting something away for it. The advent of easy consumer credit sent a message that we should not worry anymore. We learned that running out of cash wasn't the same as running out of money. As long as we had credit, it was impossible to run out of money.

We got pretty good at anticipating some things, however, like annual raises, bonuses, and tax refunds (we usually have them spent before they arrive). And oh, how about home appreciation? I always anticipated huge jumps in the value of our home, which meant, of course, more equity to play with or, to use the more professional term, to leverage.

While I'm sure you're pretty good at anticipating pay raises, bonuses, and tax refunds, it may never have crossed your mind that you could anticipate an urgent trip to the dentist. Have you ever thought you could anticipate the cost of a new set of tires, even though yours still show plenty of tread? I know how much you love that new SUV sitting in the driveway, but in your wildest dreams could you have anticipated the $800 price tag on that first required maintenance appointment?

Imagine this. You get a letter from your mortgage holder telling you that because you have been such an excellent customer, your $1,000 monthly payments will no longer be due monthly. Instead, you will make one annual payment of $12,000. Your first annual payment will be due one year from today. How do you respond?

- *Overjoyed with relief.* No more monthly pressure. It's always so hard to get that check in on time. Now you have a whole year's worth of breathing room. You will deal with that bill when the time comes.
- *Scared to death.* One thousand dollars a month is doable, but $12,000 a year is impossible. How will you ever save $12,000 from today?
- *Grinning ear to ear.* You open a special house payment account. Instead of paying your mortgage company every month, you write the $1,000 check to your special account. One year from now you look in the account to see $12,263.20. You write out the check for $12,000 to the mortgage company and pocket the difference, which is the 4 percent interest you earned on their money. Did I startle you? While 4 percent interest on bank accounts pretty much disappeared following the Great Recession, as I alluded to previously, the Fed will likely have increased rates by the time you read this. Yes, I have no doubt that 4 percent rates will return.

I believe Christmas club accounts are all but extinct, which is a shame. They were so much fun.

It was a simple concept. You gave the bank permission to transfer an amount that you stipulated (like $10 a week) from your bank account to your Christmas club account. And then you just forgot about it. As they say, out of sight, out of mind.

Right after Thanksgiving would come one big surprise: a check in the mail for all the money in your Christmas club account. Knowing you had all your Christmas shopping money in cash was such a good feeling.

I'm sure you've figured out by now that both the annual mortgage scenario and my Christmas club anecdote are leading somewhere. You are right. Both are examples of how to anticipate expenses that are real but do not occur monthly.

The Freedom Account

To treat my own case of selective amnesia, I developed the freedom account. It is a simple, personal money management tool that makes unexpected, irregular, and intermittent expenses as ordinary, predictable, and necessary as your rent or grocery bill. A freedom account eliminates financial surprises. It is not part of your 10 percent savings plan. It helps you wisely manage part of the 80 percent of your income devoted to living within your means. I have written about the freedom account in previous books, most extensively in *Debt-Proof Living*. If the contingency fund is the lifeblood of debt-proof living, then the freedom account is the heart and soul. The freedom account, not credit cards, will be your defense against financial emergencies.

Setting up and maintaining your freedom account is simple but very specific. I have tested this system thoroughly. I've tried variations and shortcuts, and I can assure you that nothing I know of works as effectively or as consistently as the steps that follow.

First, it is imperative that you understand the definition of unexpected, irregular, and intermittent expenses. This is anything that does not recur every month. Your mortgage payment, car payment, utilities, and grocery bills do not fall into this category. Gas for your car does not qualify. Preschool tuition for your child does not qualify, unless you are required to pay it on a schedule other than monthly, then of course it does. Your freedom account is a management tool for non-monthly expenses only.

Your property taxes qualify for your freedom account unless you pay them monthly by a separate check or as part of your mortgage payment. The same goes for your homeowners insurance. If you pay your auto insurance monthly, do not include this in your freedom account. If you pay it quarterly, semimonthly, or annually, include it.

Here's a list of potential candidates for your freedom account: insurance premiums, taxes, auto maintenance and repair, gifts, clothing, vacations, Christmas, hobbies, insurance deductibles (I'll explain later), household repairs and maintenance, even that new sofa you have your eye on.

How to Start

Step 1: Determine irregular expenses. Using your check registers for the past twelve months (longer if you have them), your credit card statements, your tax return, or—if all else fails—your memory, make a list of expenses that you do not pay on a monthly basis. These might come quarterly, every six months, or annually. Or they may occur so sporadically that you have no idea when they'll pop up again. You may know those expenses to the penny or not have a clue. Estimate for now. You can adjust later.

Do the math to come up with an annual estimate for each category. Now divide by twelve so you arrive at a per-month figure.

Here is an example of six typical freedom account categories:

Home maintenance/repairs
$900/year ÷ 12 = $75/month
Auto maintenance/repairs
$765/year ÷ 12 = $64/month
Life insurance premiums
$660/year ÷ 12 = $55/month
Property taxes
$864/year ÷ 12 = $72/month
Vacations
$1,200/year ÷ 12 = $100/month
Clothing
$900/year ÷ 12 = $75/month

Total $441/month

Step 2: Open another checking account. I am assuming that you have a checking account already, so open another one at the same bank or credit union. Order checks for this new account and have them personalized by adding a special line that says "freedom account." Under no circumstances should you accept overdraft protection, ATM privileges, or a debit card for this new freedom account. Why? That would make it too easy to use this account for something other than what it is designed for.

Your regular checking account will continue to accommodate your monthly expenses and typical day-to-day needs for which you presently use a checking account. You will continue to deposit your paychecks and other income into your regular account.

Step 3: Authorize an automatic deposit. At the time you open the account, request and complete an automatic deposit authorization form (some banks call this an automatic money transfer) instructing the bank to transfer the monthly total of your irregular expenses (in our example it is $441) from your regular checking account into your freedom account on a specific day of the month. The selection of your transfer date is very important because, once established, you can be sure the bank will never forget to make the transfer, nor will they be late.

Step 4: Get a three-ring binder. Or create some kind of record-keeping document. If you go with a binder, fill it with notebook paper. As far as the bank is concerned, you have a checking account, which you have titled "freedom account." But you are going to treat it as a collection of subaccounts. Prepare one page per subaccount you've designated, similar to this illustration for the Brown family (p. 188).

Fill in the title of the account, enter the amount to be deposited into that subaccount in the upper right-hand corner, and prepare five columns—"Date," "Description," "In," "Out," and "Balance"—for each subaccount.

Step 5: Manage it. Each month, on the date that you selected for your automatic transfer, deduct the amount of your freedom account deposit ($441 in this case) in your regular checking account register just as you do when you pay the mortgage payment and other bills. Don't even think about forgetting, because the bank never will. This is going to feel weird in the beginning. You won't like making this debit entry because it feels like you're throwing money away. You have this big new monthly payment with nothing to show for it. But that is not the case at all. You are managing your money. You are controlling it instead of it controlling you.

Next, go to your freedom account notebook and enter the individual deposits. Using our illustration, on the first page, which is home maintenance/repairs, the Browns would enter a deposit of $75; $64 on the next page, which is auto maintenance/repairs; $55 for life insurance premiums; $72 for property taxes; $100 for vacations; and $75 for clothing.

Referring to the illustration, let's walk through the home maintenance/repairs subaccount. Notice that the Browns have committed to a $75 deposit every month into this subaccount. They have decided what items will be handled by the subaccount, but generally they will include everything from appliances to major

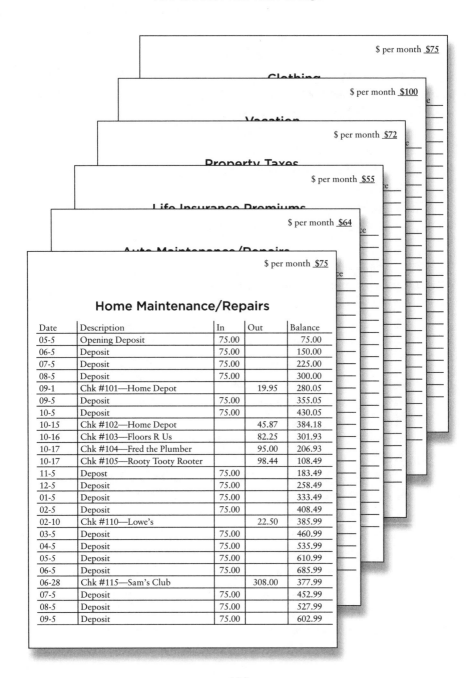

$ per month __$75__

Clothing

$ per month __$100__

Vacation

$ per month __$72__

Property Taxes

$ per month __$55__

Life Insurance Premiums

$ per month __$64__

Auto Maintenance/Repairs

$ per month __$75__

Home Maintenance/Repairs

Date	Description	In	Out	Balance
05-5	Opening Deposit	75.00		75.00
06-5	Deposit	75.00		150.00
07-5	Deposit	75.00		225.00
08-5	Deposit	75.00		300.00
09-1	Chk #101—Home Depot		19.95	280.05
09-5	Deposit	75.00		355.05
10-5	Deposit	75.00		430.05
10-15	Chk #102—Home Depot		45.87	384.18
10-16	Chk #103—Floors R Us		82.25	301.93
10-17	Chk #104—Fred the Plumber		95.00	206.93
10-17	Chk #105—Rooty Tooty Rooter		98.44	108.49
11-5	Depost	75.00		183.49
12-5	Deposit	75.00		258.49
01-5	Deposit	75.00		333.49
02-5	Deposit	75.00		408.49
02-10	Chk #110—Lowe's		22.50	385.99
03-5	Deposit	75.00		460.99
04-5	Deposit	75.00		535.99
05-5	Deposit	75.00		610.99
06-5	Deposit	75.00		685.99
06-28	Chk #115—Sam's Club		308.00	377.99
07-5	Deposit	75.00		452.99
08-5	Deposit	75.00		527.99
09-5	Deposit	75.00		602.99

repairs to replacing light bulbs—anything that has to do with maintaining and keeping a home in good condition.

On May 5, just as planned, they make a deposit of $75 and do so again in June, July, and August. They are shocked to see that in just four months they have accumulated $300 in this subaccount. On September 1, they wake to the sound of running water only to discover the toilet is in desperate need of repair. Bob grabs the freedom account checkbook or debit card for the freedom account and heads to Home Depot, where he finds not only the right toilet repair kit but also a knowledgeable guy in an orange apron who gives him a quick do-it-yourself lesson. Back home, in ten minutes, the family is back in business. Bob did the repair at a fraction of the cost of calling a plumber. Bob dutifully enters this transaction in the freedom account book, noting the check number 101, and subtracts the amount from the balance. He sees immediately they have a balance of $280.05.

Two more months go by, and now the balance in this subaccount is $430.05. And good thing, because on October 15, Sally walks into the house after taking the kids to school and is greeted by water running out from under the door. A quick inspection reveals the water hose on the washer has burst. After a dash to the main water shutoff valve, Sally calls Bob to discuss the problem. Back to Home Depot he goes, freedom account checkbook in hand, praying he'll find that same guy who was so helpful before. An hour later, with $45.87 worth of replacement parts, Bob has the job completed. But what to do about the ruined floor in the laundry room? A year ago had this happened, it would have been a crisis. With a $500 deductible on their homeowners insurance, they would not have been able to cover this expense because they were always living so close to the edge. But now things are different. They have money set aside, so the event is annoying but not devastating.

Sally finds flooring on sale and arranges for installation. The job is complete for $82.25 (it's a small room), paid by their freedom account.

Believing all is well, Bob and Sally retire for the night only to wake up to yet another water-related event. Now all the plumbing is backed up—a situation that is way beyond Bob's repair abilities. An emergency call to Fred the plumber gets the system working ($95) but not without a strong warning from Fred that they have roots in their sewer lines. Previously, they would have been reaching for credit cards, but not with the freedom account. Bob calls Rooty Tooty Rooter, who comes right out, for a charge of $98.44.

It's been a tough week in the home repairs department. Bob and Sally could have easily become discouraged with all these unexpected expenses. But having the money to cover the problems made all the difference. No sleepless nights, fights, or worries. They took it in stride knowing that home ownership does not come without its challenges.

Things in the household maintenance and repair department proceed nicely for the next few months. The subaccount quietly grows as designed. In February, Sally picks up replacement tubes for the kitchen lights as well as batteries for the smoke detectors. She could have easily paid for them from the grocery money in her purse, but that would defeat their new money management system.

In June, the clothes dryer (nearly eighteen years old) decides it's dried its last load. In the past, they would have felt compelled to buy another dryer on credit at any store that would extend it to them. But thanks to their freedom account, they have plenty of money to replace the dryer. And with cash, they can shop anywhere. They find a great deal at Sam's Club, and within twenty-four hours, that baby is drying jumbo-sized loads in half the time.

How freeing for Bob and Sally to know that the money for these kinds of unexpected, irregular, and intermittent expenses is in place and ready to go. Can you imagine how much strain and stress that relieves between a husband and wife? Having the money makes Sally feel loved and protected and makes Bob feel good that he is providing for the needs of his home and family.

While the decisions and implementation involved with your freedom account should be carried out as unemotionally as possible, part of the result is a big emotional payoff, which is to be savored with maximum enjoyment.

I've been doing this for years, but I am still amazed by the level of freedom and peace of mind that a simple $75 monthly deposit set aside for a specific purchase can bring to my life. Multiply that over several subaccounts covering several specific areas, and multiply the joy and peace of mind accordingly.

It is critical that you do not give in to the temptation of withdrawing from your freedom account for anything other than the purpose for which it has been designated. And no borrowing between subaccounts. You may feel coerced, you'll be tempted, you'll be afraid you can't stop yourself, but you can.

At times, you will be tempted to think of your freedom account as a savings account or investment. You may think it takes the place of funding your contingency fund. You may be tempted to skip your true savings in favor of your freedom account. This is not a savings account, and it is not an investment either. Your freedom account is money you have committed for a specific purpose. Remember that annual mortgage scenario earlier in this chapter? The account was neither an investment nor savings. It was simply a parking spot for money that belonged eventually to the mortgage company.

Your freedom account is going to give new meaning to the term *ebb and flow*. Some months the balance will be quite high; other times it will be very low. That's exactly the way it's supposed to work. It is strictly a financial management tool. Money should be flowing in and out at a pretty good clip if you are using it correctly.

Other Subaccounts

There are many other kinds of unpredictable expenses that can deal a crushing blow and that qualify for the freedom account.

191

Insurance Deductibles Account

An excellent way to keep insurance premiums low is to accept higher deductibles. But doing so can be devastating if you do not have that $500 or $1,000 available the moment you need to go to the emergency room or get the car repaired. The solution? A subaccount for deductibles. The subaccount should grow only until its balance is equal to the annual amount of your health, homeowners, and auto deductibles. If you are nervous about increasing the deductibles, start funding the subaccount, and when you reach that amount, you'll be in a good position to instruct your insurance agent to increase the deductibles in exchange for lower premiums.

Clothing Account

When asked to list their monthly expenses, most people don't mention clothing. Yet they seem to be dressed quite well. Where does the money come from? Probably credit cards, a quick diversion of funds from the grocery money, or delaying payment on the utilities to allow for that great twice-yearly sale.

The freedom account is the solution to the clothing problem. Now clothing becomes a legitimate monthly expense. No secrets, no sneaking the bags into the house while hoping your spouse does not notice. You may want to set up a general clothing subaccount for the family or three separate accounts: his clothes, her clothes, and kids' clothes.

Personal Accounts

I'm a huge believer that adults need some money to call their own. That's why I want to encourage you to establish a subaccount for each of you—money you can call your own.

Many years ago one of my Debt-Proof Living (formerly Cheapskate Monthly) members sent in one of the best tips I've ever heard.

She called it her $100 bill trick. She'd been quite a shopaholic, wanting everything she saw. Her debts were enormous. After much soul searching, she discovered it wasn't so much buying the stuff that gave her the joy but knowing she could. So she took a $100 bill and hid it. She told herself that $100 bill was hers to buy anything she wanted. She began to look at things differently. It was like she didn't have to prove anything anymore. She had $100 and could buy whatever she wanted. But the thought of having to run home to get the $100 bill and hand it over to a clerk always stopped her short. She says this trick changed her life.

After hearing from her, I decided to give her $100 bill trick a try. She's right. There's something about having money put away that changes everything. I told myself over and over, "You can buy that if you want . . . ," but I would invariably make the decision to pass. The same will happen for you and your spouse if you each have a subaccount in your freedom account book. You can look at your balance anytime you like. And you can spend it anytime you like. Or you can let it grow. It's safe, it's there in real money, and it's yours to do with as you please. It's not laundered money; you didn't have to skim or perform any other clandestine activity to accumulate it. It's right out in the open. You can save for that bass boat or a new sewing machine . . . anything you please! And as with the $100 bill trick, having money tucked away that you know is yours is going to make all the difference.

Dream Accounts

Go ahead and make pages in your freedom account for things you've only dreamed of. Perhaps you've always wanted to take a European vacation but fear you'll never be able to go. Make a subaccount! Even if you do not fund it right away, have the page ready. Need new carpet? Make a page. Perhaps you are stuck with an automobile lease. Make a page for your next car so you can begin saving for a car you will own.

Don't be afraid to establish lots of categories, even if you are unable to fund all of them in the beginning. It's okay to have pages with zero balances for a while. Remember, this is the start of an important plan. Even if you can fund only one or two subaccounts in the beginning, get them all in place. You can always increase your automatic deposit authorization later. Arrange the pages in order of urgency with the accounts you know you will need soon at the front of the binder.

Unscheduled Income Account

In the same way you have unexpected expenses, you get irregular and unpredictable income. It might be a $1 rebate check or $50 from your mom for your birthday. What happens to it? You put it into your pocket or bank account, and it's quickly absorbed into everyday living. Your freedom account will offer a way to capture those dollars. Maybe it's that subaccount with your name on it.

Managing the Freedom Account

You may be tempted to go high tech with your freedom account. I've heard from readers who have created an Excel spreadsheet or set their freedom account up in Quicken or the like. My only concern is that this needs to be user-friendly for both of you, not just the spouse who is more computer savvy. If both of you have access to the program and both of you are comfortable with it, then fine. But your freedom account needs to be available to and comfortable for both of you.

Once you have established the method (I still think you cannot beat my binder-with-individual-pages idea), one of you needs to take responsibility for the actual management of the pages (recording deposits and keeping current balances on each page), become the keeper of the checkbook, and also reconcile the monthly bank statements.

Few things in life are free, including your freedom account. There may be bank or credit union fees plus the cost of checks and so on. Each month when you reconcile the account (simply add up all the subaccounts and reconcile the total against the single balance the bank shows), you will need to account for any charges. I suggest that the person who manages the account should deduct these charges from his or her personal subaccount. But wait, it gets better. Any interest earned on this account should go to that person's account. That's only fair, and I say that as a freedom account manager myself.

17

You Can Get Out of Debt

The Rapid Debt-Repayment Plan

> No investment is as secure as a repaid debt.
>
> Austin Pryor, *Sound-Mind Investing*

It's time to pay off your pesky credit card balances, consumer loans, student loans, and any other unsecured debts that have you in bondage. You've been treading financial water long enough. It's time to get serious about making significant progress toward your dream of becoming debt-free. Oh, what that is going to do for your relationship and your marriage.

The Rapid Debt-Repayment Plan

Briefly, here's how my unique rapid debt-repayment plan (RDRP) works. You pay off the unsecured debt with the shortest term first, and once paid, you redirect its payment to repay other loans.

Think chain reaction and you will understand the RDRP. It's so simple and works so well and so quickly it's almost magical, if I do say so myself.

The beauty of this plan is that it doesn't require you to pay more than your current minimum monthly payments. Whatever your minimum monthly payments add up to this month is the total amount you will be paying every month until you are debt-free. What's different is that you pay that same total amount every month until you are done while committing to no new debt.

Another reason this plan works is that it is both economically sound and emotionally satisfying. The almost instant gratification of seeing a zero balance will give you a rush and the confidence to pay off the next one and the next one until you are debt-free. When the shortest debt is paid off, add its payment to the next shortest. Do the same as each debt is paid until that total amount you committed to pay each month is being applied to your last debt.

Let me show you how my rapid debt-repayment plan works using Bob and Sally Brown as our fictitious subjects. Below is a list of their unsecured debts: the current balance, the interest rate (APR), and the current minimum monthly payment.

Debt	Current Balance	Interest Rate	Current Minimum Payment
MasterCard	2,300.00	14.99%	75.00
Discover	3,800.00	18.00%	92.00
Visa 1	1,200.00	12.00%	48.00
Capital One	4,500.00	17.50%	150.00
Visa 2	2,700.00	9.99%	65.00
Totals	$14,500.00	—	430.00

The rapid debt-repayment plan is simple because there are only five rules. When you adhere closely to all five, you will get out of debt in record time. Just imagine how your life will change when you are completely free of toxic debt. It can happen and more quickly than you might have dared to dream.

198

Rule 1: No more new debt. Unless you are willing to stop adding to your unsecured debts, you're out of luck when it comes to debt-proofing your marriage. Adding new debt to your already difficult situation is like adding fuel to a fire. You might be able to manage it for a while, but you're on your way to dealing with a full-out raging inferno. This rule is simple: no more new debt.

Rule 2: Pay the same amount every month until all your unsecured debts are paid. As you know, the minimum monthly payment required by each of your creditors fluctuates each month in direct proportion to the current outstanding balance. That's because credit card companies adhere to the "falling" payment method. The minimum payment they require is an arbitrary percentage of the outstanding balance, typically 2 to 4 percent. This rule requires that you no longer pay attention to the declining minimum payments allowed by your creditors but instead choose to fix your payments at the amount they are this month. Credit card companies, unlike mortgage lenders, are required by law to accept any amount you want to send them (even if it is less than the required payment) and at any time. So if the minimum payment is $47 and you send $48, they must accept and credit it as received.

Rule 2 also requires that you agree to pay toward your rapid debt-repayment plan each month an amount equal to the total of all your current minimum monthly payments—your base amount. Ignore declining minimum monthly payments from now on. Don't listen to creditors who say you can pay less each month; stick with the amount equal to your current monthly minimum. Remember, they want you to pay less every month so you can keep paying forever. From now on, you are committed to paying this same amount every month until you complete your RDRP.

Fixing your monthly payments is a very important aspect of the RDRP. It's the second most important step you will take in your quest for financial harmony (the first is a commitment to no more new debt).

The principal balances you carry are a debt to you, but to the credit card companies they are an investment. The interest you pay is a return on their investment. That is why your minimum monthly payment is based on a percentage of the remaining balance—generally 2 to 4 percent. As the balance decreases, the minimum monthly payment decreases proportionately. Simply put, your creditors are not going to be at all happy with you when you begin to repay not only the interest but the principal too. Now they're going to have to find some other sucker. But hey, life is tough, right?

In the Browns' case, their Visa 1 payment is $48, 4 percent of the current $1,200 principal balance. Next month the required payment might drop to $47 or $46. But in keeping with rule 2, they will pay $48 every month until that debt is paid in full.

The total of all the Browns' current minimum monthly payments this month is $430. And they have agreed to continue to pay $430 every month until they are debt-free.

Rule 3: Arrange your debts so that the one with the shortest payoff time is at the top and the one with the longest payoff time is at the bottom. The reason: it is my experience that you are going to need the emotional payoff of reaching a zero balance just as quickly as possible. That is going to give you incentive and motivation to keep going.

Note that this arrangement is not done by interest rate or the outstanding balances. It is by the number of months it will take you to pay the debt in full given the payment schedule outlined in rule 2. This is going to be a little tricky because nowhere on your account statement will you find this information.

There was a time you could simply call customer service and receive an answer to this question: "If I do not add any more purchases to this account and pay $48 every month, how many months will it take me to pay it in full?" And gasoline used to cost $0.25 a gallon. In those good old days, credit card companies didn't panic at the thought of customers actually paying back their entire balances. But that was then and now is now, so back to rule 3.

If either of you is a mathematical wizard, figuring out how many months it will take you to pay your current balance (factoring in the interest each month based on the remaining balance) will be a simple exercise. If, on the other hand, both of you are like me and anything math related gives you a rash, you will need one of the following: (1) a very smart friend, (2) a good handheld financial calculator or computer program, or (3) the RDRP calculator, which we have developed specifically to help you create your individual and unique rapid debt-repayment plan.

The RDRP calculator is an online calculator, not the kind you would buy in an electronics store and hold in your hand. The RDRP calculator, along with dozens of other equally useful calculators that aid debt-proof living, is located in the members' only area of DebtProofLiving.com, which is accessible with an annual membership rate of $39. The calculator does all the work for you. All you do is input for each of your unsecured debts the current balance owed, the current interest rate, and the current minimum payment as stated on your last monthly statement.

Rule 4: Ignore the declining minimum monthly payments you will see on your statements. You will be tempted to watch your monthly statement closely, if for no other reason than to check your progress. And there will be times when you may be tempted to pay the amount you see due on your statement rather than the fixed payment on your RDRP. Let me repeat: the total amount you pay in the first month is the amount you are going to pay until your total debt reaches zero regardless of a lower amount due appearing on your statement.

Rule 5: As one debt is paid, take that payment and redirect it to the payment of the next debt in line. This rule solves the mystery of why the Browns continue to pay $430 per month toward their RDRP even after their debts begin to reach zero and fall off. When the Visa 1 amount (the debt that will be first in the lineup because it has the shortest payoff time, which is twenty-nine months) reaches a zero balance, the Browns might be tempted to believe they have $48 to spend on something else next month. Rule 5 says no. Instead, they redirect that $48 to increase the payment of the next debt in line. This is where the "rapid" part of my RDRP kicks in. By increasing the monthly payment to MasterCard (the next debt in line) to $123, it gets paid in full by month thirty-five. Then the $48 that used to go to Visa 1 plus the $75 that was going to MasterCard gets added to the $150 Capital One payment, making its total payment $273 ($48 + $75 + $150 = $273), and that gets Capital One to zero by month thirty-nine. This repeats until the last debt in line, Discover, is getting the entire $430 monthly debt payment, bringing it to zero in month forty-six. That's less than four years to get rid of all their unsecured debt.

Pay-ment #	Month/Year	Visa 1	Master-Card	Capital One	Visa 2	Dis-cover	Total
1	Jan. 2016	48.00	75.00	150.00	65.00	92.00	430.00
2	Feb. 2016	48.00	75.00	150.00	65.00	92.00	430.00
3	Mar. 2016	48.00	75.00	150.00	65.00	92.00	430.00
4	April 2016	48.00	75.00	150.00	65.00	92.00	430.00
5	May 2016	48.00	75.00	150.00	65.00	92.00	430.00
6	June 2016	48.00	75.00	150.00	65.00	92.00	430.00
7	July 2016	48.00	75.00	150.00	65.00	92.00	430.00
8	Aug. 2016	48.00	75.00	150.00	65.00	92.00	430.00
9	Sep. 2016	48.00	75.00	150.00	65.00	92.00	430.00
10	Oct. 2016	48.00	75.00	150.00	65.00	92.00	430.00
11	Nov. 2016	48.00	75.00	150.00	65.00	92.00	430.00
12	Dec. 2016	48.00	75.00	150.00	65.00	92.00	430.00
13	Jan. 2017	48.00	75.00	150.00	65.00	92.00	430.00
14	Feb. 2017	48.00	75.00	150.00	65.00	92.00	430.00
15	Mar. 2017	48.00	75.00	150.00	65.00	92.00	430.00
16	April 2017	48.00	75.00	150.00	65.00	92.00	430.00
17	May 2017	48.00	75.00	150.00	65.00	92.00	430.00
18	June 2017	48.00	75.00	150.00	65.00	92.00	430.00
19	July 2017	48.00	75.00	150.00	65.00	92.00	430.00

Pay-ment #	Month/Year	Visa 1	Master-Card	Capital One	Visa 2	Dis-cover	Total
20	Aug. 2017	48.00	75.00	150.00	65.00	92.00	430.00
21	Sep. 2017	48.00	75.00	150.00	65.00	92.00	430.00
22	Oct. 2017	48.00	75.00	150.00	65.00	92.00	430.00
23	Nov. 2017	48.00	75.00	150.00	65.00	92.00	430.00
24	Dec. 2017	48.00	75.00	150.00	65.00	92.00	430.00
25	Jan. 2018	48.00	75.00	150.00	65.00	92.00	430.00
26	Feb. 2018	48.00	75.00	150.00	65.00	92.00	430.00
27	Mar. 2018	48.00	75.00	150.00	65.00	92.00	430.00
28	April 2018	48.00	75.00	150.00	65.00	92.00	430.00
29	May 2018	44.00	79.00	150.00	65.00	92.00	430.00
30	June 2018	0	123.00	150.00	65.00	92.00	430.00
31	July 2018		123.00	150.00	65.00	92.00	430.00
32	Aug. 2018		123.00	150.00	65.00	92.00	430.00
33	Sep. 2018		123.00	150.00	65.00	92.00	430.00
34	Oct. 2018		123.00	150.00	65.00	92.00	430.00
35	Nov. 2018		106.00	167.00	65.00	92.00	430.00
36	Dec. 2018		0	273.00	65.00	92.00	430.00
37	Jan. 2019			273.00	65.00	92.00	430.00
38	Feb. 2019			136.00	202.00	92.00	430.00
39	Mar. 2019			0	338.00	92.00	430.00
40	April 2019				338.00	92.00	430.00
41	May 2019				75.00	355.00	430.00
42	June 2019				0	430.00	430.00
43	July 2019					430.00	430.00
44	Aug. 2019					430.00	430.00
45	Sep. 2019					341.00	341.00
46	Oct. 2019	Debt-free!				0	0

If the Browns had stopped adding any new debts but followed the creditors' preferred method of repayment, paying only the minimum monthly payments on each debt, it would have taken them twenty-four years to reach zero. Twenty-four years and $15,237 in interest on top of the $14,550 they owed.

Following the Rapid Debt-Repayment Plan as I described above, they reach zero in less than four years and pay $4,711 in interest, saving themselves $10,526 in interest!

Let's Recap

To get out of debt so quickly and to avoid paying over $10,000 in interest, the Browns follow all five rules. (1) They stop incurring new debt; (2) they pay the same amount every month (the total of the minimum monthly payments required in the first month of their plan); (3) they place the debt with the shortest number of months at the top of the list; (4) as they get their statements each month, they enjoy looking at the declining balances but ignore the new minimum monthly payments, referring instead to their RDRP, which shows how much to send to each creditor; and (5) as one debt is paid, they take the amount of that payment and add it to the payment of the next debt in line, thereby accelerating the payoff plan.

I just love it when a plan comes together! Bob and Sally can see exactly when they will finish paying their debts. And should they decide to accelerate their plan even more, they can simply add to the amount they pay to the debt at the top of the chart.

Let's say the Browns—out of their commitment to get out of debt as quickly as possible—do this and add an additional $50 to their RDRP from the very start so that their total monthly debt payment becomes $480. This booster amount will reduce their out-of-debt time by an additional six months and lop off another $635 from the interest they would otherwise have to pay.

Once the Browns are debt-free in forty-five months (or thirty-nine months if they decide to boost their RDRP monthly payment by $50) as their plan prescribes, they should immediately redirect the entire $430 (or $480 as the case may be) to some other specific purpose (see chap. 18).

I ran the numbers and discovered that if Bob and Sally invest the $430 debt payment each month once they are debt-free and earn an average of 8 percent interest (not an unreasonable expectation if invested carefully for a long period of time), in twenty years they will have a tidy sum of $253,293.[1] That is not a typo.

That's more than a quarter of a million dollars just because they stopped debting, repaid their unsecured debts, and then redirected that same amount each month to themselves, not into the pockets of the consumer credit industry. Amazing!

While this information is fresh in your mind, I hope you stop now and put together your own RDRP. At the very least, you need to know exactly what your new monthly debt payment figure is. Simply add up the minimum monthly payments you are required to make this month. You can determine this by looking at each of your monthly statements. Once you have this number, get it fixed in your mind. Remember it, think about it, imprint it on the inside of your eyelids—whatever it takes for you to see this total amount as your monthly debt payment in the same way you think of your mortgage or other major monthly fixed payment. It will be this same amount this month and every month until you have paid all your unsecured debts in their entirety.

Thankfully, by following your new RDRP, that day is going to come much sooner than you ever thought possible.

18

Telling Your Money Where to Go

The Spending Plan

I've had an opportunity to study how my clients got rich. A few got lucky, but most just stopped spending every penny they had.

Michael Stolper, *Wealth: An Owner's Manual*

My husband is an avid woodworker. While I've been writing this book in my upstairs office, he's been downstairs remodeling. It's like we are racing to see who finishes first.

The first thing he did was gut the living room and the dining room, and I am talking about taking it right down to the stud walls that hold up the second story. He then commenced to build again from the ground up. The feature element for the living room will be wall-to-wall, floor-to-ceiling built-in bookshelves surrounding the front window, which will have a window seat. I believe all of this will be gorgeous, based only on his sketches.

Partway into the process, he assured me that all the elements were completed—stacked all over the room like the pieces of a puzzle. I trusted him, but I could not begin to imagine how all the pieces could fit together and end up looking anything like his sketches. He kept saying that any day now (an apparent reference to the Scripture passage that says, "With the Lord . . . a thousand years [is] as one day" [2 Pet. 3:8 KJV]) the new window would go in, and then he would install his masterpiece.

In the same way Harold painstakingly crafted and then put together the pieces of our remodeling puzzle, you need to put together the pieces of your money management system: a spending record, a spending plan, a contingency fund, a freedom account, and a rapid debt-repayment plan. In this chapter, you'll see the sketch for the entire project and understand how the pieces fit together.

Let's look again at Bob and Sally Browns' first monthly spending record from chapter 14, which I have copied here so you won't have to keep flipping back.

Bob and Sally's Monthly Spending Record

Month 1

Category	Week 1	Week 2	Week 3	Week 4	Total
Groceries	237.50	150.78	83.00		471.28
Fast food	74.75	35.50	42.00	24.00	176.25
School lunches	18.50	18.50	18.50	18.50	74.00
Restaurant meals	265.56	52.00	34.79	114.75	467.10
School expenses	15.00				15.00
Credit card payments		115.00	90.00	225.00	430.00
Gasoline	144.00	40.00	42.35	44.68	271.03
Auto maintenance/ repairs	72.50			53.00	125.50
Cell phones	178.00				178.00
Cable TV/internet	145.00				145.00
Newspaper	1.50	1.50	1.50	1.50	6.00

Category	Week 1	Week 2	Week 3	Week 4	Total
Pharmacy	35.79			25.00	60.79
Gifts	39.52			25.00	64.52
Housekeeper	90.00		90.00		180.00
Beauty shop and barber	97.00			27.50	124.50
Clothing and dry cleaning	141.87		45.88		187.75
Utilities (gas, electricity, water, refuse)		117.00	27.50	84.00	228.50
Mortgage payment				975.00	975.00
Home maintenance/ repairs	23.98		78.00		101.98
Car payment			273.00		273.00
Miscellaneous	92.00	232.00	108.00	248.00	680.00
Totals	1,762.47	762.28	934.52	1,865.93	5,235.20

Average monthly income: $5,114.00
Less total spent this month: $5,235.20
Amount <overspent> or underspent: <$121.20>

The information on this spending record came directly from Bob and Sally's daily spending records. They did a great job tracking their spending and then merging all those daily records into weekly spending records at the end of each week and finally into this monthly spending record.

Look at the bottom line. The Browns lived beyond their means—they spent $121.20 more than their monthly income. Seeing this was like turning on a light in a dark room.

Overspending, of course, is a real problem. But more than that, the Browns made no provision for giving, for saving (a retirement plan like a 401[k] that uses before-tax dollars does not count as saving for our purposes), or for irregular and unexpected expenses they will undoubtedly encounter in the future. The Browns overspent, but the larger picture is much worse than that. They do not have any emergency savings. They live close to the edge. They are overspending by paying with credit—digging their debt pit a little deeper. And because the Browns are carrying credit card balances, the $121.20 they added to their debt will take years to be repaid and will cost a ton in interest. That's bad, but they've set themselves up for much worse debt problems in the future.

For example, how will they pay for maintenance and repairs on their cars, the family vacation, or next Christmas? If they wait until those things happen and then search for ways to deal with them, it's a foregone conclusion what will happen. More debt. Unless they have a secret stash somewhere (clearly they don't or why would they be overspending and carrying all that consumer debt?), they're looking at a lifetime of debilitating consumer debt, and we know how adversely that can affect their relationship and their marriage. Further, if they continue spending all they have plus some they don't have yet, as they did this month, they will join many others who will enter retirement with few assets and a negative net worth.

Once the Browns finished their first monthly spending record, they sat down together to analyze it. They didn't need me to point out that $176 for fast food in one month was way over the top, given their income. Because they incurred new debt this month (they overspent their income by $121.20), it's likely they will be paying for those fast-food indulgences for some time to come. That sobering thought made the Browns decide to exercise more discipline as they plan their spending for the next month. Ditto for the restaurant meals. They were shocked to see how much they spent for food in all the categories of groceries, fast food, school lunches, and restaurant meals—$1,188.63, or over 20 percent of their available income. No question that was a huge leak they needed to plug immediately.

The Browns agreed that professional housecleaning was a luxury they couldn't afford, so they canceled that service. Now they're looking to change plans for their cell phones and considering pulling the plug on cable TV, keeping their high-speed internet, which will allow them alternative entertainment like Netflix and Hulu for a lot less money.

Thankfully, things are about to change for the Browns. They've decided to buckle down and debt-proof their marriage. Using this information, the Browns are ready to put all the puzzle pieces together into another document, the Spending Plan.

The Spending Plan

Unlike the spending record, which is compiled *after* the spending occurs and simply shows what happened, the spending plan maps out what will happen—the ways the Browns will choose to spend their income. The Spending Plan says, "We have this much money to manage, and this is how we intend to do it." It is really nothing more than prespending your paycheck on paper before you actually spend any of it. It's you telling your money where to go!

The first thing you should notice is that in this monthly spending plan I have changed the "total" column to "plan to spend this month" and added "actual spent this month." The plan to spend column gets tallied up at the start of the month, and the actual spent column will be for comparison at the end of the month. With this information filled in, you'll have a better handle on how to plan your spending for the next month. You'll see where you went over, where you came in way under—all important information as you become a better money manager.

Because Bob is paid twice a month, on the first and the fifteenth, some of their expenses have been listed to reflect that schedule. For example, they plan to give 10 percent of their net income, rounded to $500 per month, half in the first week and half in week 3. They plan the same for their Contingency Fund deposit of $500 (two semimonthly payments of $250 each).

Because their mortgage payment is due on the fifth of the month, they plan to pay that from their first paycheck of the month, and they will make their Freedom Account and Rapid Debt-Repayment Plan contributions from the second paycheck of the month in week 3.

Bob and Sally's Spending Plan

Month: _____

Category	Plan to Spend Week 1	Plan to Spend Week 2	Plan to Spend Week 3	Plan to Spend Week 4	Plan to Spend This Month	Actual Spent This Month
Contingency fund	250.00		250.00		500.00	
Giving	250.00		250.00		500.00	
Freedom account			441.00		441.00	
RDRP			430.00		430.00	
Mortgage payment	975.00				975.00	
Car payment	273.00				273.00	
Gasoline	40.00	40.00	40.00	40.00	160.00	
Groceries	100.00	100.00	100.00	100.00	400.00	
Food away from home	30.00	30.00	30.00	30.00	120.00	
Utilities (gas, electricity, water, refuse)	65.00	120.00	20.00	117.00	322.00	
Cell phones	178.00				178.00	
Cable TV/internet			145.00		145.00	
Babysitter	30.00	30.00	30.00	30.00	120.00	
Kids' allowances	16.00	16.00	16.00	16.00	64.00	
Auto insurance			53.00		53.00	
Pharmacy	25.00				25.00	
Newspaper	1.50	1.50	1.50	1.50	6.00	
Miscellaneous	50.00	50.00	50.00	50.00	200.00	
Totals	2,283.50	387.50	1,856.50	384.50	4,912.00	

Average monthly income: $5,114.00
Less total spent this month: $4,912.00
Amount <overspent> or underspent: $202.00

Their new Freedom Account with fixed monthly payments of $441 takes the place of several categories on the Browns' monthly spending record. Auto maintenance and repairs will no longer show up as a separate category, nor will clothing and home maintenance. All those items are now managed through their Freedom Account.

Their Rapid Debt-Repayment Plan takes the place of individual credit card payments. They are now covered in the single entry of $430.

Next they list their mortgage and car payments. So far all the Browns' entries are fixed and predictable. Then comes the food. The Browns took a long, hard look at this problem category and decided to have only two food-related categories: groceries and food they eat away from home. They also listed amounts for utilities, cell phones, kids' expenses, and so on.

With their first spending plan, Bob and Sally are ready to face their first month of planned spending with the understanding that at the end of the month they'll again analyze and brainstorm. They will undoubtedly need to make adjustments.

They will continue with their daily and weekly spending records so that by the end of the month they can easily fill in missing information on their spending plan.

Managing Day by Day

Creating a spending plan is one thing. Managing it, the freedom account, the contingency fund, and the rapid debt-repayment plan is quite another. Managing your money can be overwhelming at first, not because any of this is unreasonable but because it is all so new.

In the beginning, you may feel you are spinning plates and juggling chain saws as you move from your old ways of spending all you have and then using plastic to finish out the month. The transition period may be challenging, particularly if you are behind in your bills or facing initial expenses that are greater than the amount of money you have to work with. While I cannot anticipate every possibility, I can tell you that you can do this. You can start with small steps (but please push yourself to the maximum effort possible). For example, if you simply cannot save and give 10 percent in the first month, give and save something! Make it 5 percent, then next month push it to 6, and so on.

One of you is better with organization and math, so you should be the one to handle the physical task of writing out the checks,

213

balancing the bank accounts, tracking the rapid debt-repayment plan, making the deposits into the contingency fund, and filling out next month's spending plan. You will both continue to keep daily spending records and to develop them into weekly spending records.

You may be thinking this sounds like way too much work—a lot of trouble. Perhaps that is true if you compare debt-proof living to the way you have been managing your money in the past. I can only assume that since you're reading this book, you are looking for a new way. Compared to having no system, debt-proof living does require time and effort. However, when you realize you are potentially taking care of millions of dollars in your lifetime, you will have to agree that once you have your system up and running, the small amount of time and effort debt-proof living requires is minimal compared to the payoff. And if you keep your accounting simple and both of you have input on at least a weekly basis, this is going to run so smoothly you'll wonder how you ever got along before.

Many Ways to Budget

For me, just the word *budget* was like fingernails on a chalkboard. I'm not sure why, but I think it had to do with my dark financial days, when I chafed at the directive that I needed to get on a budget. It was like a straitjacket someone else created and into which I had to be locked. A budget was sure to force me into something that didn't fit, wasn't comfortable, and was not very attractive either.

I've managed to grow up, financially speaking, and now I see that a budget is simply a method by which to plan one's spending. Sure, you can purchase ready-made budget forms that look an awful lot like a straitjacket to me. I don't want anyone telling me I can spend only 38 percent on housing and 27 percent on transportation. What if I want to spend 10 percent on housing because I have no mortgage but 37 percent on transportation because I travel all over the world visiting my grandchildren? None of that is true (except

214

the no mortgage part). I'm just trying to point out the absurdity of trying to live according to another's budget.

Your budget needs to be tailor-made for your income and your expenses. And it is likely to change every month because that's how our lives are.

There are many ways to budget money. And in the beginning, any budget is like training wheels. You need it to get going! It keeps you upright and making progress getting from here to there. The more you practice, the better you get. You can relax, enjoy the scenery, and consider just how fond you are of this ride. Eventually, you won't need the training wheels so much. Managing your money will become nearly instinctive. But until then, you need to strap on the training wheels, the helmet, the knee and elbow pads too. You will fall. You'll even get a few scrapes along the way as you get used to this new way of traveling through life.

While I am fond of the spending plan way of budgeting, I know of people who are fond of other methods. So rather than telling you that you must use one specific method, I'd like to introduce you to others just in case one of them more closely fits your style, personality, and temperament.

What I will not tell you is that getting on a budget is optional. It is not, at least not in the beginning. If you plan to debt-proof your marriage and take control of your money, you need some way to manage your money that puts both of you at ease, does not create undue stress on anyone, and makes your lives—and your marriage—better.

Your choice of money management system may change over time. You may go through many revisions. You may find that the best money management system is for each of you to have your own system. Some spouses have their own money, which they manage separately, and then share expenses. Budgets should never become financial prisons. Rather, they should be the best tool in your financial tool chest.

Another system involves using envelopes—one for each spending category in your spending plan. You cash your paycheck and divvy up the money among the envelopes as stated in the plan. If you plan to spend $100 for groceries because that is what your plan directs, then you take $100 in cash and place it in the envelope labeled "groceries." When you go to the supermarket, you take that envelope—not your checkbook or plastic. You spend from the envelopes (which you are keeping in a very safe place, not carrying around with you). When an envelope is empty, there is no more spending until the next fill-up.

For payments you must send through the mail, you can either retain your regular checking account or purchase money orders from the post office or another source. Yes, it is a pain, and it takes time to stand in line to buy a money order, but you cannot bounce a money order and you cannot overdraw an envelope. If you have demonstrated that you cannot yet manage a checking account responsibly, you should consider the envelope method.

At the end of the month, play the zero-sum game. Place whatever amount remains in the envelopes into savings to zero out your account instead of seeing the extra money as found money you can just blow. The goal is to leave no dollar unallocated.

Savings Levels

The day will come, and sooner than you think, when your contingency fund reaches the goal you have set. So you may be wondering, can we stop saving money then? No, never! Always and forever you must pay yourself 10 percent of your net income. You simply move from one savings level to the next.

Savings level 1: fund your contingency fund. When you save money, you are building a wall of protection between you and the edge. The first level of your wall of protection is your contingency fund. Every dollar you place in that account is like another brick that will keep you from tumbling over the edge. And each time you dip into the Contingency Fund to cover emergencies, it's like removing a brick. When that happens, you have to replace the bricks and then move quickly to catch up. Every month you add more and more bricks to stand between you and financial crisis. Once you have accumulated enough money so that you could pay all your bills for six months without a paycheck, you will stop funding your contingency fund and will move on to the next level.

Savings level 2: boost your freedom account. Your freedom account has been up and running all along as you have been building your contingency fund, but it's possible you have been funding only the first two or three subaccounts. Or you may have been funding many subaccounts but with such small amounts each month that they have grown slowly.

At savings level 2, your 10 percent savings becomes an additional deposit into your freedom account to temporarily give it a second source of funding. You should stay at level 2 until you are comfortable that each of the subaccounts in your freedom account is funded adequately up to one year in advance. If, for example, your property taxes are $3,000 a year, you would want to see a balance of at least $6,000 in that subaccount—enough to pay the bill that will arrive any day and also the one that will arrive a year later. Likewise, your Christmas or holidays subaccount should have a balance equal to what you intend to spend on that in the coming year.

Savings level 2 is your opportunity to fund all the subaccounts you designed that were inactive because you were unable to increase your monthly contribution to include them. Once you reach the fully funded goal, you are ready to move on to level 3 (while still making your regular freedom account deposits each month).

Savings level 3: finish your RDRP. At savings level 3, your 10 percent savings should go to your RDRP to speed up the process of getting debt-free. For example, if your 10 percent savings is $400 a month and your regular monthly RDRP payment is $339, you would redo your RDRP to reflect monthly payments of $739. Once you complete your RDRP so that you are debt-free, you can go right on to level 4.

Savings level 4: create an investment portfolio. By the time you reach savings level 4, you will have your contingency fund fully funded in a safe place, you will have a fully funded freedom account (can you even imagine how wonderful that will be?), and you will be free of all unsecured debt. Wow, you made it! And now the fun begins.

In savings level 4, you begin building wealth for yourself, your family—your future! You have so many options at this level. For example, with your 10 percent savings you can:

- accumulate a down payment to buy a house
- prepay the principal on your present mortgage
- start building an investment portfolio of stocks, bonds, and mutual funds
- create a combination plan in which you are both prepaying your mortgage and investing

Savings level 4 is where you will settle in for the rest of your income-producing life, except for times when you will need to return to previous levels for a season. For example, if you use your contingency fund to live during a season of unemployment, once you go back to work, you will return to savings level 1 to restore and rebuild it. Or there may be a time when you will need to move back to savings level 2 for a season to build a subaccount for college tuition or to pay for a wedding.

Frequently Asked Questions

Q: We need 100 percent of our paychecks just to get by. We can't save 10 percent. What should we do?

A: Saving 10 percent of your income is the goal. If you can't start with 10 percent, start with 5 percent. Still can't do it? Even if it's only $5 a week, that's enough to get your contingency fund up and running. Now start reducing your expenses dramatically until your lifestyle fits within 80 percent of your income.

Q: We can't do both, so which should we work on first, a contingency fund or a freedom account?

A: You can do both if you start out small. It costs nothing to set up your freedom account binder, prepare the subaccount pages, and determine the monthly deposit required for each. This exercise will clear the fog and give you a boost because you are taking steps in the right direction. If you absolutely cannot begin funding both, the contingency fund should come first. As expenses come up that would normally be paid from your freedom account, it would be better to cover them from your contingency fund than to use credit. If you do this, you should quickly repay your contingency fund so you do not lose ground.

Q: We contribute to our employers' 401(k) retirement plans. Can we just make one of them our contingency fund?

A: No, because retirement accounts are not liquid. You cannot make arbitrary withdrawals. But that's only one problem. Cashing in a retirement account can be very expensive because of the penalties and taxes. Your retirement account is a frozen asset that is out of reach for now. If you cannot build a contingency fund under your current circumstances, consider reducing your 401(k) contributions temporarily to free up the money you need to do that.

Q: Isn't it dumb to let $10,000 or more sit in a bank when it could be invested in mutual funds or the stock market?

A: No, not when you consider that this is primarily an emergency fund, not an investment. If you become suddenly unemployed,

219

you want to have the funds available and intact. There are a variety of safe places to put your contingency fund where it is immediately available, safe, and still earning the highest rate of interest available.

Q: It does not make sense to put any of my money into a contingency fund while I am in debt and paying double-digit interest to credit card companies. Shouldn't I use all of my available money to pay my debts first, then start saving?

A: If you do not have an emergency fund, what are you going to do next month when your car breaks down and requires an expensive repair? If you have no emergency source, you'll be forced to use credit. If you keep following that pattern every time an unexpected expense comes up, you will never get out of debt. If, on the other hand, you diligently build this wall of protection level by level, one brick at a time, you will be able to repay your debts quickly while building a contingency fund and a freedom account. With those, you can keep your promise to incur no new debt and still keep your boat afloat. And you will be well on your way to reaching savings level 4.

Part 3

Unique Solutions
for Common Dilemmas

19

Finding Money
You Didn't Know You Had

Forty Ways to Live below Your Means

Spending less is easier than saving more.
Bill and Mary Toohey,
The Average Family's Guide
to Financial Freedom

B ob and Sally Brown took control of their reckless overspending and created a contingency fund and a freedom account. They developed their rapid debt-repayment plan, and in their first month of planned spending (a mere thirty days), they funded all three of their new management elements, they gave, they paid themselves, and they ended the month with money in the bank, also known as a surplus.

I made it sound so easy, didn't I?

Well, it ain't.

First of all, the Browns are a figment of my imagination. And even then, their situation is not true to life. Did you notice they have no category for entertainment? That means no date nights and nothing for movies or occasional fun activities. If they came to me with this spending plan, I would gently point out that omission.

My point is that it's unrealistic to think they will stick with a plan that is so rigid there's no room for the joys of life. Sure, they'll be able to get along for a few months, but if the plan is so strict they have no breathing room, they won't stick with it. One or both will become resentful, and they'll be right back where they were many chapters ago.

They're going to have to agree to extreme sacrifice in many areas of their lives, at least until they get debt-free, but they need to be realistic before they completely eliminate entertainment from their family life. On the bright side, there are many activities and events that don't cost a lot of money.

Creating your spending plan is a lot like finding the perfect pair of jeans. You have to really suck it in to get them zipped, but wow, they make you look spectacular. You get them home, wash them a couple of times, and before you know it, either they've shrunk or you've grown. If you can get them zipped, you can't breathe. All of a sudden, these jeans feel a couple of sizes too small.

This is exactly what will happen with your spending plan if you are not careful. You might be able to cram yourself into that tight plan for a few months, but when you realize you can't breathe, you'll feel like giving up altogether. The way to make the spending plan not just comfortable but downright roomy is to reduce your spending. It all comes down to this: if you are ever going to accumulate enough assets to make a difference in your marriage and provide responsibly for your future, you must spend less than you earn. And if you don't have high-paying jobs and you do have a bunch of kids, make that considerably less.

As you begin to challenge every expenditure, in time your spending plan will begin to fit more comfortably. And as your income increases and if you are diligent not to see that as an excuse to expand your lifestyle, you will begin to see big things happen. Your finances will start to improve . . . considerably.

As you have learned (or will soon) from tracking your spending and analyzing your daily, weekly, and monthly spending records, money is leaking out of your life. Some of my favorite letters are from couples and individuals who are startled by what they learn when they begin to track their spending. Plugging those leaks is the way they find money they didn't know they had.

If you think of yourself as a financial plumber, you'll soon realize that some leaks are easily detected and plugged while other areas will be far more challenging. Take credit card interest for example. You may not have a clue the exact amount of credit card interest you are paying. Sure, you know the total of your monthly payments, but how much of that is pure, horrible interest?

I heard from one woman who calculated just the interest portion of all their monthly debt payments and then divided it by thirty to get a daily figure. She discovered they were paying $11.51 a day in interest on their unsecured debt. That's one gigantic money leak! But it's a leak that cannot be plugged overnight.

For most couples, money is leaking from every area of their lives, even if only a little bit. By detecting and plugging those leaks using every possible ingenious tactic, they will see their bottom line change dramatically. No longer will you think saving $10 here or $5 there is not worth the effort. Of course, it is! Some of us five- and ten-dollared ourselves into a big mess, and the same every-little-bit-counts attitude will get us out.

There are so many ways to reduce your spending and plug your money leaks that I could fill a book. Wait! I did. It's called *Cheaper, Better, Faster*. And I will be filling others in the future. And I load up my website with clever and often painless ways to save too.

Expense cutting and leak plugging is a two-step process. First, you have to retrain your brain, and then you have to find all kinds of clever ways to live on less.

Retrain Your Brain

So much of this money management thing is about attitude rather than money. Living within your means is a state of mind. You have to stop believing what you have is a leverage to get everything you richly deserve. Sure, you want something, but that's not a good excuse for buying it. Contrary to what television ads would like you to believe, you don't deserve it all. You're not entitled to have it all now and pay for it some other time. That's just a bunch of baloney, and the sooner you retrain your brain to believe the truth, the sooner you'll be on your way to living beneath your means.

This retraining process means seeing frugality as your ticket to success. Embrace the idea of fixing things, using what you already have, or (gasp!) doing without rather than buying new. There are thousands of ways to live on less, and that does not mean living a life of misery. Some people think there are just two choices: living deeply in debt or living like a pauper. Believe me, there are many stages in between.

Seek inspiration from others who've been in debt and are now living on less. There are thousands of us who find inspiration from one another. We push, prod, and encourage one another. We share our ideas and strength. You need to join us and learn all you can. Become a closet cheapskate at first if you must. You'll soon learn to live beneath your means with dignity and style. You'll learn handy phrases like, "Let's eat at home for a change," "I think I'd like to wear this coat for one more season," and "Let's take a stay-at-home vacation!" It's less embarrassing than you'd think because there is this delightful payoff called margin—that space between you and the edge, also known as a surplus.

If you learn to keep a lid on your expenses by controlling your spending, something amazing will happen. You will reduce your needs. As you reduce your needs, you will cut expenses, and that means you will have more of your income to invest in your future.

Live on Less

While this space will not allow for an exhaustive treatment of all the ways to slash your expenses, here for your plumbing pleasure are forty fabulous ways to get started on your quest to find the money you didn't know you had.

1. *Shop with cash*. Adopt a policy of cash only. No checks, no plastic. You will find it difficult to turn over good, old-fashioned paper money. Credit cards, debit cards, ATM cards, even your checkbook are stand-ins for your money for the sake of convenience and "safety." We've been fed that marketing hype for so long we've come to believe it. The truth is checks and plastic feel like play money, and that's the problem. They are too convenient. Parting with your money should be inconvenient, even painful. As much as possible, stick to cash. Statistically speaking, you'll spend 30 percent less over time. Why do you think merchants and retailers are so eager to accept your debit, credit, and ATM cards as payment? Because they know you are likely to spend 30 percent more than if you were shopping with cash only. Leave the plastic and the checks at home and take only the amount you intend to spend. You will be a different kind of shopper because you will not be so apt to fall for all the impulsive opportunities ready to trip you up.

2. *Toss the catalogs*. Mail-order catalogs are the most insidious form of spending temptation known to humankind. Keep a recycling bin close to the door and toss them out before you are tempted to take a look. Or shred them. They make dandy packing material.

3. *Get free checking.* Have you figured out how much you're paying to have access to your own money? You shouldn't be paying a cent! Some credit unions still offer free checking with few, if any, conditions or limitations; however, it is getting more and more difficult to find a truly free account.

You can still get a free checking account at USAA Federal Savings Bank (usaa.com). To open an account, you must have a membership number, which you can get by calling 1-800-531-3410. You can request an account application be mailed to you, or you can open an account online at www.usaa.com. When you first log on, it will appear you must be in the military to qualify for USAA services. While some USAA Federal Savings Bank services are for active military only (insurance, for example), the banking services are available to the public. You can become a USAA member no matter where you live or how often you move. There is no monthly service fee—none! They pay interest on balances over $1,000, and quick cash is as close as the nearest ATM. Funds are easily transferred, at no charge, to and from other financial institutions. And you can access account information and pay bills in the comfort of your home or office. There is no charge for the first ten ATM withdrawals per monthly statement cycle; additional withdrawals are $1 each. USAA Federal Savings Bank will rebate up to $1.50 for each of the first ten domestic ATM surcharges per account per statement cycle.

4. *Buy checks direct.* You do need a checking account, and if you still prefer paper checks, get them at a rock-bottom price. (USAA will give you your first batch of personalized checks free). Don't order them from your bank, even if you have a free account. Go directly to a check printer, such as checksunlimited.com or checksinthemail.com, or look in the advertising inserts in your Sunday newspaper. You'll find ads for check printing companies with specials for first-time orders.

5. *Call your insurance companies.* If you carry homeowners, renters, and automobile insurance, call those companies this

month. Tell the agent you want to find out if you qualify for any additional discounts. Perhaps your youthful drivers qualify for good-grades discounts or you've moved to a new zip code. Prod the agent to help you discover how to reduce your premiums, and make sure he or she knows you're shopping around for lower rates.

6. *Play games with your money.* For example, don't spend coins. If your bill comes to $4.02, hand the checker $5, and you'll end up with $0.98 in change. At the end of every day, empty your pockets, wallet, and purse into a collection center like a jar or drawer. If you are diligent, you'll accumulate $20 a month easily and painlessly. Once you're into the coinage groove (it is habit forming), add dollar bills to the rule. Then fives. As soon as your container gets full, take it to the bank or credit union to get the coins rolled.

7. *Become fee phobic.* Don't pay a $3 or even a $1.50 ATM fee when you could walk two blocks to your own bank. Refuse to stay in a hotel that charges a $4 "connectivity fee" or $14 a day for the fitness center whether you use it or not. Don't accept a credit card that has an annual fee. Go to indexcreditcards.com to find the best no-fee cards currently available (but only after you read chap. 20).

8. *Find cheap internet service.* A number of companies offer cheap internet services, but qualifying depends on where you live. And qualifying may depend on your financial situation. Here are some options for your consideration.

Advertised as free high-speed internet from FreedomPop, this may be an option if you are not a heavy internet user. Just know that there will be some cost to get this "free" service. Go to freedom pop.com, where you'll need to provide your zip code and email address to see if they serve your location. If they do, you'll need to buy the $89 Freedom Hub Burst home modem, which you simply plug in. You'll be ready to go with instant internet connectivity. FreedomPop is a non-contract service that provides 1 gigabyte (GB) of data per month for free, which is adequate for sending and receiving emails and surfing the web. You can buy more if you want to share photos, stream movies, and so on. The rate is about $18 per month for 10 GB.

If you can't get FreedomPop, other providers offer high-speed internet at a low cost. NetZero and Juno now have DSL plans for about $10 per month for the first six months (the plan jumps to about $18 a month after that) with no data restrictions, provided you live in their service areas and you have a home phone line. Understand going in that these services create revenue through ads. You're likely to see plenty. But if this is a way you can have internet access within your means, it could be a great tradeoff.

9. *Use secret codes.* Most online merchants provide a place during the checkout process to enter a promotional code. Type it in and your total amount is automatically adjusted. Or you might get free shipping. Getting those promotional codes is easy provided you know where to look. Some websites do nothing but collect codes and online coupons: currentcodes.com, coolsavings.com, dealcatcher.com, edealfinder.com, and dealhunting.com. Where do these sites get the codes? From retailers looking for free advertising. Promotional codes are distributed by the retailers to improve sales. Many people who are regular customers of these stores get the codes by email or regular mail. The retailers hope their marketing efforts will expand as the recipients pass the information on to friends. Warning: if you have a spending problem and/or you do not pay your credit card bill in full each month, sites like these can be deadly to your financial well-being.

10. *Clean it yourself.* Many manufacturers, wanting to carry the least amount of liability or responsibility for mislaundering, slap on a "dry clean only" tag to cover themselves. Few fabrics are damaged by water. Let your common sense be your guide, but don't always believe what you read either. For sure your husband's $1,200 Italian suit should go to the dry cleaner (you did pay cash, right?). But most items in your closets can be laundered. And given the rates at dry cleaners these days, that's saying a lot. I know of

one woman who spends a minimum of $60 a month just on dry cleaning. She even includes cotton items that would be better off laundered in soap and water. Why? She's lazy, likes that freshly pressed look, and would rather throw things in the dry cleaning bag than hang them up for another day's wear. I don't know about you, but I could find a better place for $720 each year. At the very least, learn how to remove spots and how often clothes need to be cleaned (a man's suit that's worn regularly, properly hung between wearings, and aired outdoors occasionally needs professional cleaning only twice a year. That's assuming normal, commonsense hygiene and that he doesn't have a major catastrophe over lunch).

11. *Use self-talk.* Before you spend, ask yourself, Do we need it, or do we already have something that would work just as well? If we do need it, do we have to buy it now, or can we wait for a while? If we absolutely cannot wait, have we found the best deal? Once you can answer yes to that final question, put the item on hold and wait a full twenty-four hours before making the purchase. You won't believe how many times you will not close the deal because you've given yourself plenty of time to think things through. By stepping back and taking time, you will often change your mind. And save yourself from some pretty stupid purchases.

12. *Don't overpay your taxes.* You love to get a big, fat refund from the IRS. The fact is, however, you're lending money to the government interest free. You need to go through your tax return, assess your current income situation, and make appropriate adjustments so you get to December 31 owing or being owed as little as possible. That way you can use your money now, or you can put it into your contingency fund and earn interest. There is nothing patriotic, noble, or righteous about overpaying your taxes and then waiting for Uncle Sam to send money back to you.

13. *Prepay to shop online.* If you are committed to adding no more new purchases to your credit cards because you have revolving debt and you are committed to pay it off—and you are aware that

it is very dangerous to shop online with a debit card—there is a way you can shop with cash without incurring any fees (prepaid debit cards charge ridiculously exorbitant fees!). Go to just about any chain drugstore or supermarket and purchase an Amazon gift card with cash. You will not pay any fees, and the gift card will not expire. Now you can shop online at Amazon, paying for your purchases with your gift card. You will have all the benefits of quick shipping and returns using your gift card just as you would if you were paying with a credit card. Bonus: no worries about identity theft!

14. *Dump PMI.* If you bought your home with less than 20 percent down, you are probably paying a lot for the dreaded PMI. PMI (private mortgage insurance, not to be confused with mortgage insurance, which is a specific type of life insurance that pays off the mortgage upon death of the borrower) is insurance that protects the lender in the event the borrower defaults on the loan. Once your equity reaches 20 percent of the current market value, you should be able to dump your PMI. You may have to pay for an appraisal to substantiate market value, but that will be significantly cheaper ($300 is typical) than those horrible PMI premiums that could be $1,000 or more per year buried in your monthly payment. Don't know if you're paying for PMI? Make a call to find out. If you have an FHA mortgage, the PMI has been built into the interest rate. You cannot get rid of it; it's part of your loan for the duration.

15. *Bank your raise and windfalls.* You may find that measly 3 percent or 5 percent cost-of-living raise to be insultingly shabby. Or that $3 rebate for the lightbulbs you bought to be pocket change. Well, change your attitude. Bank your raises, rebates, refunds, and windfalls. In time, even that pocket change will add up to something significant.

16. *Learn to cook.* If you're eating out because you're too busy to cook or too lazy to learn how, we need to have a little talk. Both excuses are costing you a bundle. The average family of four spends

upward of $5,000 a year eating out. So make some big changes. Eat at home most of the time. Reserve eating out for special occasions, and everyone will value it as the special occasion it should be. Get out your cookbooks, tune into a few cooking shows, ask a friend to give you a lesson. Whatever it takes, learn how to cook at home, and then take pride in the meals you learn to cook. Change your attitude about cooking, and you'll change your bottom line too.

17. *Go meatless.* If you can go meatless three days a week, you could save $25 or more each week on your grocery bill. That's about $100 a month or $1,200 a year.

18. *Never pay full price.* If you must shop, make sure you're waiting for sales or buying from a discounter or bargain website. My theory is that everything eventually goes on sale, and if it doesn't, I probably don't need it.

19. *Know your bulks.* Contrary to popular thought, just because you're buying from a discount warehouse club doesn't mean something is a bargain. You have to know your unit costs and then be able to compare effectively. However, you can be confident that milk, cheese, and eggs will always be more cost effective at a warehouse club. Everything else is probably cheaper unless it can be purchased on sale at the supermarket.

20. *Get supermarket savvy.* Want to know the most impulsive place on earth? Your supermarket. If you only knew the lengths to which marketers, distributors, and retailers go to grab your attention and persuade you to buy something you'd not planned to buy when you walked in. Everything from the music over the sound system, the width of the aisles, the color of the walls, the arrangement of the products, the smells from the bakery, the stuff piled high at the end of an aisle, and the placement at eye level of the most expensive products is designed with your impulsivity in mind. Your best defense? Shop with cash. And carry only the amount you have decided ahead of time to spend. Go with a list and buy what's on the list. If you find a bargain too good to pass

up, come back later when you have more cash. As long as you know in your heart that you can write a larger check or simply swipe the plastic, all that really good-looking stuff is going to sabotage your best efforts every time. That's just human nature. So use your human intelligence to trump your nature, and you'll win at the grocery game.

21. *Grocery shop less frequently.* Do not allow yourself to run to the grocery store every time you get the urge. Every time you step foot in that place it's an impulsive act waiting to happen. Ever run into the store to pick up milk and come out with $50 worth of stuff you had no idea you really "needed"? My point exactly. If you shop every week, stretch it to eight days. Next week, make it nine days. Before you know it, you'll be making stuff last at home and using up what you have . . . and putting two weeks or more between grocery shopping trips. Your bill might be a little higher than it was for one week but not double.

22. *Try store brands.* Store brands, economy brands, generic brands . . . all words that used to make our kids go "Yuck!" But times have changed. And while not all store brands are worth your consumption, many are. Do you hear me? Many! Here's the deal. Chains that have their own label do not have their own manufacturing and processing plants. They make deals with the plants that process name-brand food items and deliver a stack of labels with their name on it. The label is the only difference between most store brands and their name-brand cousins. Well, there is one more important difference: the price. Why? Because 80 percent of the cost of food items in your supermarket goes for marketing and advertising. Store brands require far less of that, which is reflected in the price. Your job is to decide which products are the same. Experiment! Try a variety of items. And check at the front counter of the market. Do they advertise satisfaction guaranteed? Well then, if you're not satisfied with the store brand caviar, return it for a full refund. Start taking

full advantage of all that your market offers you, its valuable consumer.

Hint: There are only five major turkey-processing plants in the United States. There are a gazillion brands of turkeys. Does that tell you anything? They're all from the same place and processed in the same way! So go for the cheapest turkey you can find. Never pay the big bucks again for a name brand. Another hint: Frozen turkeys are much fresher than fresh turkeys. Really. That's because modern equipment flash freezes a turkey within minutes of processing. But the fresh one? The FDA rules allow processors to take them to a temperature at which the liquid in the bird freezes while the meat remains soft. They can butcher those gobblers two weeks before they reach the market and allow them to sit there for a few more days until you go in and pick up your "fresh turkey." But the frozen turkey is as fresh as the moment it hit the flash freezer. Freezing does not change the taste or quality of turkey.

23. *Match coupons with sales.* Manufacturer coupons are not by themselves much good for saving money. But if you can hold on to a coupon until the item goes on sale, you can get quite a bargain. Teri Gault has turned the art of couponing into a science that she teaches to anyone willing to learn. You can check this out at her website, www.thegrocerygame.com.

24. *Stock up when it's cheap.* Most major grocery chains work on a twelve-week cycle. That means, generally speaking, every category of food product will go on sale every twelve weeks. The key to savvy grocery shopping is to wait until the items you need go on sale and then buy enough of them to last until the next sale. The grocery store is the last place you want to get caught paying full price.

25. *Buy cheap shampoo.* All shampoo, whether it's a 99 cent grocery store variety or a $24 salon brand, is 80 to 90 percent water, 9 to 19 percent detergent, with just a few drops of fragrance and other additives and preservatives. As long as you know how to read

the ingredients label and know your detergents, you can stop paying the big bucks for shampoo. Here's the lowdown on shampoo detergents: ammonium lauryl sulfate—very harsh; ammonium laureth sulfate—harsh; sodium lauryl sulfate (SLS)—still harsh; sodium laureth sulfate (SLES)—mild, great choice; TEA lauryl sulfate—gentle, good choice; TEA laureth sulfate—gentle, also a good choice. When buying shampoo, think price and detergent. Buy the cheapest one you can find that has the detergent that's right for your hair. Baby shampoo (no tears) is great for babies but way too gentle for adult hair, particularly if you use gels, mousse, or hairspray. You will not be satisfied with the results if you use it on a regular basis. Check out Altruism Biomedical Network (hair. shampoo.com) for more information.

26. *Find the library.* Think libraries lend only books? Think again! These days many public libraries lend videos, DVDs, VCRs, even character cake pans! Become a friend of your library. Stop buying books you'll read just once. Stop buying magazines the library stocks. Spend time at the library, then borrow books, movies, music, and even cake pans to make your kids' birthday cakes! But please, no overdue fees.

27. *Liquidate.* Have you looked through your home lately? I mean really looked? In the attic, basement, cupboards, closets, and garage? Yikes, you've got a lot of stuff! Perhaps now would be a good time to turn some of your stash into cash. Figure out what you haven't used during the last year, and if it's not Grandma's vintage sterling silver flatware, get rid of it. Sell it through your local classifieds, at a garage sale, or on an internet auction site.

28. *Buy used, late model, domestic.* There's nothing quite as expensive as a brand-new car. There are times, rare though they be, when buying new might be advisable. But generally speaking, the cheapest way to own a car is to buy a late model, used, domestic car with cash. Don't dismiss the thought so quickly. Anyone can do this, but you have to work up to it. You start with the best clunker

236

you can buy with the cash you have. Let's say that's $1,200. Not a pretty set of wheels, but if it runs, hey, that's transportation. Now, let's say you believe you could cover $200 payments on a new car. Great. But start making them to yourself. Put $200 every month into your car account. At the end of one year, sell that heap of steel for $900. Add that to the $2,400 you've saved and go buy the best $3,300 clunker you can find. For cash! Keep making those $200 payments to yourself. At the end of a year, sell that better clunker for $3,000 and add that to the $2,400 in the bank. Now go buy the best $5,400 car you can find. Keep doing this every year until you have enough cash to buy a brand-new car with all cash. But wait, you say. Isn't that a poor use of money? It sure is . . . and you never would've asked that question unless you had $25,000 cash in your hand. It doesn't feel good to spend that much on a new car that will be worth about $20,000 the minute you drive it home. So take your cash and buy the best late model, domestic (cheaper to repair and maintain than a foreign beauty), used car you can find. Keep making those payments to yourself, and you will be an all-cash car buyer for the rest of your life.

29. *Empty the trunk; fill the tires.* Want to know the biggest enemy of good gas mileage? Weight. The heavier your car, the harder that engine has to work to push it around town. So give your car a break and empty all the excess weight from the trunk. It is not a mini-storage unit! All that should be in there on a regular basis is the spare tire and required safety equipment. You'll fill up less often, and when you do, be sure to check the air pressure in your tires. Keep them at optimum pressure (look on the tire itself for the correct psi rating). These two simple tactics will improve your gas mileage by about 10 percent, and that's considerable given today's gasoline prices.

30. *Make your own fast food.* Keep a batch of this dry muffin mix in the pantry, and you'll have fresh, hot muffins for breakfast in less time than it takes to hit the drive-thru.

5 cups	all-purpose flour
1 cup	whole wheat flour
1 ½ cups	sugar
1 cup	instant nonfat dry milk powder
¼ cup	baking powder
2 tsp.	salt
1 tbsp.	cinnamon
½ tsp.	ground cloves

Mix in a large bowl and store in an airtight container. To bake muffins, place 2 cups mix in a large bowl. Add ⅔ cup water, 1 slightly beaten egg, and ¼ cup oil. With a fork, mix only until dry ingredients are moistened. Fill paper-lined muffin cups half full. Bake at 400 degrees for 10 to 15 minutes or until muffins are puffed and a toothpick comes out clean.

31. *Stop shopping.* Do you find yourself wandering around malls and bargain centers looking for, well, bargains? Stop! When you need something, refer to 11 above, find what you need, and buy it. Then leave. That's called planned spending, and it is light-years from shopping till you drop.

32. *Think secondary market.* In our affluent society, the secondary market has grown immensely. I'm talking about thrift stores, consignment shops, auctions, estate sales, and so on. Add these to internet auction sites and you can find just about anything you need or want in a gently used condition with a huge discount off the new price.

33. *Use free fitness.* Do you really have enough money to devote $20, $30, or more per month to your local gym or fitness center? If so, God bless you, provided you're actually making use of the facilities. If not, don't worry. You have an even more ideal fitness opportunity for free. It's called your legs and the great outdoors. Start walking, my friend!

34. *Expect satisfaction.* When something doesn't fit right, doesn't operate to your satisfaction, or doesn't stay together, don't

just throw it away. Take it back! Ask for a refund or a replacement. Expect to be a satisfied customer. No one has the right to take your money without your permission, and you should not grant that permission until you are fully satisfied. Be assertive but always remain a pleasing fragrance. Never become an odor.

35. *Do it yourself.* It's so easy to call a housekeeping service or agree to pay more for installation. But if you can do some of those things yourself, or learn how, you should. Just think of all the money you can save while knowing the job has been done right.

36. *Make one big, bold move.* Whether its downsizing to a smaller home, getting a second job, or renting out a spare room (using a great deal of caution), there's one really big thing you can do to give your expense-cutting mission a mighty jump start. Mine was selling my car. After thirty-five years of having my own car (something I would have told you was more essential than just about anything in my life), we sold it and became a one-car family. Truth be told, our plan was to replace it once we saved enough cash. But that didn't happen. Once we counted what we were not spending in terms of insurance, fuel, maintenance, repairs, licensing, washing, parking, to name only the basics, we decided not to buy one. Besides, I got spoiled having a driver and not having to pump, wash, and worry about all the mainte- nance and getting a ticket every other Friday when I forgot about neighborhood street sweeping. Sure, my husband and I worked in the same office, which made our situation somewhat unique. But we also lived in California, the land of virtually no public transportation. So how did we do it? With a lot of planning ahead, compromising, and most valuable for me, a great deal of just not going. I can't begin to count how many mindless trips to the store or garden center I delayed, postponed, and eventu- ally forgot about because I just didn't have a way to get there. By the time I went through the hassle of arranging transport, the thrill of the shop had worn off. Don't misunderstand. My

husband is the most cooperative guy in the world. But our days often took us in opposite directions, and that put quite a crimp on my compulsive trips to buy stuff. Becoming a one-car family turned into a double bonus for us. The primary effect was $800 or so a month right off the top of our expenses. But the secondary effect, and one we'd not anticipated, was that many opportunities to spend money mindlessly were thwarted purely as a matter of logistics. We are now almost twenty years into our single vehicle situation. It's our way of life, and not one that every family can adopt. But I know there is one really big, bold move you could make for at least a short while. Ka-ching.

37. *Learn to cut hair.* I am not advocating goofy-looking kids or frumpy moms and dads. I'm the first to appreciate a quality cut and fashionable hairstyle. But I also know that anyone with a little patience and the willingness to learn can perform hair trims to increase the time between professional cuts. You need the right tools, and that will represent an initial investment of less than $25. But even if learning this new skill reduces your family's hair salon bill by only 50 percent (not at all difficult), you could be looking at savings of $500 or more per year. Check the library for a good how-to book or find a YouTube video.

38. *Turn down/up the thermostat two degrees.* In the winter, lower your thermostat by just two degrees; in the summer, increase it by two degrees. Experts say you can reduce your heating and air-conditioning bills by 5 to 10 percent by simply moving the thermostat two degrees.

39. *Make your own.* The next time you need household cleaning supplies, take a trip to your pantry, not the store. You can even make some of your own groceries too! Here's an example of both.

All-purpose spray cleaner: 2 cups rubbing alcohol, 1 tbsp. liquid dishwashing detergent, 1 tbsp. household ammonia, 1 tbsp. white vinegar. Mix the ingredients in a gallon jug. Fill the jug with warm water and shake to combine. You can dispense this in a spray bottle and use as you would Windex. It's great for cleaning windows, chrome, and bath fixtures.

Sports drink (like Gatorade): 1 packet any flavor unsweetened Kool-Aid or similar product, 8 tbsp. sugar or 10 packets Equal, ⅜ tsp. salt, ⅛ tsp. salt substitute (contains potassium chloride), 2 qt. water. You can make your own sports drink in any flavor you desire, and the ingredients will be very similar to the popular ones on the market. The cost is 3.75 cents per 8 oz. glass or 30 cents for two quarts. The same amount of commercial Gatorade retails for $2.99.

40. *Extend useful life.* If you know a few tips and tricks, you can make your perishable food items last longer or at least until you can consume them. When opening a container of milk, drop in a generous pinch of salt. Salt retards the growth of bacteria and will allow your milk to stay fresh for about a week longer than you're used to. Once you've opened a container of sour cream or cottage cheese, put the lid back on and store the container upside down in the refrigerator. It will last several weeks longer. Want to keep your chips, crackers, even marshmallows fresher longer? Store them tightly closed in the freezer.

20

Credit: The Good, the Bad, the Ugly

Credit Cards, Credit Reports, Credit Scores, and Credit Repair

Credit is like a rope. You can use it as a tool or tie it into a noose to hang yourself.

Mary Hunt

To say that I have a love/hate relationship with consumer credit would be a huge understatement. On the one hand, without consumer credit, Harold and I would not be homeowners. Few people can afford their first home without some kind of home mortgage.

On the other hand, we will always wonder what might have been had we not spent so many years of our marriage getting into unsecured debt (twelve years) and digging our way out (thirteen).

It is sad to think it took us twenty-five years to get back to zero. It breaks my heart to watch consumer debt destroy marriages, blow families apart, and ruin lives.

While all forms of consumer credit can be deadly if used inappropriately, I believe credit cards are among the most dangerous. Credit cards are available to anyone of any age without regard for employment or the demonstration of a reasonable way to repay the debt. Too bad we cannot treat them like the poisonous creatures they are and simply ban them from our lives. While occasionally I'll meet someone who has managed to do that, I can tell you it is not easy, nor is it advisable. So I put credit cards in the same category as insurance and taxes. You gotta have them, so make sure they work for you and enhance your life—but do not ruin it.

Credit Cards

Ideally, you need one good, all-purpose credit card for the two of you—one account in both your names. Such a card has no annual fee (you can find a current list of no-fee cards at indexcreditcards. com), has at least a twenty-five-day grace period (the time between the purchase and when interest begins to accrue), and is accepted in the greatest number of places (that would make it either Master-Card or Visa). Technically speaking, you do not care about the interest rate because you are never going to carry a balance on this card. However, if you have a choice, opt for the lowest rate. This one good, all-purpose credit card is to be a tool, not an instrument of debt. You will not use it to finance anything but rather as a means to secure a rental car, to reserve a hotel room, or to order something by mail order or the internet. Always and without fail, any purchases that end up on this account will be paid for during the twenty-five-day grace period so that you never accrue interest. You may not need to acquire this new card; you may already have it in your current portfolio of cards.

I suggest that neither one of you carry your one good, all-purpose credit card with you. You are not going to use it for shopping. It is too tempting. Put both of the cards for this account into a safe place that both of you know about. Make a promise that before using the account you will let the other person know, and the decision will be mutual.

Here's a way to make a cool vault for your credit cards. Get a large, empty coffee can. Fill it halfway with water. Freeze. Lay your credit cards facedown on the ice. Fill it to the top with water. Refreeze. Replace the plastic lid and return the can to the freezer for safe storage. Now the cards are safe from you and from would-be burglars. If you know you need to rent a car or buy an airline ticket (it's nearly impossible to buy a ticket with cash these days), you will have enough notice to thaw the vault. You will feel silly standing at the sink with the hot water running and will have plenty of time to rethink that twice-yearly sale that got your attention.

But what about an emergency? I know what you're thinking. But, Mary, what if we're driving across the desert in the middle of the summer and our radiator blows a hole the size of Detroit and we don't have $950 cash for the tow truck driver? We'll need our one good, all-purpose credit card! Even though most what-ifs never happen, I understand your concern, so I have a solution. Before you freeze your cards, do this: write the credit card number, expiration date, three-digit security code, and toll-free number for customer service in a secret place in your wallet, day planner, or address book—some place only you will know. Encrypt it (do not call it "My Visa") by calling it "Blu-Ray Serial Number" or something far more silly. Now when you're stranded in that hot desert sun with that gaping hole in the empty radiator and Toby the tow truck driver is standing there wringing his hands, you can simply call customer service and get approval right over his phone.

Take all your other credit cards and divide them into two piles: those with zero balances and those that have a revolving balance.

If you have any with zero balances, put them into an envelope and seal it well. Hand it off to a trusted friend or relative if you cannot trust yourself not to use them. Or put it in a safe place that is far away from you. In time, you will want to close those accounts, but for now just leave them be so you can concentrate on the credit card debt you have that is revolving from month to month.

Next, take the cards on which you are carrying a balance. You do not have to close these accounts officially, but you must close these accounts to you—emotionally. Cut the cards up with a scissors. For extra fun, place the pieces in a pile on a piece of aluminum foil and put it in a 300° F oven. Remember Shrinky Dinks? That's similar to what will happen. You may come out with a very unusual sculpture suitable for wall hanging—something to serve as a reminder of why you don't want to go through this again! Keep your eye on it, please. No fires because you got distracted, okay?

Credit Reports

If you've been looking forward to this section about as much as a root canal, congratulations! You are perfectly normal. Most of us would prefer just about anything to a face-to-face encounter with our credit report due to:

- *Fear.* Many people are so afraid to know what's in their credit report that they choose denial over reality. As long as they don't know for sure what's there, the possibility remains that it's not that bad.
- *Ignorance.* Many people simply do not understand what a credit report is, that they have one, where it is, who can look at it, or why it matters.
- *Blind faith.* There are some who naively trust the supreme credit bureau in the sky to have their best interests at heart. These people believe that because they pay their bills on time

their credit report is automatically a mirror image of such exemplary behavior.

I want to encourage you to push past your fear, ignorance, and misplaced trust and get a current copy of your credit report.

What Is a Credit Bureau?

A credit bureau is a nongovernmental profit-making company that gathers credit information about individuals. Credit bureaus collect, compile, analyze, and sell that information to banks, mortgage lenders, credit unions, credit card companies, landlords, and employers. Banks and businesses voluntarily subscribe to the services of the credit bureaus; they are not required by law to do so. Companies that buy information from credit bureaus use it to supplement applications for credit, insurance, housing, employment, and to market their services and products to new customers.

Credit bureaus are regulated by the Federal Trade Commission under the provisions of the 1971 Fair Credit Reporting Act (FCRA). The FCRA is designed to protect consumers and to impose limitations on creditors and credit bureaus. Most states have similar laws that impose additional limitations.

By law, credit bureaus are required to share the information they gather with one another, so theoretically, while the format in which the information is presented can vary from one bureau to the next, the contents of your credit file at Experian should be the same as the file with your name on it at Equifax, TransUnion, and others. You should, however, never rely on that theory.

What Is a Credit Report?

Think of your credit report as a rap sheet about you containing information that may or may not be true. Compiled by a credit bureau from information received from untold sources, it is a list of allegations others have made about the way you conduct your financial life.

A credit report includes personal information: your name, former names if any, past and present addresses, Social Security number, and employment history, including current salary. Credit bureaus get this information from creditors who get it from you every time you fill out a credit application. Whether you are married, separated, divorced, or single, your credit file should contain information about you only. Information about others, including your spouse, will appear only where that person is legally obligated with you on an account.

Accounts reported monthly. Most creditors, including banks, credit card companies, mortgage companies, student loan lenders, oil and gas companies, and large department stores, provide monthly reports to credit bureaus showing the status of your account with them. They report your payment activity (or inactivity as the case may be) for that month. They report if your account is turned over to a third party collector, if the account has been discharged in bankruptcy, or if you are disputing any charges. They also report any special arrangements they've made with you or a credit counseling organization you may have hired to work for you (more on credit counseling to follow).

Accounts reported in default. Some businesses report to credit bureaus only when an account is past due or has gone to collection. There are no laws or guidelines that insist companies must report anything at all to the credit bureaus.

Public records. Public information maintained by government agencies is accessible to anyone. Credit bureaus hire private companies to search public records for information on lawsuits, court judgments and liens, foreclosures, bankruptcy filings, tax liens, and criminal arrests and convictions. And it all ends up in individual credit reports.

Inquiries. Inquiries are made by individuals and companies to which you have given permission to look at your credit report.

248

These may be companies who mailed you a preapproved application that you signed and returned. Your signature gives permission for them to make an inquiry. Inquiries are recorded and then show up on your credit report.

Who Has a Credit Report?

Every adult has an individual credit report in his or her name. For the very young adult, that report might be blank, but you can be sure there's a file with his or her name and Social Security number on it, poised and ready to receive data.

How Do You Get Your Credit Report?

By law you are entitled to receive one free copy of your credit report from each of the three credit bureaus every twelve months. The only way you can get your free reports is by going to annual creditreport.com or by calling 1-877-322-8228.

How Do You Read Your Credit Report?

At the top of the report, you should see your name and unique report number. Whether your report is two or twenty-two pages long, everything on it has contributed to your current level of credit worthiness. Experian divides this information into two categories: potentially negative items and accounts in good standing. Experian, unlike its competitors, includes important information about each creditor: its name, address, and each account or court case number for all accounts, both negative and those in good standing. To protect your privacy and lessen the risk of identity theft, Experian does not include the full account number (the final few digits are missing). Also, if you ordered the report online, your Social Security number does not appear.

For each account on your report, you will see the date it was opened, how long the creditor has been reporting this account to the credit agency, the date of last activity on the account, the type of account, the payment terms, the monthly payment amount, who else if anyone is responsible for paying the account, the original amount borrowed, the credit limit or highest balance, and any recent balance or payment. The comments paragraph tells the status of the account, such as "in collection" or "never late." If the account is past due, you will see information about when this negative item is scheduled to disappear.

Finally, Experian shows who's been snooping in your credit file. Inquiries are divided into two categories:

1. those you've given permission in writing to review your report
2. your current creditors, who are allowed to keep a close eye on you, and companies who bought your information in an attempt to snag you as a new customer

Experian tells you how long each of the category 1 inquiries will remain on your record. This is important because they are negative entries. It is not wise to allow many inquiries on your credit report. Inquiries paint a picture that you are desperate, so you are applying all over town for credit. Category 2 inquiries are of no consequence and for your information only. They show up only on your copy of your report.

What's the Consequence?

Credit bureaus are allowed (but not required) by law to report your negative information to potential creditors and others who want to know about you. The result can be devastating, all the way from being charged unreasonably high interest rates to losing out on a great apartment or job. While it might feel like those ugly blemishes will remain forever, they cannot. The law provides for specific time limits.

Bankruptcies: up to ten years from the date of the last activity on the bankruptcy filing.

Past-due accounts, charge-offs, collections, tax liens, judgments, and lawsuits: up to seven years from the date of entry even if the damage is reversed or the account is brought current and/or paid off.

Inquiries: up to two years from the date of inquiry.

All negative information, including bankruptcies, lawsuits, paid tax liens, accounts sent for collection, and criminal records, may be reported indefinitely when you apply for $150,000 or more of credit or insurance or if you apply for a job with an annual income of at least $75,000.

You Are the Managers

Credit bureaus collect between 2 and 3 billion pieces of information every month. Even if that information is shuttled into individual credit files at a nearly flawless error rate of only 1 percent (doubtful), that translates to 20 million mistakes per month. No wonder studies indicate nearly 70 percent of all credit reports contain errors. It is doubtful that yours has escaped. And no one checks.

There are no agencies or consumer advocates checking up on the information creditors supply or even if that information gets into the right file. No one cares whether your report is accurate, except you and your spouse. That is why you must take on the job of manager.

Your first task as manager is to conduct a thorough review of your report. Get three different colored highlighters. Choose one color to highlight all items that are correct. Use another color to highlight entries you know for sure are incorrect. Use the third color to highlight the mysteries.

Question everything, including the spelling of your name and other personal information. Remember, your credit report is nothing more than a list of allegations that may or may not be correct.

Credit Scores

Credit bureaus not only compile and sell credit information but also analyze that information by subjecting it to a complicated computerized scientific method developed by the Fair, Isaac Company that spits out a numerical score. Also known as a FICO score, this is a three-digit number ranging from a pathetic 340 at the bottom up to 820, 850, or 900 on the high end depending on the credit bureau.

Until recently, consumers were not allowed to know their credit scores. Lenders were sworn to secrecy, so it was virtually impossible for consumers to find out their scores, let alone understand how the scores were determined and what could be done to improve them.

Things have changed, thanks to the unrelenting pressure piled onto credit bureaus by consumers. Consumers are now allowed (for a fee) to know their FICO credit scores (myfico.com). Some websites, such as creditkarma.com, offer free credit scores or credit report cards, but they are not FICO scores. Think of them as wannabe scores that will give you a ballpark idea of where you stand.

Some credit card issuers are now including credit scores with each statement, and yours may even be your FICO score.

If you ordered your credit score with your Experian credit report, take a look at it now. Close to the top you will see your score followed by an analysis that shows your percentile as compared to the "US credit-active population," which of course means every adult person in America who has a pulse. Generally speaking, 720 is a decent score—not excellent but okay.

Credit Repair

The first step in repairing your credit report is to know exactly what's in your file. If you've secured a copy of your credit report and are satisfied with what you found, you are among the fortunate few. If you've taken that step and are not satisfied, read on.

Chances are great that yours is among the 70 percent of all credit reports that contain some piece of information that is incorrect, obsolete, or no longer verifiable. Federal law gives you the right to challenge that information, no matter how serious or minor, through a process called disputing.

If you have a nitpicking kind of personality or tend to be controlling (who me?), you are going to love the disputing process. If not, you may not find the process enjoyable, but it is tolerable and something you must force yourself to do. It is that important.

Learning the Jargon

CR: If you've ever applied for a credit card, a personal loan, insurance, or a job, somewhere there's a file about you. This file contains information on where you work and live; how you pay your bills; whether you've been sued, been arrested, or filed for bankruptcy; and, some would accuse, how often you mow the lawn. This is called a credit report (CR). You have the right to know what's in your CR but only if you ask. You should also think of your CR as your character report. It is a snapshot the world sees that reflects who you are and how you choose to conduct your financial life.

CRA: Companies that gather and sell individuals' credit information are called Consumer Reporting Agencies (CRAs). The most common type of CRA is the credit bureau, and the largest and most well-known CRAs are Experian, TransUnion, and Equifax. CRAs have specific responsibilities under the law to report only true and accurate information.

IP: Information providers (IPs) are businesses that supply information about you to CRAs. These include banks, lenders, credit card companies, insurance companies, department stores, and other credit grantors. IPs are required under the FCRA (below) to provide only true and accurate information to CRAs.

FCRA: The federal law that protects you in all of this is the Fair Credit Reporting Act (FCRA). It says you have the right to dispute any remark on your report that you believe to be inaccurate or incomplete. You may have additional rights under your state laws. Contact your state attorney general or local consumer protection agency for more information.

FTC: The Federal Trade Commission (FTC) enforces the FCRA and works for consumers to prevent the fraudulent, deceptive, and unfair business practices of CRAs. The FTC provides information to help consumers spot, stop, and avoid these kinds of activities that, unfortunately, go on all the time. You are encouraged to file complaints directly with the FTC. The FTC cannot intervene in individual disputes or act as your lawyer, but the information you provide about your experiences and concerns is vital to the enforcement of the FCRA because it may indicate a pattern of possible law violations that require action by the commission.

ECOA: The Equal Credit Opportunity Act (ECOA) requires creditors to specify why your credit application was denied if you ask. The ECOA also requires creditors to consider additional information you might supply about your credit history.

YOU: The most important piece of this credit repair puzzle is YOU. You are the manager and the only member of the cast who cares if your CR is a true reflection of who you are. You are the only one who has the right by law to approve and/or dispute what is in your CR. If you don't do it, no one else is going to do it for you.

Disputing an Item

It is very important that you follow these strict guidelines when disputing any item in your credit report.

1. Make a detailed list of the items you believe to be false, inaccurate, incomplete, or obsolete. They can be as minor as a misspelled name or as serious as an item that doesn't even belong to you. Let's say you have a reasonable belief that you owe $948

on an account that is currently in default and threatening to go to collection. Your CR shows it as $1,048. This is inaccurate, and you have the right to dispute the entire account.

2. Complete a request for a reinvestigation dispute form and return it to the CRA that issued the report. This form should have been enclosed with the CR and can be completed in handwriting. Just make sure it is neat and legible. If you do not have the form, you can prepare a letter that includes this information: the name of the CRA that issued your CR, your full name, Social Security number, address, telephone number, and date of birth. Prepare this on a computer (handwritten letters on plain paper are often given minimal attention).

Begin your letter with something like this: "Please begin an investigation of the following items listed on my credit report that do not belong in my credit file." In the body of the letter, include for each item you are disputing the company's name (also called the subscriber), the account number, and the reason for the dispute or why you believe the item is being reported incorrectly.

For incorrect personal information, write, "The following personal information about me is incorrect." Then state which information is erroneous followed by the correct information.

For accounts that are not yours, write, "The following accounts are not mine." Then include the creditor's name, the account number, and an explanation, if you have one (i.e., "This is a premarital debt of my wife, Susan Jones," or "I've never had an account with Pedicures A-Plenty").

For account information that is incorrect, write, "The account status and/or details are incorrect for the following accounts." Include the creditor's name, the account number, and the correct status.

For inquiries you do not recognize and did not authorize, write, "The following inquiries were not authorized by me." List the creditor's name, the date of inquiry, and an explanation (i.e., "I did not apply for credit with Big Bucks Bank, nor did I authorize them to conduct a credit check on me").

For any other incorrect information, provide a complete explanation as to why that information on your CR is incorrect or obsolete. For example, "It has been more than seven years since this item was reported." Or "Citibank account 123456 is listed twice with two different balances, one showing a delinquency. Only the first entry is correct, and I have never had a late payment with this creditor."

Finish your communication with the following: "Please update my credit report and send me a copy at the conclusion of your investigation." Optional: "Send the results to the following organizations that have reviewed my credit report in the past six months and/or to employers that have reviewed it during the past two years" and then list them. End with, "Thank you for your help and prompt attention in this matter."

Once the CRA receives your request for reinvestigation, by law it must:

- contact the creditor reporting the information you dispute within five days of receiving your dispute
- review and consider all relevant information submitted by you
- remove all inaccurate and unverified information
- adopt procedures to keep the information from reappearing
- reinsert removed information only if the provider of the information certifies that the information is accurate and you are notified within five days of the reinsertion
- provide you with the results of its investigation within five days of completion along with a new credit report

3. Keep track of the date the dispute form was sent. And now the fun begins. I suggest you get a calendar and some kind of notebook or binder. The FCRA requires the CRA to investigate

all disputed items within "a reasonable period of time," which has been interpreted by the FTC as thirty days. If the bureau finds that the information was incorrect, obsolete, or could no longer be verified, it must correct or delete the information.

4. Follow up. If you do not receive a response within six weeks, send a follow-up letter on this order even though you might be tempted to use more colorful language: "On [date], I sent you a request to investigate certain items on my credit report that I believe to be incorrect or inaccurate. As of today, six weeks have passed, and I have not yet received a response from you. Under the Fair Credit Reporting Act, you are required to respond within a reasonable time. If the information cannot be verified, please delete it from my credit report. I would appreciate your immediate attention in this matter, and please inform me of the result." Be sure to include your name, address, telephone number, Social Security number, and a copy of your original dispute.

5. Wait four more weeks. While most credit bureaus will notify you of the result of their investigation within the first six weeks along with a copy of your updated credit report, you may have to go through another cycle, especially if you are trying to dispute during the credit-busy holiday season. Repeat until you receive satisfaction.

6. Keep excellent records. Make copies of all credit reports, disputes, replies, and responses. If the reply is by telephone, note the date and the time of the call, the name of the person who spoke with you, and a summary of the conversation.

7. If the CRA continues to violate your rights by refusing to investigate, send a final letter. In this letter, repeat what you said in the follow-up letter but also threaten to take legal action. Send copies of your letters to the FTC and to your local office of the attorney general.

8. If the CRA responds that the IP verified its accuracy and that, therefore, the information will remain on your file, you will need

to take more aggressive action to clean up your report. Understand that this may be frustrating and time consuming. If you still have an honest and reasonable belief that the information is incorrect and inaccurate, you should contact the IP directly with the incorrect information and demand that it tell the CRA to remove the information from your CR. Write to the customer service department, vice president of marketing, and president or CEO.

9. If the IP agrees with you that the information is incorrect, forward a copy of the letter you received from the IP to the CRA. Follow up in thirty days to make sure the CRA has removed the disputed information from your CR.

10. Consider adding a brief statement to your CR. If you are still unable to successfully dispute the item(s), under the FCRA you have the right to add to your CR a statement of up to one hundred words regarding any item(s) you wish to clarify. This statement, or a version of it, will then appear on all subsequent reports sent to your credit grantors. You should consider doing this only if you have many positives but only a single negative item in your CR. Sometimes a statement in your account draws more negative attention than the item itself. But there are times it can be helpful. Here's an example: "Attention! This is not my account. I have never owed money to Pedicures A-Plenty. Apparently a mistake was made during reporting."

21

Tell the Middleman Thanks but No Thanks

How to Pay Off Your Mortgage Early

"I have a confession. I just did something that feels Un-American. I paid off my mortgage . . . my husband and I couldn't be happier about our decision. I love the fact that my monthly housing costs (including my taxes and utilities) now mirror what I paid back when I was living alone in a studio in my early 20s."

Stacey Bradford, CBS MoneyWatch

If you're like most homeowners, you may wake up in the middle of the night in a cold sweat and ask, "Are we doing enough to avoid paying insane amounts of interest on our mortgage?" Your spouse, being your complete opposite and less than appreciative of your middle-of-the-night outbursts, encourages you to go back to sleep.

And then, wouldn't you know it, in the mail comes a confusing, albeit compelling, offer from your mortgage company. They are dying to give back a big load of the interest they were so intent on charging you in the first place. What gives?

The Biweekly Mortgage Payment

Carl and Sandy received one of these letters in the mail from their mortgage company. By switching to the company's Equity Accelerator program, the letter informed them, they could pocket the last $32,000 of mortgage interest they are obligated to pay. Should they accept?

If the Wheelers accept, they will stop mailing their regular monthly payments and authorize the mortgage company to electronically deduct about half of one mortgage payment from their checking account every two weeks (biweekly). The letter says this simple change will speed the growth of equity (the difference between what they borrowed and what they still owe), reduce the time it takes to pay the loan in full, and save Carl and Sandy a pile of dough.

If you have a mortgage on your home, it's likely you've been offered something like this from your mortgage company or, more likely, a third party or middleman.

The biweekly mortgage payment has become quite popular, not because your mortgage company or that middleman company cares a whit about your financial situation but because it is another way to increase its profits.

Only a fool would say this doesn't sound like a good deal. Who wouldn't be interested in saving $32,000 of mortgage interest? Nevertheless, before Carl and Sandy jumped on the Equity Accelerator bandwagon, they had some questions.

Why does this work? The plan is based on the difference between monthly payments and biweekly payments. One mortgage payment each month means twelve payments in a year. If you make a half payment every two weeks, you will make twenty-six biweekly payments or the equivalent of thirteen monthly payments in the same period. This one additional payment each year is the secret to what makes this plan work.

Paying half a payment every two weeks is a painless way to make an extra monthly payment every year—a strategy that is not new by any means. The problem is that under normal circumstances few mortgage holders are ready or willing to accept and process half payments. Mortgages are different from open-ended credit contracts like those of credit cards and other lines of credit. Your mortgage contract requires full payments "or more" each month. Therefore, if you send anything less than that, the mortgage company will either return the partial payment as insufficient or hold the funds until the other half shows up.

By reading the fine print on the Wheelers' offer, I discovered their mortgage company is not willing to accept partial payments, even for those who enroll in their Equity Accelerator program. It says the company electronically deducts the half payments every two weeks but holds the money to accumulate and then makes appropriate payments on the customer's regular monthly payment date. In essence, the company is setting up a subcompany to collect and hold these partial payments for people who opt for the Equity Accelerator plan.

What is it going to cost the Wheelers to save all this money? This program requires an initial "onetime lifetime program fee" of $195, which is collected with the first payment (I have seen similar programs with a $395 or even $495 initial fee). But wait! There's more. All these programs charge a fee by the month or a certain amount on each biweekly electronic transaction. In the Wheelers' case, the company's "participation fee" amounts to $5.42, withdrawn electronically along with each of those half payments.

Even though the Equity Accelerator program would reduce their mortgage payback time to 23.9 years, the Wheelers would end up paying $3,562.99 in fees ($195 plus [$5.42 x 26 x 23.9]).

What's in this for the company? For starters, $3,562.99 (the total of the initial fee plus the biweekly fees until the mortgage is paid in full). However, there's more than that. Banks and lending institutions rely heavily on something called "float" to determine the present value of money. The float is the daily interest they earn on the money they hold on account. By collecting half payments every two weeks from many customers, they increase their deposits and earning power significantly. Moreover, they are assured on-time payment.

These programs are always presented to make the company look compassionate and concerned about the customer's financial situation—as if the banks and lending institutions are going to great lengths to do all they can to help out. Don't believe it. Every mortgage holder is interested in only one thing: increasing its bottom line.

So is this Equity Accelerator program a scam? No. It is a fact that making the equivalent of thirteen monthly mortgage payments each year will significantly reduce the time it takes to pay off a mortgage and at the same time reduce the amount of interest. There is nothing immoral or particularly unethical about the Wheelers' mortgage company introducing the plan and then interjecting themselves into the deal with the expectation of remuneration, provided, of course, there is full disclosure. I do not doubt the Wheelers' bank fully disclosed all aspects of this plan. However, the Wheelers are not obligated to accept.

A Do-It-Yourself Plan

The Wheelers can do this deal by themselves. They do not need a middleman, and they do not have to lock themselves into a biweekly schedule. The Wheelers can accomplish the same objective as the Equity Accelerator program and do it far more efficiently than if they were to join the program. They can create and manage their own thirteen-payments-a-year program to painlessly and rapidly repay their mortgage.

By doing it themselves, the Wheelers will not have to fill out paperwork, seek permission, make a long-term commitment to a new payment plan, pay a cent in fees, or even stick with it if their financial picture changes in the future. Their mortgage company will also cooperate with them if they do it themselves—guaranteed. The key is to understand that nearly all mortgages allow the customer to pay more than the required payment, but never less. (It is rare these days for a residential mortgage to contain a prepayment penalty clause.)

How would the Wheelers create this type of plan on their own? Each time they make their regular mortgage payment, they should write a second check equal to one-twelfth of one payment (read that carefully). I get lots of letters from people who misread that as one-half of one payment. It is one-twelfth. On the memo line of that second check, they should write "principal only." At the end of twelve months, they will have made the equivalent of thirteen monthly payments. No fees, no contracts, and no middleman demanding a commission.

The Wheelers can make this deal even sweeter if they increase that second check by the $5.42 fee they won't be paying to the Equity Accelerator middleman. Even the smallest amount put toward prepayment makes a remarkable impact.

And what about that $195 onetime lifetime program fee the Wheelers won't be paying for the privilege of switching to the Equity Accelerator program? If they've got it (apparently they do since they asked me if they should do this), they should send it with their next payment as yet another principal-only pay down and cheer as their mortgage shrinks even faster.

By creating their own equity acceleration plan, the Wheelers remain in control of their situation. If in the future they encounter a financially difficult season, they can always pull back to their original payment schedule. They're not locked into the company's Equity Accelerator program. And when they find they are able to increase their contribution, they can do that too. They are in charge!

Best of all, every cent they devote to their principal prepayment plan will go to work for them, not line the pockets of their mortgage holder.

Pay Down or Pay Ahead?

When sending in extra money for your mortgage, or for any other debt for that matter, it is very important that you understand the difference between paying down and paying ahead.

There are two common reasons that borrowers send extra cash to their mortgage companies: (1) to pay down the principal balance or (2) to pay ahead on payments that will be due in the future.

Sometime ago we refinanced our mortgage. The transaction closed in December with the first payment due in February. We did what I would always advise you to do when either starting a new mortgage or refinancing. Rather than taking a month off from making a house payment (the lender typically collects the first month's interest through the escrow closing process), we made the equivalent of one payment in January (even though it was not required) to reduce the principal right off the bat. We were careful to write "principal prepayment" on the check along with our account number.

In just a couple of weeks, we received a detailed statement that correctly reflected the starting balance and showed that we made the unscheduled payment in January and that it had been credited in its entirety to reduce the principal. Exactly right.

The next day another statement arrived showing they had reversed the transaction and applied the total amount of that unscheduled payment to the February payment, which wouldn't be due for another month.

I called customer service with a simple question: "Why did you do that?" The lady on the other end of the line said someone must have assumed we wished to "pay ahead" when what we wanted to do was "pay down."

I know why they did this. Do you? Interest. Applying that unscheduled payment to the principal was not at all profitable for the lender. Simply put, every dollar we prepay is a dollar the mortgage company cannot collect interest on every month. They want as many dollars to remain on the principal balance as possible. Prepaying the equivalent of an entire month's payment represents a big chunk of money they cannot collect interest on for the next fifteen years. Prepaying any amount of principal at the beginning of a mortgage saves huge amounts of interest and shortens the payback time.

This single principal prepayment, when applied correctly to pay down the principal, will save us more than $4,000 in interest, and we'll own our home three months sooner. On the other hand, applying it to the February payment would have put most of the $4,000 into the lender's pocket in the form of interest.

Pay Down the Principal Balance

When you send an additional amount to pay down the principal balance, your loan balance goes down. But you still have to make the next scheduled payment.

Let's say it's April, and you make your regular mortgage payment this month plus the equivalent of three extra payments. You enclose a note that the additional payments are to pay down the principal balance. You will still have a payment due in May, June, and July as scheduled.

Pay the Account Ahead

On the other hand, let's assume for a moment that you sent those three extra payments for a different reason. You are going to Europe for the summer and don't want to worry about making mortgage payments. In this scenario, you want to pay ahead.

Attaching a note to the additional payments will tell the lender to apply them to the May, June, and July payments. You'll be back before the August payment is due.

If you were not clear how you wanted those three extra payments handled, the employee who happens to be handling incoming payments that day might assume you want to pay down the principal balance. You leave the country assuming you've made your mortgage payments. Of course, you don't get the late notices because you're not around. You arrive home only to learn that your home is in foreclosure.

You cannot assume the mortgage company will automatically pay your account ahead if you do not send clear instructions. Nor can you assume they will know to pay down the principal balance. Never assume they will read your mind correctly.

Some lenders, I'm told, will simply return additional payments if they are not clear on how you wish for them to be handled. Others automatically apply additional sums to future payments, defaulting always to the lender's benefit.

Give Crystal Clear Instructions

Whenever you send more than the amount of your regular payment to your mortgage holder, or to any creditor, you should write instructions in the memo area of the check and also include a note explaining what it is for. Do not staple your instructions to your check. Use a paper clip instead.

Don't stop there. Follow up in a couple of weeks to make sure the company handles the transaction per your instructions. If you get a monthly statement, wait for the next one unless you're leaving on that European vacation! If all you have are a stack of coupons and your lender sends a statement once a year, make sure your account was handled properly. Many mortgage lenders now offer online account information. This is a great way to keep an eye on your account. As a bonus, just seeing those numbers in print will motivate you to make sure that balance keeps going down as rapidly as possible.

22

How to Stay on Track
with a Roller-Coaster
Income

The Thrill and the Agony
of Self-Employment

A big mistake consultants make is that they have a $10,000 month,
so they assume they make $120,000 a year.

David L. Bach, *Smart Couples Finish Rich*

I f you are among the millions of people in this country who don't
know how or when they will see another paycheck, chances are
you're either unemployed or self-employed.

If you are a freelancer or a consultant or you work in sales or
the arts and you don't know when or how or how much you'll get
paid from month to month, the word *roller coaster* probably brings

more to mind than something in an amusement park. And I would not be surprised if because of said status you have dismissed much of what you have read thus far as inapplicable to your situation. Having been self-employed most of my working years, I know exactly the justifications you may have for being unable to plan ahead or to stick with anything close to a spending plan. You feel out of step with your lucky friends and relatives who have "real jobs" with regular paychecks.

The majority of those who fall into the irregular income category live in constant uncertainty. Some months there is absolutely no income, and then a deal closes or a big account comes through with a good-sized check. Somehow when the big deal closes, we forget the lean months we just survived and the fact that there may be many more ahead.

"Feast or famine" sums it up pretty well. For many, at least in the beginning, self-employment is survival on a daily basis. I hear from many self-employed people who usually conclude it is impossible to come up with any kind of reasonable spending plan or to live within their means when the means are so unpredictable. But that's a potentially dangerous conclusion.

Commissioned salespersons, freelancers, and small business owners make a huge mistake when they fail to become their own strict and unbending employer. If you are self-employed, you have to learn how to wear two hats—you the employer and you the employee.

You the employee need to determine the lowest reasonable amount you can accept from you the employer as monthly compensation. Now that's a new twist. Usually self-employed people ask, "What is the largest amount I can possibly pull out of this business every month?"

Let's say, for example, that your rock-bottom, absolute minimum, bare-bones, just-the-essentials figure is $3,000 a month, based on your monthly spending plan. You may intend to bring $10 million into the business this year, but determining your reasonable monthly requirement has nothing to do with that. You the employer are going to have to determine if the business is able to commit to this $3,000 monthly salary for you the employee. Let's assume that it can.

If you are a typical small business owner, you probably have a business checking account separate from your personal checking account. As a freelance artist, writer, or commissioned salesperson, you may be in the habit of depositing your checks directly into your personal account. This is a problem! Even though you do not have a formal small business complete with a business license, you must still see yourself as operating a business. No matter your form of self-employment, you need to have a separate checking account for your self-employment income.

By opening another checking account, you will be able to take control. Example: You receive a $10,000 commission check in January, nothing in February, and nothing in March; in April, you receive four checks for $550, $1,200, $3,000, and $850. Not so bad. That's $15,600 for four months, which should more than cover your expenses of $3,000 a month. The problem is that in January you might have had to play catch-up on all the holiday bills you couldn't pay because December was a dry month. And then there were all those great after-Christmas sales, and you felt as if you had extra money, so you splurged a bit here and there. Then along came February and March and no income. The personal checking account was depleted, the credit cards were called into action, and it was desperation time until April.

The $5,600 you receive in April barely gets you caught up, and then you remember you have to file your taxes on April 15 and make another estimated tax payment. You file for an extension on your taxes and take a cash advance from your one and only remaining credit card limit, and so goes the ride on the roller coaster. You get stuck in survival mode even though on paper it looks as if you should be doing pretty well.

With the separate business checking account method, here is what should happen. You deposit the January $10,000 check into your business checking account. You the employer guard this account as any good employer or business owner would. On payday—a predetermined day that you the employer set each month—you write yourself, the employee, a paycheck for $3,000, regardless of the balance in that account. After all, you the employee certainly cannot expect a raise every month. It's $3,000 on payday and not a day before, and that's it. On February 1, you write you the employee your $3,000 monthly paycheck. On March 1, you write yourself a $3,000 paycheck. On April 1, you deposit the $5,600 and write yourself a $3,000 paycheck and so on each month.

If your self-employment work is sufficient to support you and your family, you should not have to worry. The business checking account serves as a holding tank, and the income you deposit into it must exceed the paychecks you withdraw. As the holding account becomes healthy, you will have more of a cushion in the form of reserves to carry you through the lean times. No longer will you see a great month that produces $10,000 as the signal to put in the pool you've always dreamed of.

In time, as things continue to go well and you build sufficient reserves, you the employer might even consider sitting down with you the employee to negotiate a raise, but don't be too hasty. Weigh the pros and cons. Consider the position of the prudent employer against the needy employee. Employers cannot deal from emotion. They need to consider the best interests of both the company and the employee. The wise employer knows that if the company goes under, that will be infinitely worse for the employee than a pathetically small raise.

Your success as a self-employed person lies in your ability to discipline yourself and be a fair but strict employer and at the same time a grateful, restrained employee. You must become ultraconservative and fanatically frugal and make your irregular cash flow as predictable as possible.

It's not easy to be self-employed. It's one month after another of holding on and waiting until "then." But "then" never comes. So you have to believe that "then" is now and figure out how to fit your regular spending plan and your real life into your irregular income and (most difficult of all) how to step back and make a nonemotional assessment of how this is really working out.

If it wouldn't land us both in dire need of a heavy dose of anti-depressants, I'd share with you a few of the letters I've received from couples who are in desperate financial situations because they stayed in a self-employment situation long after they should have turned it back into the hobby it was. And now they have huge amounts of debt and IRS liens to carry into the future.

You can smooth out the extremes of the self-employed roller-coaster ride if you live on the very least, not the most, you possibly can, underestimate the income the business will produce, and overestimate the expenses (double them and you'll probably come out just right).

23

What to Do When You've Fallen and You Can't Get Up

Credit Counseling and Debt Negotiation

> When you get in a tight place and everything goes against you, till it
> seems as though you could not hold on a minute longer, never give
> up then, for that is just the place and time that the tide will turn.
>
> Harriet Beecher Stowe[1]

Not every couple in financial trouble needs to call a bankruptcy attorney. Even if you feel you are drowning in debt
and there is no hope, credit counseling may be the lifeline that
can pull you to safety.

Credit counseling is a service that helps people in serious financial peril before their situation deteriorates into bankruptcy. While

273

there is definitely a humanitarian motive at the center of what this industry does for people, credit counseling is about business too.

Credit counseling works because it benefits all three parties involved:

1. The consumer gets back on track and avoids bankruptcy.
2. The creditor gets his money.
3. The counseling organization receives funding that allows it to continue its good works.

Reputable credit counseling firms are nonprofit organizations, a designation that can be quite confusing. "Nonprofit" does not mean the company must be run by volunteers and is not allowed to make money. On the contrary, nonprofit organizations can operate very much like a for-profit corporation. They can charge for their services and build up millions of dollars in cash reserves. They can pay handsome salaries; their executives can drive fancy company cars and operate out of luxurious offices. They can advertise and participate in slick marketing campaigns.

The main difference between a for-profit corporation and one with a nonprofit status is that no one can own a nonprofit organization. Employees cannot receive stock options, and profits are not distributed to individuals at the end of the year. Some nonprofits are tax exempt and some are not. This chapter is about tax exempt, nonprofit, charitable organizations that perform credit counseling services.

Credit Counseling

What Is It?

Credit counseling is intervention in the form of confidential counseling and negotiation with a client's creditors in an attempt to freeze penalties, reduce interest, and create a monthly debt repayment plan that is mutually beneficial to all involved. The principal owed is not the subject of negotiation but rather the interest and punitive fees. The borrowers are not trying to stiff their creditors and get out of repaying what they borrowed. Credit counseling addresses the add-ons and the payment structure. Theoretically, credit counseling is a moral and ethical way to manage a situation that has become unmanageable.

Counseling can also include help with rent and mortgage issues, transportation needs, student loans, and bill paying. The typical counseling organization deals primarily with credit card debts. Some counseling organizations offer educational programs to help their clients learn how to manage their money well, live within their means, and embark on the road to financial recovery with an excellent chance for success.

Creditor-approved repayment plans are administered through the counselor's debt management program. While enrolled, the client makes a single payment each month to the counseling organization, which then distributes payments to each of the creditors.

How Does It Work?

Typically, the troubled consumer calls the credit counseling organization to set up an appointment. If married, the consumer and his or her spouse are required to attend this initial orientation.

At the first meeting, a counselor sits down with you and goes over your financial situation. You fill out an application and reveal everything about your financial situation. You must disclose everything in terms of income, expenses, debts, and the contents of your credit report. Be prepared to hand over all your credit cards. Many counselors cut them up on the spot and assist you in canceling the accounts, a requirement to be accepted into counseling.

Most credit counseling organizations have minimum requirements, such as you must have a steady income and there must be a reasonable expectation that with counseling and the payment schedule they can negotiate with your creditors you can get out of unsecured debt within three to five years.

The counselor, if he or she feels you are a likely candidate, then contacts all your creditors to inform them you've entered a counseling program. He or she asks your creditors to reduce interest rates, to waive fees and penalties, and to accept a different payment schedule based on what the counselor suggests you can afford and will be able to pay on a regular basis. Once the creditors have made their adjustments (some will cooperate, others will not, but all will be informed that you have entered counseling), the counselor will come up with a repayment plan for you. This could take a few days, a few weeks, or longer.

Once you agree, instead of paying your creditors individually each month, you will send one payment to the credit counseling firm each month and then trust that it will pay your creditors according to the agreed-upon payment schedule.

Who Pays for It?

Credit counseling organizations receive the bulk of their income from your creditors. Through a cooperative arrangement called the Fair Share Program, creditors rebate to the counseling firms a small portion of the money they collect. Think of it as a commission. There are some who criticize the credit counseling concept because, they say, the counselors have a conflict of interest. However, as long as all of this is disclosed, it's up to you to decide if the counselor is working more for the creditors than for you.

In addition to the Fair Share Program, some counseling organizations charge their debt management clients a modest administrative fee plus a monthly fee for services rendered. Others don't charge a fee but encourage voluntary tax-deductible monetary contributions. Whatever this amount turns out to be (it could be as low as $6 per month or up to $30, $50, or more depending on how many accounts you have), it is included in the one amount you send to the counseling organization each month.

The credit counseling industry has and continues to go through a season of change. Banks and creditors that cooperate with credit counseling agencies have cut the Fair Share rebates from a high of 15 percent to 8 percent, with industry leaders suggesting this will probably bottom out at 6 percent. Not good news for the credit counseling industry. As a result, credit counseling firms are scrambling to attract new clients to their debt management programs in an effort to increase business and make up for the shortfall.

Who Needs It?

Credit counseling is a serious remedy with unavoidable consequences. It is not the right choice for everyone. Effective as it can be, credit counseling is not a clever way to reduce high interest rates. It is not a cool way to reduce your bills so you have more money to buy more stuff.

Think of credit counseling as you would think of chemotherapy. It offers an excellent chance for recovery if you have a potentially terminal illness but is certainly not a treatment you would choose if you had other choices. You would never agree to chemotherapy if you have the flu. If you have any other choice than filing for bankruptcy, credit counseling is probably not the route you should take.

Typically, a couple who is a good candidate for credit counseling is experiencing some or all of the following: past due bills, the inability to make the minimum payments on credit card accounts, borrowing from one card to pay another card, using credit for necessities such as groceries and gasoline, a damaged credit report, creditors calling, and an overall feeling of despair.

Most credit counselors are caring, sensitive individuals who truly want to help their clients find solutions to their financial problems. Your initial session will include an interview to help the counselor understand your situation. This experience should not be dehumanizing but rather encouraging and filled with hope.

Is There a Downside?

While the fact that you are in credit counseling and a debt management program will be reported to the credit bureaus, this is not necessarily a negative on your credit report.

There is some disagreement in the industry as to how negatively this will impact your future ability to qualify for credit. The best scenario is that future employers, landlords, and credit granters will see that you took responsibility for your situation and sought professional help. At the worst, it will be seen as a blemish on your ability to stick by your financial promises and moral obligations.

If you want to look into credit counseling, I highly recommend the National Federation for Credit Counseling (nfcc.org), which certifies Consumer Credit Counseling Services (CCCS) offices across the United States. You can connect with a local office where you live by going to nfcc.org or by calling 1-800-338-2227.

Debt Negotiation

Sometimes referred to as "arbitration" or "accord and satisfaction," debt negotiation involves cutting a deal with a creditor to make a one-time cash payment that is considerably less than the current amount owed. But there's a small matter of having to come up with a big chunk of cash if the creditor agrees to settle.

At first glance, this sounds pretty cool: run up a big balance and then negotiate a greatly reduced cash settlement. The truth is it is anything but cool. For starters, negotiation and settlement will result in the destruction of your credit score. But there's more.

It is important to understand that debt negotiation is not a regulated profession, so there are no rules. Anyone can call himself or herself a debt negotiator. There is no training, no certification, and no licensing required. And the scariest part? Most debt negotiators require their clients to deposit huge sums into their equally unregulated company trust accounts before negotiations can commence.

Basically, this is how it works. You hear or read some slick and compelling ad that promises you can stick it to your creditors by paying a lot less than you owe. You meet with the debt negotiator in person or by phone. You list your outstanding balances, and they come up with an amount they believe your creditors will accept. Typically, it's 50 to 60 percent of the total and could be thousands of dollars. Next, you must give that amount to the negotiator.

If you don't have that kind of cash lying around the house (show me someone in dire financial straits who does), they set up a monthly payment plan. Of course, they add in their fee, which can be anywhere from 20 to 30 percent of what they hope to save you or 11 percent of your total outstanding debt. No matter how you look at it, we're talking about a lot of money in fees.

Next, if you are not behind on your payments, the negotiator will likely hint (wink, wink) that your creditors will have little motivation to arbitrate for a less-than-full payoff unless you are two or three months behind on payments and they believe recovery is not likely. They will suggest that instead of making your payments for the next few months, you deposit that money with them to be held for your settlements.

When the full amount is on deposit, the negotiator commences to contact your creditors with offers to settle. In theory, each of your creditors jumps for joy upon hearing of your offer, the negotiator writes out all the checks, and you end up debt-free. If only it were that simple.

A few years ago a debt negotiation company (which shall remain nameless due to pending litigation) took the Southern California radio airwaves by storm and other areas of the country as well.

Based on a tip from an angry client of this company, I checked it out with the Better Business Bureau. I learned the following.

This company has an unsatisfactory business performance record, including a pattern of complaints alleging the company failed to negotiate debts, failed to pay creditors, and failed to provide adequate service. A few complainants alleged that while in the program they were sued by creditors or debts were arbitrated under the cardholder agreements. Some customers complained that creditors continued to contact them or they were turned over to collection even though they were led to believe by the company this would not occur. A few complainants alleged they were instructed not to pay their debt, as this would improve the company's ability to negotiate settlement.

A local talk show host recently spoke on air with several people who had been clients of this company. One man told his truly sad story of taking more than $30,000 from his 401(k) retirement account to deposit with the company for his settlement program. When the company failed to deliver on their promised settlements, he ended up filing for bankruptcy. If that wasn't bad enough, he got hit with a big IRS penalty for dipping into his 401(k).

Another guest told of writing checks to the company totaling over $17,000, from which it took $12,000 as its fee. When the company would not stand behind its promises and the situation dragged out for many months, he ended up settling his debts on his own. The company refused to refund any of its fee, and he walked away having learned a very expensive lesson.

I've read dozens of similar accounts from people who worked with this firm and others. Over and again these clients said they were misled and misinformed. They were instructed that their lenders wouldn't be motivated to settle unless they were at least two to three months behind. When their settlements didn't come through, they were in a real mess.

What Negotiators Won't Tell You

1. If you're maxed out and stop making payments on your credit card accounts, you're going to get hit with late fees and over-limit fees every month. When you combine those with your already outrageous double-digit interest rate, your effective APR could zoom to 40 percent or more.

2. A creditor can agree to a settlement, but even after you've paid that amount, that creditor can (and probably will) pursue the balance at a later date by turning it over to collection. Settlement can be tricky.

3. Lenders report settlements to the credit bureaus as "settled." This will appear on your report as an R9, which is a low rating just one notch above bankruptcy. It will stay there for seven years from the date of final payment.

4. You can negotiate your own settlement directly with your creditor. One woman reported that when she called on her own behalf, she was treated rudely, but when she had a friend call as her representative, her friend was treated professionally and eventually negotiated a settlement.

5. If the amount forgiven by settlement exceeds $600, expect to hear from the IRS. Most creditors are required by law to report the forgiven amount as taxable income. You will receive a form 1099 showing the amount you must claim as income on your next tax filing.

If You Decide to Use a Negotiator

Debt negotiation is so problematic that it should be seen as a last resort, and only after giving credit counseling a fair chance.

I will concede that there may be circumstances when negotiation is an appropriate course of action. Examples might be when both the creditor and the debtor are eager to reach a compromise, such as with an old forgotten debt, an "inherited" debt from something like a cosigning that went bad, or a large medical debt.

I hope it never happens, but if you should find yourself in need of a debt negotiator and you cannot represent yourself, do your homework and then carry a big stick. Here are some guidelines to follow:

- Check out the company with the Better Business Bureau in your area as well as with your state attorney general.
- Make sure you know the fee structure. Is there a monthly charge? A setup charge? A penalty for leaving the program? Are these fees mandatory?
- Make one of your deal points that the lender will report "paid as agreed" to the credit bureaus.
- Do not stop making payments in an effort to trick your creditor into negotiating more aggressively.

Better Alternatives

Under normal circumstances of just too much debt, you have much better and more ethical alternatives.

First, develop your rapid debt-repayment plan. You know how to get yourself out of debt quickly and honorably without paying a penny in fees or stiffing a creditor for even a dime. It's exciting and it works. Go back and read chapter 17 again.

If you are behind, cannot get caught up, and are continually unable to make even your minimum monthly payments, seek the help of a reputable credit counseling organization.

Beyond the logistics of how debt negotiation works is the matter of ethics and right living. Lenders have the legal and moral right to full payment under the terms to which you agreed, regardless if you've now soured on those terms. Paying your debt is the moral thing to do.

If by chance you are tempted to sign on with a debt negotiator—and have the ability to plunk down 60 percent of what you owe in cash—why don't you do the right thing and pay down your debts with that money now?

24

A Call to Faithfulness

An Eternal Perspective on Wealth

Most people fail to realize that money is both a test and a trust
from God.

Rick Warren, *The Purpose Driven Life*

My first real job paid $110 a week. Of course, that wasn't enough. I needed $200 a week to solve all my problems. It would take something like $500 a week, I thought, to make me wealthy. To me, "wealthy" meant having so much money I could buy anything I wanted, anytime I wanted it, without having to even think about it.

More money was always what I needed to be happy. When I reached the $500 a week level, something happened—it was no longer enough to make me happy, let alone wealthy. The truth is more was never enough. You read chapter 1, so you know what I mean when I say that back then more money would've never been enough, because I was expecting money to fill my life and satisfy my soul in ways it cannot.

I am not saying that money isn't important or that I don't enjoy earning it and spending it. It is, and I do. But things are different for me now that I've discovered the secret of true wealth and how to achieve it.

Wealth is an elusive thing. One minute you're sure you know what it means, and just when you believe you're about to grab on to it, it escapes your grip and disappears from sight. So what does it mean to you to be wealthy? How much money would that be? An additional $50,000 a year? $100,000? Millions?

True wealth is a holistic sense of overall well-being that no amount of money alone can buy. Money is just a tool we can use to become wealthy. This sense of well-being gets to the deeper issues of our lives—our personal values.[1]

I believe God is the author of universal rules and principles that govern every aspect of life, including money. In fact, the number of pages the Bible devotes to money is second only to love. It is the owner's manual for how we are to live and contains the principles and rules on which we are to base our lives.

- *On charity and giving*: "It is more blessed to give than to receive" (Acts 20:35 KJV); "The righteous give generously" (Ps. 37:21).
- *On debt repayment*: "The wicked borrow and do not repay" (Ps. 37:21).
- *On money's place in our lives*: "For the love of money is a root of all kinds of evil" (1 Tim. 6:10).
- *On debt*: "The rich rule over the poor, and the borrower is slave to the lender" (Prov. 22:7).
- *On saving*: "The wise have wealth and luxury, but fools spend whatever they get" (Prov. 21:20 NLT).

- *On investing*: "Take a lesson from the ants, you lazybones. Learn from their ways and be wise! . . . They labor hard all summer, gathering food for the winter" (Prov. 6:6, 8 NLT).

- *On diversification*: "Plant your seed in the morning and keep busy all afternoon, for you don't know if profit will come from one activity or another—or maybe both" (Eccles. 11:6 NLT).

- *On risk management*: "A prudent person foresees danger and takes precautions. The simpleton goes blindly on and suffers the consequences" (Prov. 27:12 NLT).

- *On financial planning*: "Know the state of your flocks, and put your heart into caring for your herds" (Prov. 27:23 NLT).

- *On giving back*: "'Bring all the tithes into the storehouse so there will be enough food in my Temple. If you do,' says the Lord of Heaven's Armies, 'I will open the windows of heaven for you. I will pour out a blessing so great you won't have enough room to take it in! Try it! Put me to the test!'" (Mal. 3:10 NLT).

- *On stewardship*: "Moreover it is required in stewards, that a man be found faithful" (1 Cor. 4:2 KJV).

One of the universal laws of money is that everything you own is on loan from God. "What do you have that God hasn't given you? And if all you have is from God, why act as though you are so great, and as though you have accomplished something on your own?" (1 Cor. 4:7 TLB).

And just as you might expect, the principles of stewardship (responsibility, faithfulness, growth, and potential) apply to the money you receive the same as to your time and talents.

What you receive has a correlation to how much God knows he can trust you with. "Those who are trusted with something valuable must show they are worthy of that trust" (1 Cor. 4:2 NCV).

I once worked for a man who owned rental units. Whenever we had vacancies, we would run ads and then wait for the phone to ring. When applicants called, I would ask them to come to the office to fill out a rental application.

While I was interviewing the hopeful renters and they were busily filling out the application, my boss would excuse himself and step into the parking lot to take a look at the candidates' cars. He didn't care at all about the age or model of the car they arrived in. He wanted to see how they took care of their possessions. If the car was dirty, the seats torn, the windows smudged, and the floors and backseat strewn with trash, he wouldn't consider renting to them. He didn't care how they looked on paper, because he knew they could manipulate that with selective references and a failure to disclose certain information from their past. He was convinced that the way people cared for their cars was an excellent predictor for how they would care for his property. In fact, he put more weight on what he discovered in the parking lot than he did on anything else. Great references could not trump a grungy car. But a car that showed it was well cared for could tip the scales in a candidate's favor, even if he or she had other deficiencies.

After years of working together, we discovered predictable patterns that led to this correlation: the people with the unkempt automobiles were usually the ones with rotten credit reports. Irresponsible and untrustworthy people didn't take care of their cars or their money.

By refusing to rent to people with filthy cars, laden with trash and showing obvious signs of deferred maintenance, we had very few problems with tenants trashing our buildings. Only on rare occasions did we resort to eviction. The same care our tenants gave to their cars they extended to other things they managed. We learned that people who had demonstrated they could be trusted with little were much more likely to be responsible when given the chance to handle much more.

On the other hand, people who had really blown it in the past (a poor credit report, a history of evictions, a car that looked more like a pigsty than a vehicle) had to work twice as hard to restore the damage they'd done in terms of both cleaning up their credit reports and proving they could be trusted with caring for another's property. They had to prove they could change, that they could be good stewards in managing what did not belong to them but had been entrusted to their care.

Every day of your life on earth is a test to develop you for eternity. Nothing is insignificant in your life, and not a single dime that God entrusts to your care goes unnoticed. Even the smallest way you handle your money has significance for your character development. You don't have to worry about having enough money. God promises to supply all your needs if you obey his laws and rules. You will have enough. That is a promise you can count on! "And my God will meet all your needs according to the riches of his glory in Christ Jesus" (Phil. 4:19).

The more God gives you, the more responsible he expects you to be. But even more than that, God says that if you delight yourself in him, he will also give you your desires: "Take delight in the LORD, and he will give you the desires of your heart" (Ps. 37:4).

God uses finances to teach us to trust him to supply all our needs. For most of us, money is the greatest test of all. He watches how we use money to see how trustworthy we are. "And if you are untrustworthy about worldly wealth, who will trust you with the true riches of heaven?" (Luke 16:11 TLB).

God is not ignorant of your needs or your desires. He never falls asleep on the job or misses a due date. He cares about you and what's going on in your life more than you could possibly imagine. All he asks is that you obey his laws, trust his Word, and handle the money he entrusts to you by following the rules and principles he has given you. Those who do and go on to demonstrate they can be trusted with more are blessed beyond what they deserve or what they could possibly imagine.

God is long-suffering and patient. He allows us to make our stupid mistakes, to not trust him, to think we know best, to run ahead of him, and to try to take care of our lives and our emergencies by ourselves. We try to level all the bumps in the road. And when we stumble and fall despite our foolish efforts, he doesn't give up on us. Never! He forgives and gives us another chance. And another, and another.

You can count on God to keep his promises. Now the question is, can he count on you to be faithful?

Epilogue

Well, my friend, we have come a long way together. I hope you have found this material helpful. More than anything else, I hope you are excited about your future and all the possibilities ahead. No matter what your financial situation looks like right now, remember it can and likely will change dramatically in the future as you begin to take steps to strengthen your relationship and debt-proof your marriage.

In a way, I feel like I did the day our oldest son left our home to live on his own. All of a sudden, I had thousands of things I needed to say, things I might've forgotten to tell him or that he didn't hear in the years he lived with us. Did I teach him how to change the sheets? Would he remember to vacuum and turn the mattress quarterly? Of course, my anxiety had little to do with matters of housekeeping and more to do with whether we'd adequately prepared him for life.

I grieved for a while but then had to let go and trust that we had done the best we could and that he would be okay. He would remember and he would figure some stuff out on his own.

I'm feeling that way about you. You are about to leave to go out on your own. Have I explained all of this adequately? Did you get the really important stuff . . . the part about love being a choice, not only a feeling? Did you understand the magic of choosing to meet your spouse's deep emotional needs even when he or she is being somewhat unlovable? Did you really understand the part about the two of you being different and that that's the way it's supposed to be? Embrace your differences and don't try to change each other.

Do you fully comprehend what it meant when you agreed to forsake all others? Do you know that when you really experience debt-proof living and emotional intimacy, wonderful things will happen in your marriage? That as you begin to trust and be trusted, conflicts over money will begin to melt away?

Yes, I have to believe that you got it and that you are ready to put this information to work in your life and your marriage.

Writing this book has been personally transforming. More than a writing process, it has been life changing, and I mean in my life. All the books I read, the people I interviewed and with whom I corresponded, and the stories I shared have deeply affected my life and my marriage.

I've never enjoyed saying good-bye, so I am not going to do that now. Instead, I'm inviting you to join me at DebtProofLiving.com. You will find lots of current and relevant information as well as a wonderful community of couples who like you have embarked on a journey to debt-proof their marriages. Please drop by Everyday-Cheapskate.com as well, which is my blog. I post every weekday, and you can even get those posts in your email inbox each weekday morning. I hope you will join us at both sites soon and often!

Acknowledgments

I am deeply indebted to so many people for their support. To my editor and friend, Vicki Crumpton, who has routinely over the years extended to me patience and personal affirmation beyond the legal limit, many thanks for what you do so well.

To my Debt-Proof Living and Everyday Cheapskate staff, thanks for making the office run so smoothly, even when it seems that I am missing in action.

To all the wonderful people at Revell and Baker Publishing Group, thanks for believing in this project and giving it your all. I'm honored to be part of your rapidly growing family.

To my children, Jeremy and Tawny, Josh and Wendy, who continue to color my life and motivate me to live it well. And to my precious grandsons, Elijah and Samuel—you are the sunshine of my life.

To my husband, Harold, thanks for loving me and keeping everything balanced, and I don't mean just the checkbook. Our boat would have capsized long ago had it not been for your steady ways, constant support, and unconditional love.

My heartfelt thanks to every person who's been part of my Debt-Proof Living family since the first issue of the newsletter (formerly Cheapskate Monthly) back in January 1992. Thank you for your undying support, constant encouragement, and amazing loyalty.

Notes

Chapter 1 This Is My Story and I'm Sticking to It

1. www.traveling9to5.com/2013/07/10-inspirational-quotes-from-donald
-miller-to-write-a-better-story-for-your-life/.

Chapter 2 A Stiff Dose of Reality

1. Alex Kuczynski, "The Curse of the InStyle Wedding," *InStyle Weddings*, Spring 2001, as reported in the *New York Times*, June 2, 2002, www.nytimes
.com/2002/06/02/fashion/02WEDD.html.

2. Elizabeth Marquardt, David Blankenhorn, Robert I. Lerman, Linda Malone-Colón, and W. Bradford Wilcox, "The President's Marriage Agenda for the Forgotten Sixty Percent," *The State of Our Unions* (Charlottesville, VA: National Marriage Project and Institute for American Values, 2012), nationalmarriageproject
.org/wp-content/uploads/2012/12/SOOU2012.pdf.

3. Linda J. Waite and Maggie Gallagher, *The Case for Marriage* (New York: Broadway Press, 2000), 67.

4. Laurence J. Kotlikoff, Philip Moeller, and Paul Soloman, *Get What's Yours: The Secrets to Maxing Out Your Social Security* (New York: Simon & Schuster, 2015), 115.

5. Howard Markman et al., *Fighting for Your Marriage* (San Francisco: Jossey-Bass, 1994), 1.

6. Natalie H. Jenkins et al., *You Paid How Much for That?* (San Francisco: Jossey-Bass, 2000), 15.

7. Ragnar Storaaski and Howard Markman, 1991, University of Denver, Center for Marital and Family Studies, DU Graduate School of Professional Psychology, 2450 S. Vine St., Denver, CO 80208, 303-871-3873.

8. Judith Wallerstein, *Surviving the Breakup: How Children and Parents Cope with Divorce* (New York: Basic Books, 1979), 46–50.

9. Ibid., 211.

10. The National Marriage Project, "The State of Our Unions," 1991: The Social Health of Marriage in America (New Brunswick: National Marriage Project, 1999), 8.

11. Linda J. Waite et al., "Does Divorce Make People Happy?" americanvalues.org/catalog/pdfs/does_divorce_make_people_happy.pdf

12. Jenkins et al., You Paid How Much for That?, 40.

13. Tom Strohl, president, Marriage Works Learning Center, www.divorce reform.org.

14. National Survey of Families and Households by the University of Wisconsin, in Waite and Gallagher, The Case for Marriage, 148.

15. Waite and Gallagher, The Case for Marriage, 40–41.

16. Glenn T. Stanton, Why Marriage Matters (Colorado Springs: Pinon Press, 1997), 11.

Chapter 3 Marriage Is like a Dirt Road

1. thinkexist.com/quotation/the_real_voyage_of_discovery_consists_not_in/144224.html.

2. The Million-Dollar Highway derives its name from the low-grade gold ore present in its roadbed.

3. Michele Weiner Davis, The Divorce Remedy (New York: Simon & Schuster, 2001), 59.

4. Ibid., 211.

Chapter 4 The Currency of Life

1. Gary Smalley and John Trent, Two Sides of Love (Colorado Springs: Focus on the Family, 1990).

2. Myers-Briggs Type Indicator developed by the mother-daughter team of Katherine Cook Briggs and Isabel Briggs Myers.

3. David Keirsey, Please Understand Me II (Del Mar, CA: Prometheus Nemesis, 1998), 26.

4. Ray Linder, What Will I Do with My Money? (Chicago: Northfield Publishing, 2000), 46.

5. Ibid.

6. www.pbs.org/kcts/affluenza/show/about.html.

7. Linda J. Waite and Maggie Gallagher, The Case for Marriage, 33.

Chapter 5 News Flash: You Are Different

1. Leah Ariniello, "Gender and the Brain" (Washington, DC: Society for Neuroscience, 1998). Obtained via ProQuest, an information service by Bell & Howell.

2. Ibid.

3. Leon James, Aggressive Driving Analyzed: The Effect of Age, Gender, and Type of Car Driven across the States, 1999, www.drdriving.org/surveys/interpretations.htm.

4. Nancy Ammon Jianakoplos and Alexandra Bernasek, "Are Women More Risk Averse?" *Economic Inquire* 35, no. 4 (October 1998): 620–30.

5. Bernice Kanner, "Are You a Normal Guy?" *American Demographics* 21, no. 3 (March 1999): 19.

6. James C. Dobson, *Love for a Lifetime* (Portland, OR: Multnomah, 1987, 1993).

7. Lillian Glass, *He Says, She Says* (New York: Perigee, 1993), 33–34.

8. Bill and Pam Farrel, *Men Are like Waffles, Women Are like Spaghetti* (Eugene, OR: Harvest House, 2001), 12–14.

9. Willard F. Harley Jr., *His Needs, Her Needs: Building an Affair-Proof Marriage* (Grand Rapids: Revell, 1986), 15.

10. David Macaulay, *The Way Things Work* (Boston: Houghton Mifflin, 1998), 294–309.

11. Harley, *His Needs, Her Needs*, 16.

12. Ibid., 25.

Chapter 7 For Husbands Only

1. www.goodreads.com/quotes/31894-they-do-not-love-that-do-not-show-their-love.

Chapter 8 Getting It Together

1. Linda J. Waite and Maggie Gallagher, *The Case for Marriage*, 57.

Chapter 9 Debt-Proof Living

1. US Census Bureau, Median Income 4-Person Family, www.census.gov/hhes/www/income/data/statistics/4person.html.

Chapter 10 Till Debt Do Us Part

1. www.theobserver.ca/2012/02/19/dead-dog-offered-credit-card.

2. www.indexcreditcards.com.

3. www.bankrate.com.

4. "Do Big Cities Help College Graduates Find Better Jobs?" libertystreet economics.newyorkfed.org/2013/05/do-big-cities-help-college-graduates-find-better-jobs.html

Chapter 11 You Are Here

1. Joe Dominguez and Vicki Robin, *Your Money or Your Life* (New York: Penguin, 1999).

2. Thomas J. Stanley and William D. Danko, *The Millionaire Next Door: The Surprising Secrets of America's Wealthy* (Atlanta: Longstreet Press, 1996).

Chapter 12 Getting Where You Want to Be

1. www.brainyquote.com/quotes/quotes/c/cslewis132782.html.

Chapter 13 A Life-Changing Formula

1. izquotes.com/quote/96088.
2. George S. Clason, *The Richest Man in Babylon* (New York: Signet, 1926), 19.

Chapter 14 Knowledge Is a Powerful Thing

1. www.amazon.com/The-Beacon-Book-Quotations-Women/dp/0807067830/ref=sr_tc_2_3?ie=UTF8&qid=1420528038&sr=1-2-ent.

Chapter 15 You Want Security? I'll Show You Security!

1. Go to americancentury.com and click on "Individual Investors." Then scroll to the bottom of the page and click on "Money Markets & CDs" listed under "Investment Products."
2. Go to usaa.com and click on "Our Products," then "USAA Mutual Funds" under the listing "Investing," then "Money Market Funds" under the listing "Overview." They don't make it easy, do they?

Chapter 16 You Want Freedom? I'll Show You Freedom!

1. www.searchquotes.com/quotes/author/Johnny_Carson/2/.

Chapter 17 You Can Get Out of Debt

1. The RDRP calculator at DebtProofLiving.com figures this for members too. Just input how many years you will invest the freed-up money you've been sending to creditors once you are debt-free.

Chapter 23 What to Do When You've Fallen and You Can't Get Up

1. thinkexist.com/quotation/when_you_get_into_a_tight_place_and_everything/150745.html.

Chapter 24 A Call to Faithfulness

1. Ray Linder, *What Will I Do with My Money?* (Chicago: Moody, 2000), 197.

Mary Hunt is an award-winning and bestselling author, a syndicated columnist, and a sought-after motivational speaker who helps men and women battle the epidemic of consumer debt. She is founder and publisher of the interactive website DebtProofLiving .com, which features financial tools, resources, and information for her online members. Her books have sold more than a million copies, and her daily newspaper column, "Everyday Cheapskate," is nationally syndicated through Creators Syndicate and is enjoyed by hundreds of thousands of readers. The author of several books, including 7 *Money Rules for Life*, *Debt-Proof Living*, and *The Financially Confident Woman*, which won a Gold Medallion Book Award, Hunt speaks widely on personal finance and has appeared on shows such as NBC's *TODAY* and *Dr. Phil*. She and her husband live in Colorado. Learn more at DebtProofLiving.com.

Debt-Proof LIVING

Debt-Proof Living is a great big wonderful community offering help and hope to anyone who wants to learn how to manage their money more effectively. If you want to get out of debt—or stay out—and learn how to live below your means, Debt-Proof Living is the place to be.

Debt-proof living is a way of life where you spend less than you earn; you give and save consistently; your financial decisions are purposeful; and you work toward your goals by following a specific plan.

DebtProofLiving.com is the home of the debt-proof living philosophy. It is primarily a members-only website with features including money management tools, articles, resources, community forums, consumer tips, recipes, and more. Here you'll find, in continuous publication since 1992, the DPL newsletter, which is published in an online format available to all members of this website.

Visit DebtProofLiving.com today to find out how you can debt-proof your life!

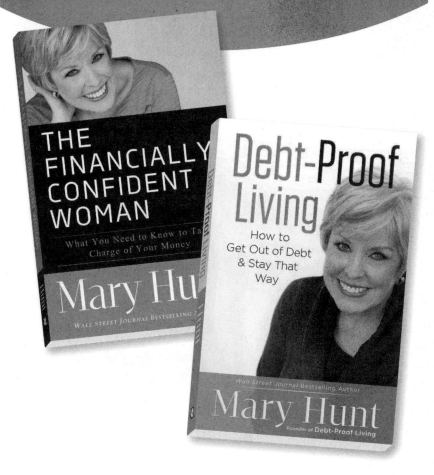

Make Your Money
WORK FOR YOU

7 How to Take Control of Your Financial Future

Money Rules for Life

Mary Hunt

Live Your Life for **1/2 THE PRICE**

Mary Hunt

WALL STREET JOURNAL BESTSELLING AUTHOR

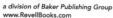